FRED BASSET YEARBOOK 2012

Summersdale Publishers Ltd
46 West Street
Chichester
West Sussex
PO19 1RP
UK

www.summersdale.com

Printed and bound in the Czech Republic

Drawings by Michael Martin

ISBN: 978-1-84953-172-6

2012

Ha ha – I won!
You blinked!

Substantial discounts on bulk quantities of Summersdale books are available to corporations, professional associations and other organisations.
For details contact Summersdale Publishers by telephone: +44 (0) 1243 771107, fax: +44 (0) 1243 786300 or email: nicky@summersdale.com.

M000048793

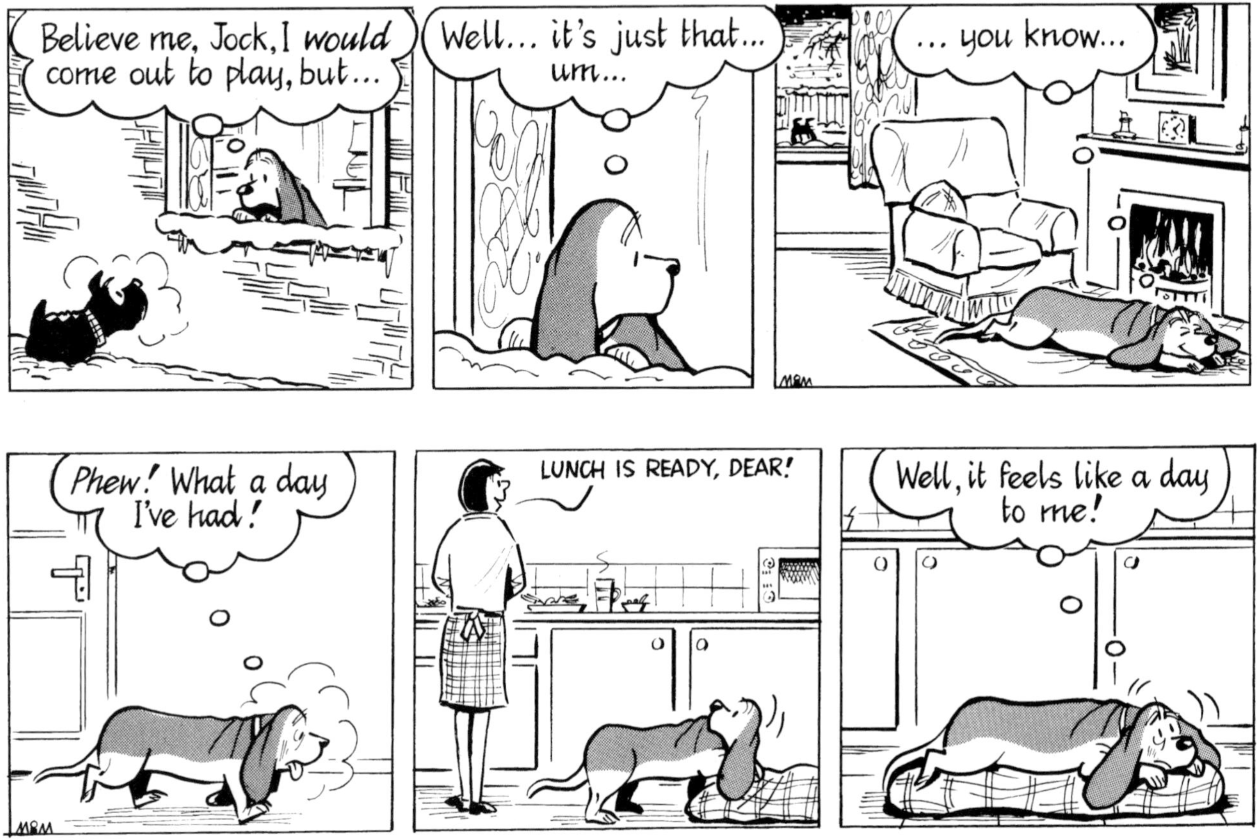
Believe me, Jock, I *would* come out to play, but...
Well... it's just that... um...
... you know...
M&M
Phew! What a day I've had!
M&M
LUNCH IS READY, DEAR!
Well, it feels like a day to me!

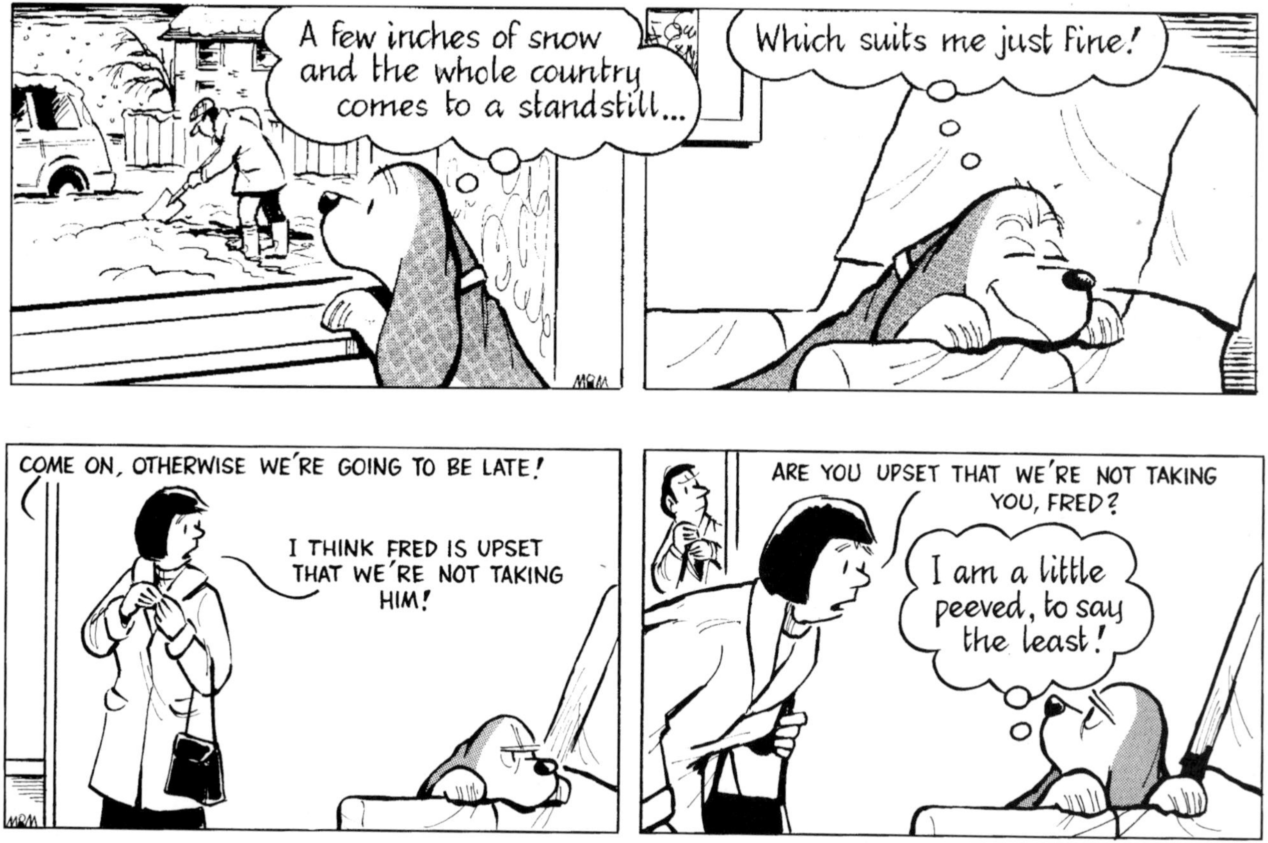
A few inches of snow and the whole country comes to a standstill...
MRM
Which suits me just fine!
COME ON, OTHERWISE WE'RE GOING TO BE LATE!
I THINK FRED IS UPSET THAT WE'RE NOT TAKING HIM!
MRM
ARE YOU UPSET THAT WE'RE NOT TAKING YOU, FRED?
I am a little peeved, to say the least!

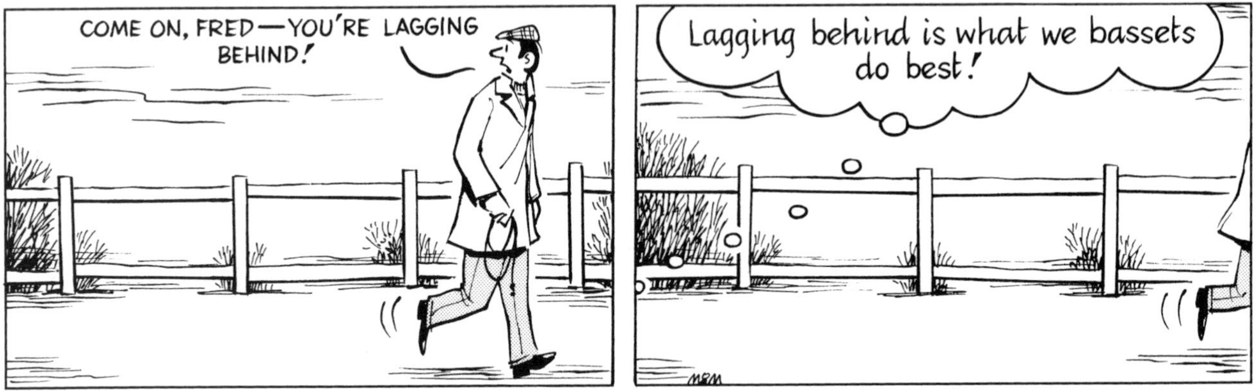
COME ON, FRED—YOU'RE LAGGING BEHIND!
Lagging behind is what we bassets do best!
MSM

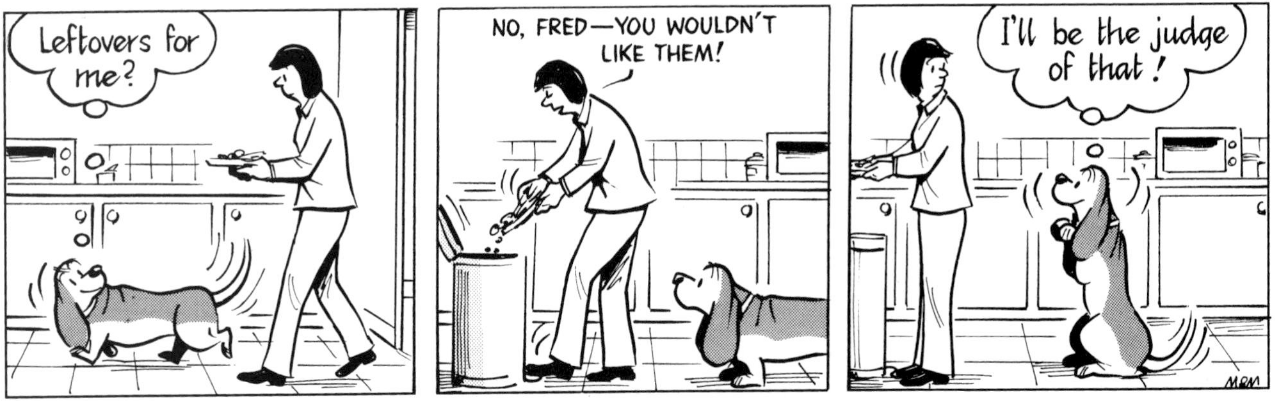
Leftovers for me?
NO, FRED—YOU WOULDN'T LIKE THEM!
I'll be the judge of that!
MSM

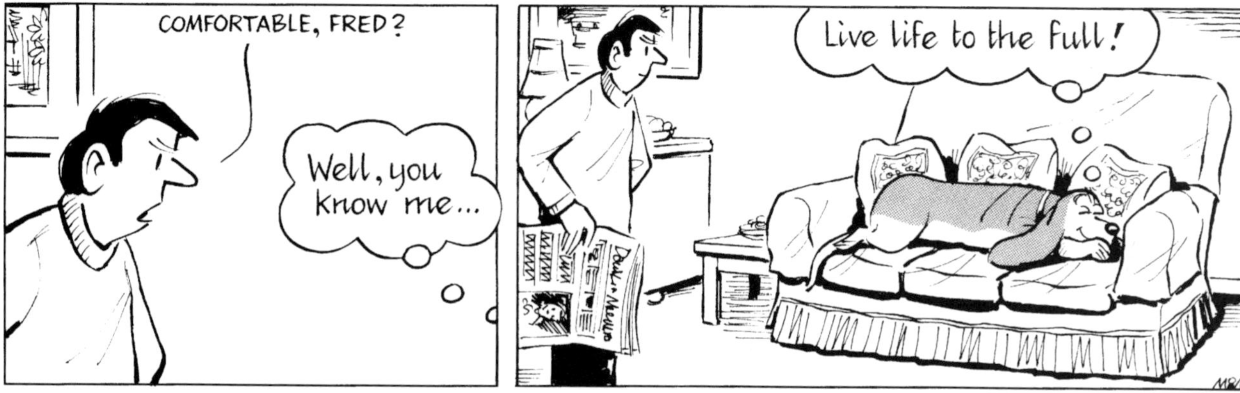
COMFORTABLE, FRED?
Well, you know me...
Live life to the full!

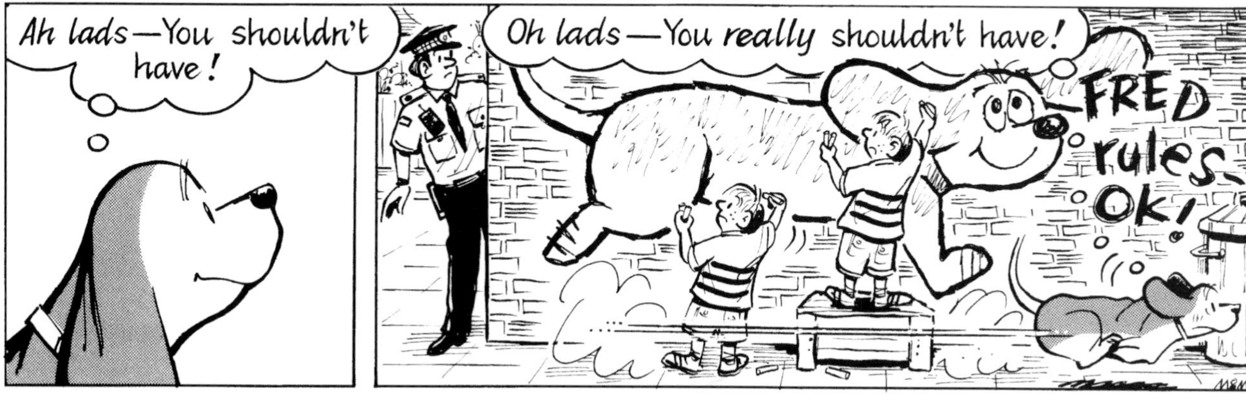
Ah lads—You shouldn't have!
Oh lads—You really shouldn't have!
FRED rules OK!

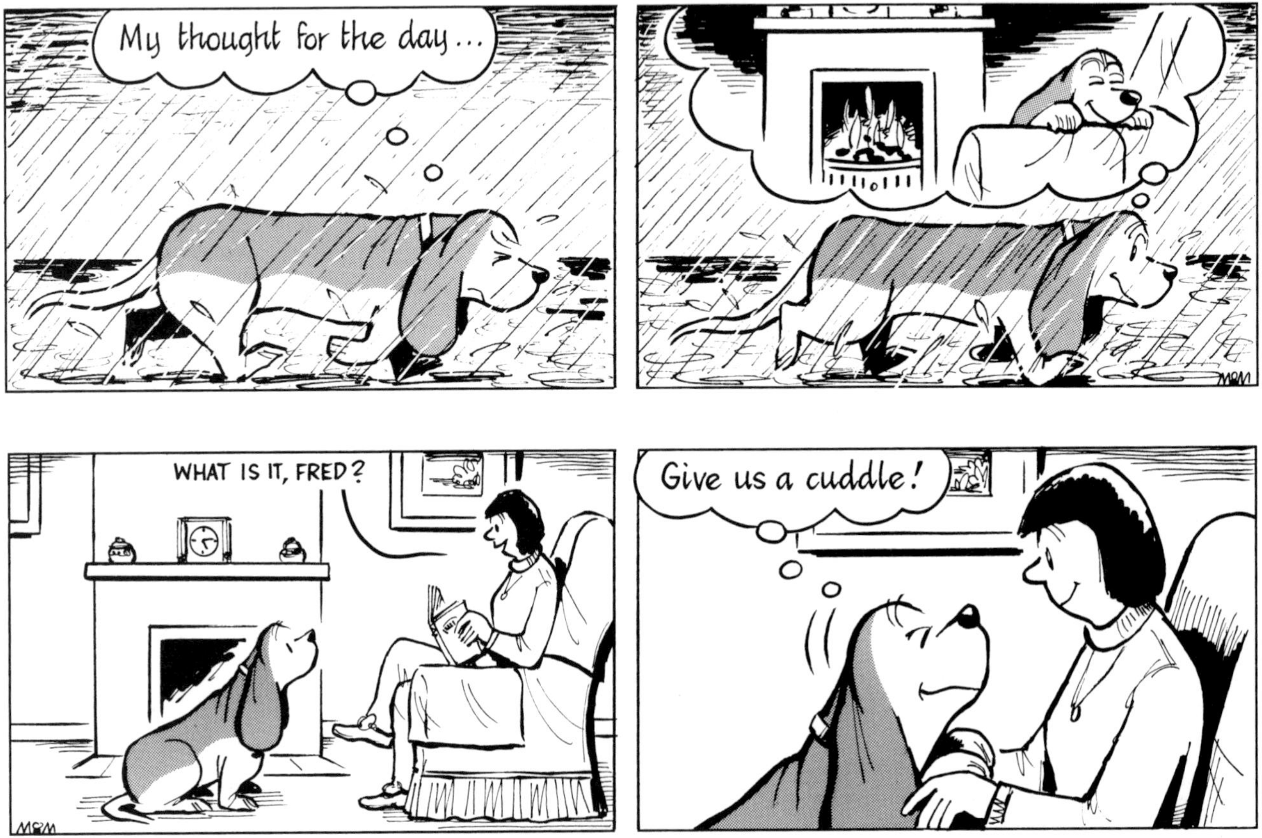
My thought for the day ...
WHAT IS IT, FRED?
Give us a cuddle!

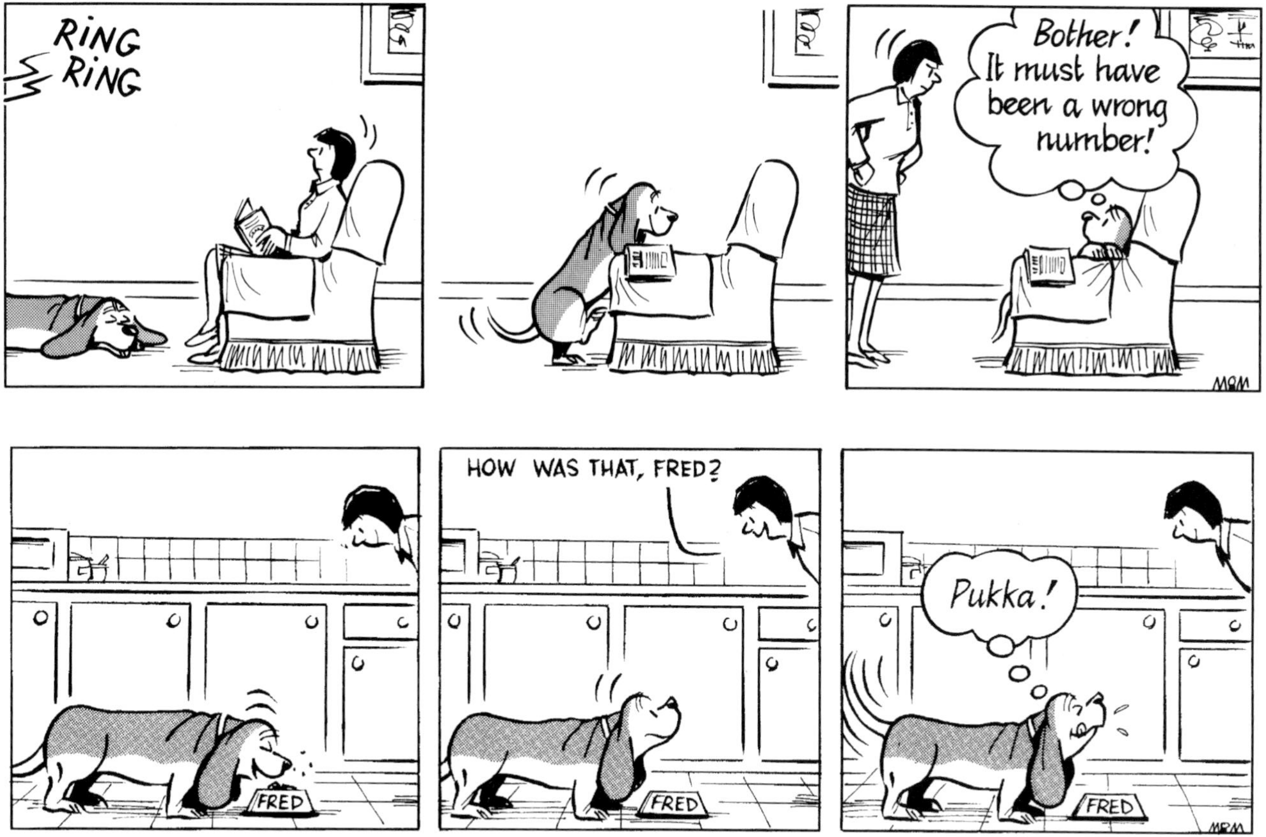
RING
RING
Bother! It must have been a wrong number!
MGM
HOW WAS THAT, FRED?
FRED
FRED
Pukka!
FRED
MGM

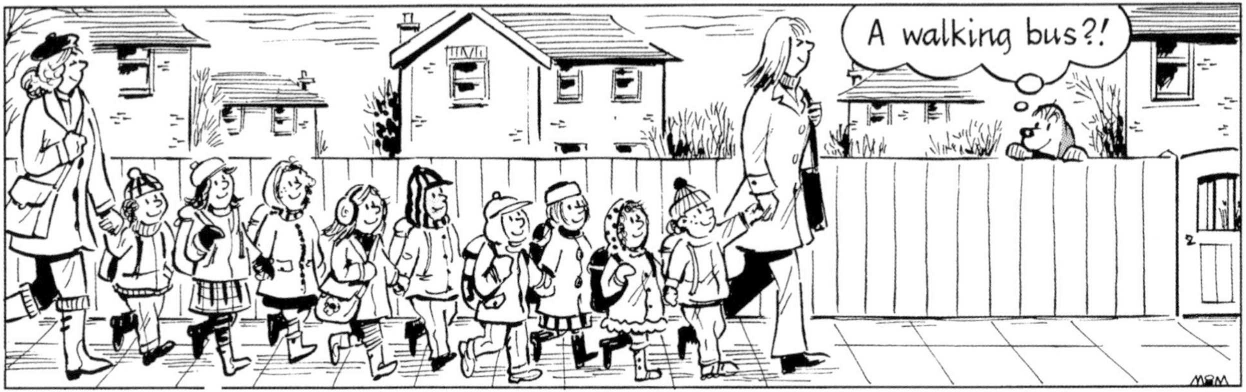
A walking bus?!

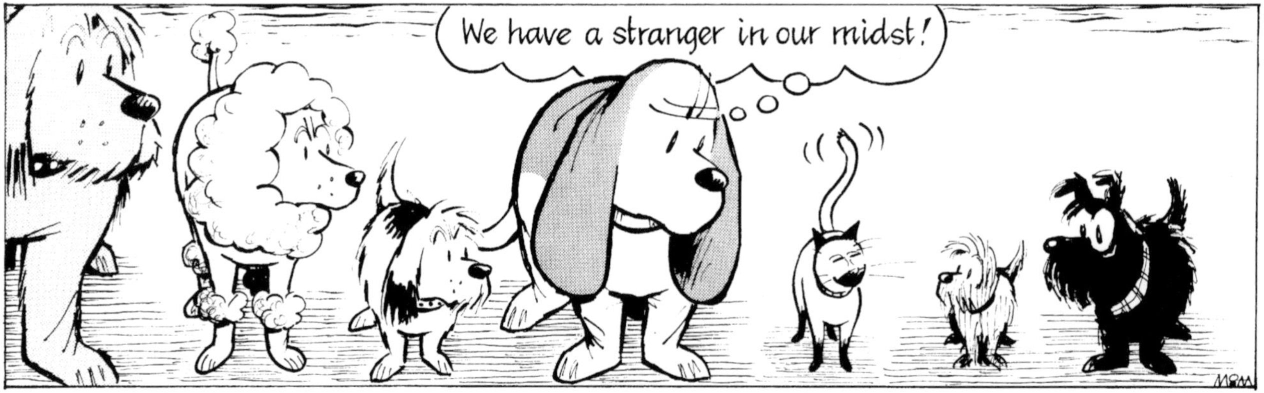
We have a stranger in our midst!

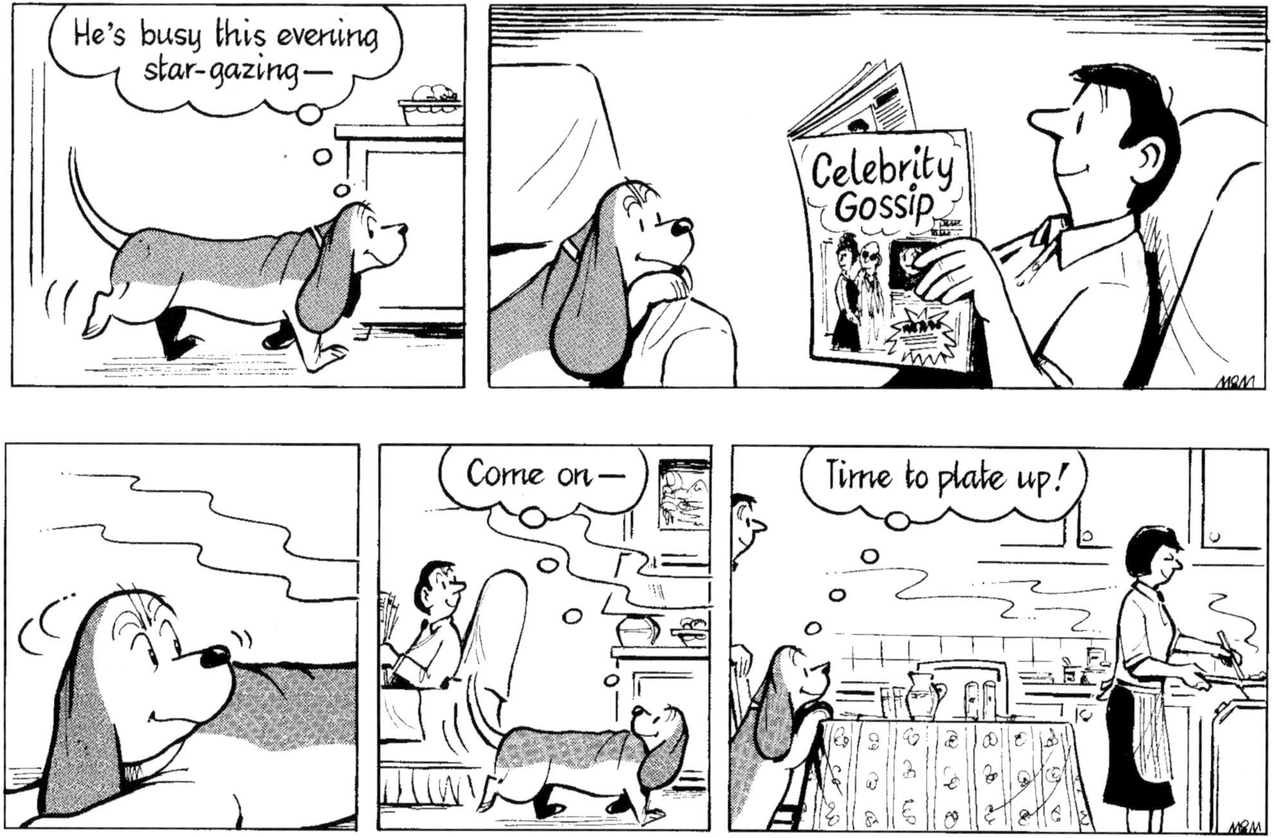
He's busy this evening star-gazing—
Celebrity Gossip
Come on—
Time to plate up!

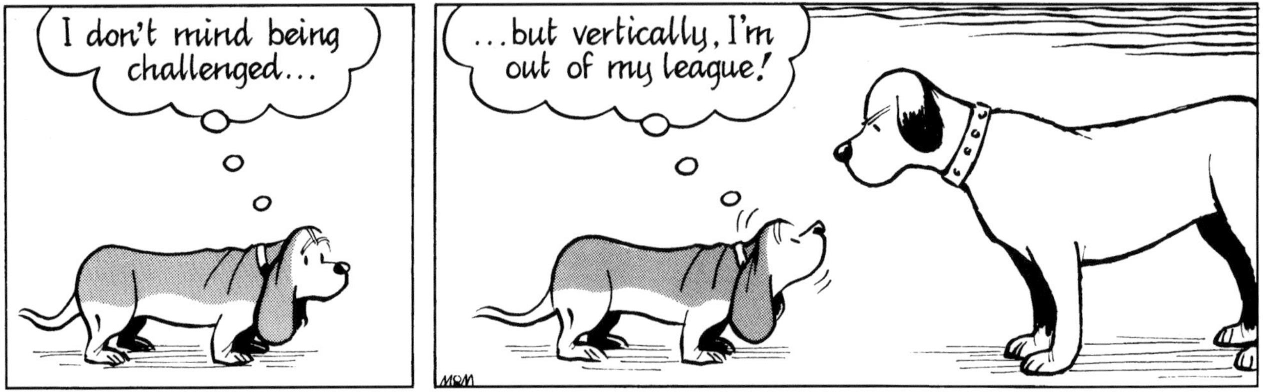
I don't mind being challenged...
...but vertically, I'm out of my league!
M&M

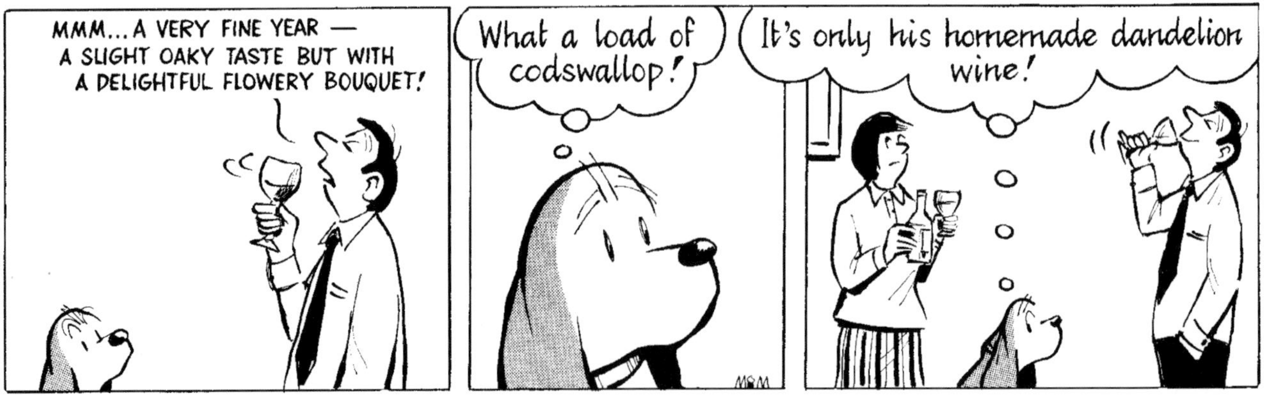
MMM... A VERY FINE YEAR — A SLIGHT OAKY TASTE BUT WITH A DELIGHTFUL FLOWERY BOUQUET!
What a load of codswallop!
M&M
It's only his homemade dandelion wine!

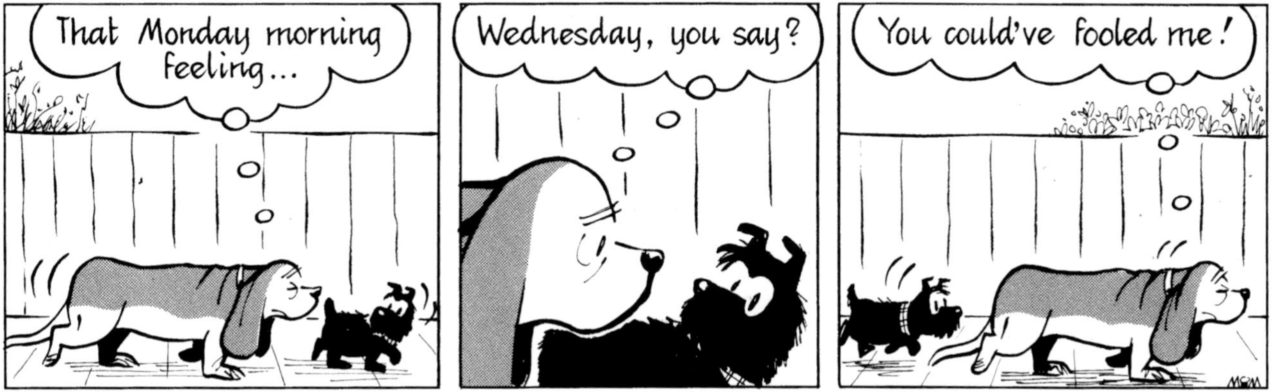

That Monday morning feeling...
Wednesday, you say?
You could've fooled me!
M&M

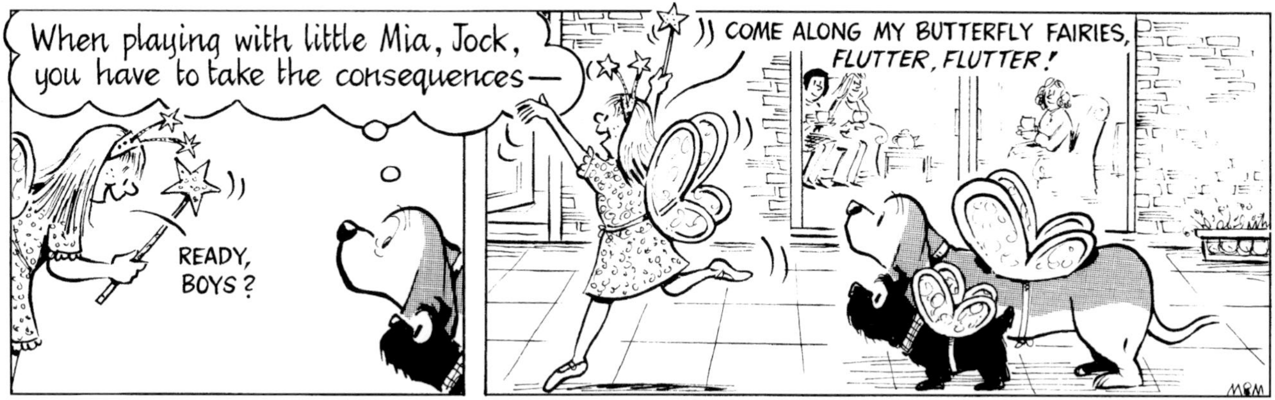

When playing with little Mia, Jock, you have to take the consequences—
READY, BOYS?
COME ALONG MY BUTTERFLY FAIRIES, FLUTTER, FLUTTER!
M&M

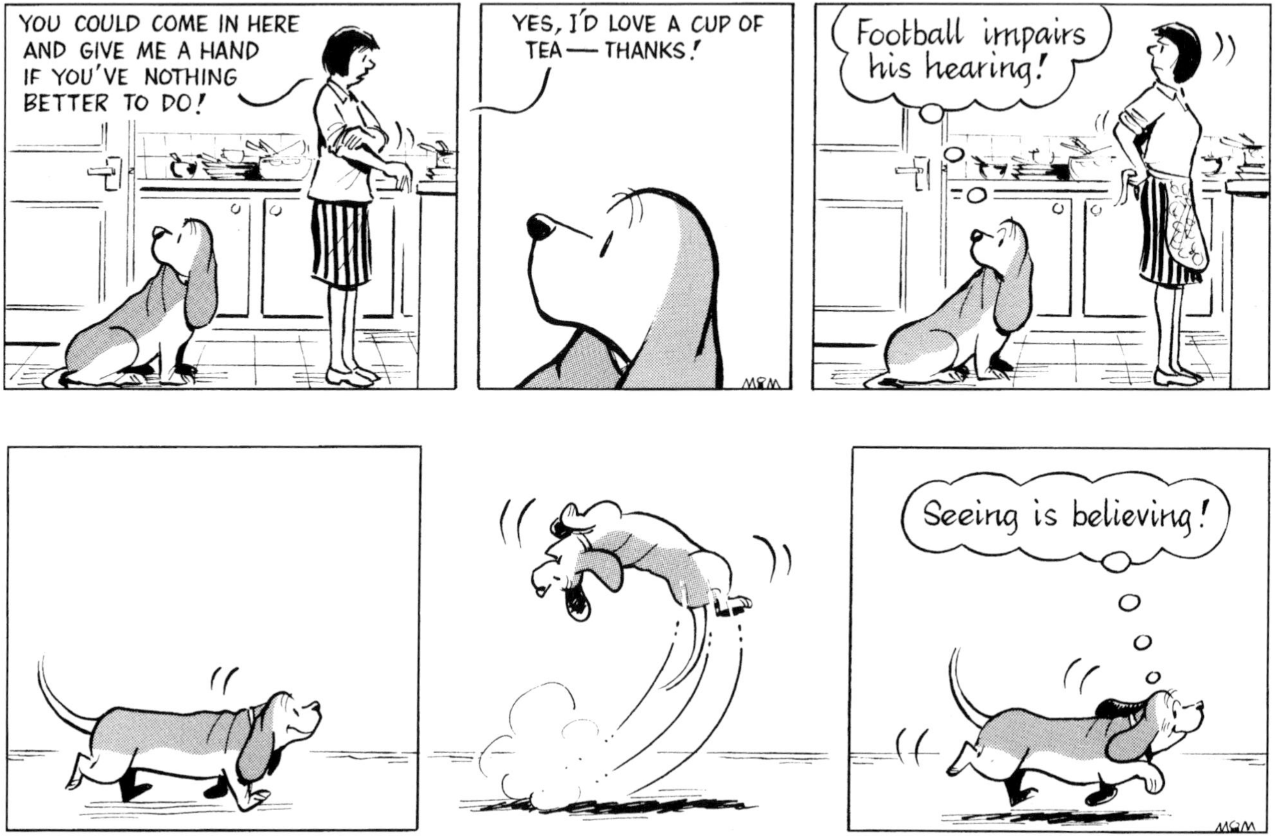
YOU COULD COME IN HERE AND GIVE ME A HAND IF YOU'VE NOTHING BETTER TO DO!
YES, I'D LOVE A CUP OF TEA — THANKS!
MGM
Football impairs his hearing!
Seeing is believing!
MGM

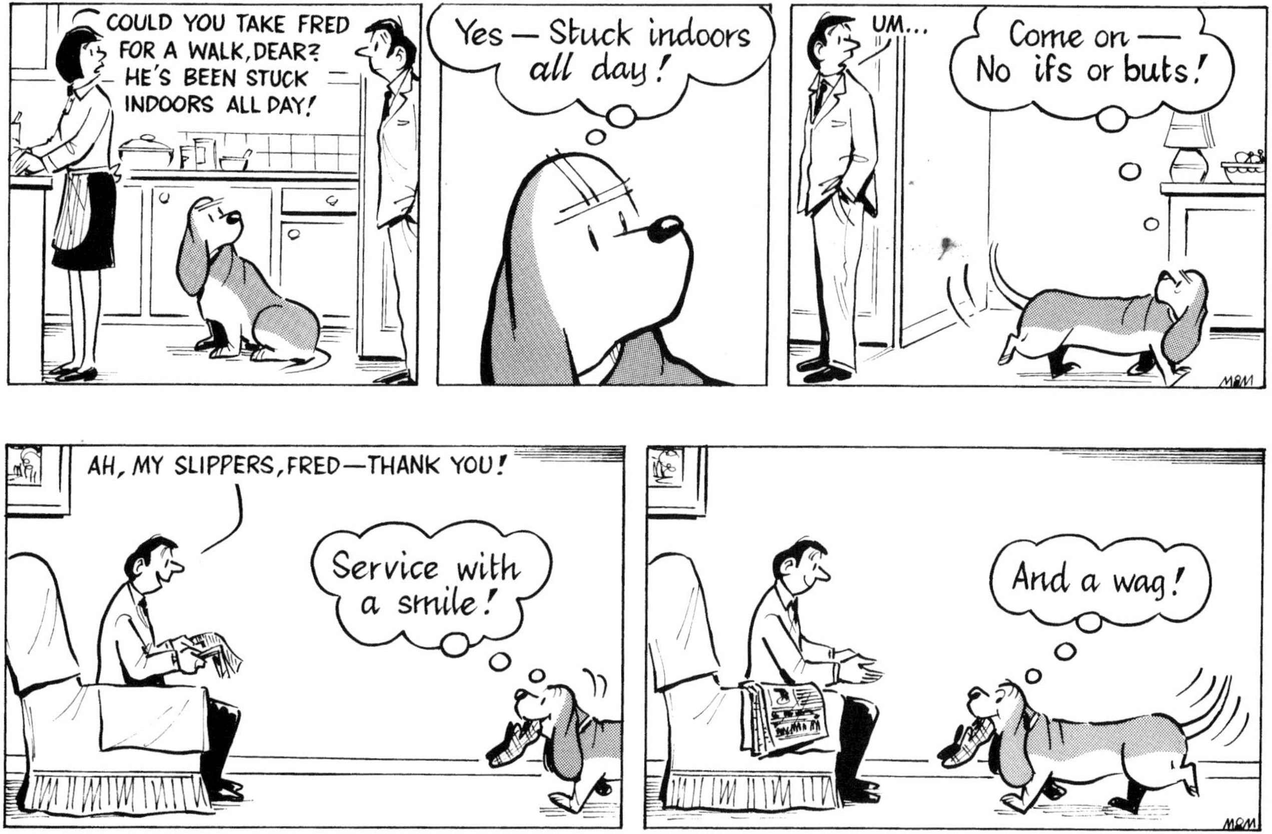
COULD YOU TAKE FRED FOR A WALK, DEAR? HE'S BEEN STUCK INDOORS ALL DAY!
Yes — Stuck indoors all day!
UM...
Come on — No ifs or buts!
MGM
AH, MY SLIPPERS, FRED—THANK YOU!
Service with a smile!
And a wag!
MGM

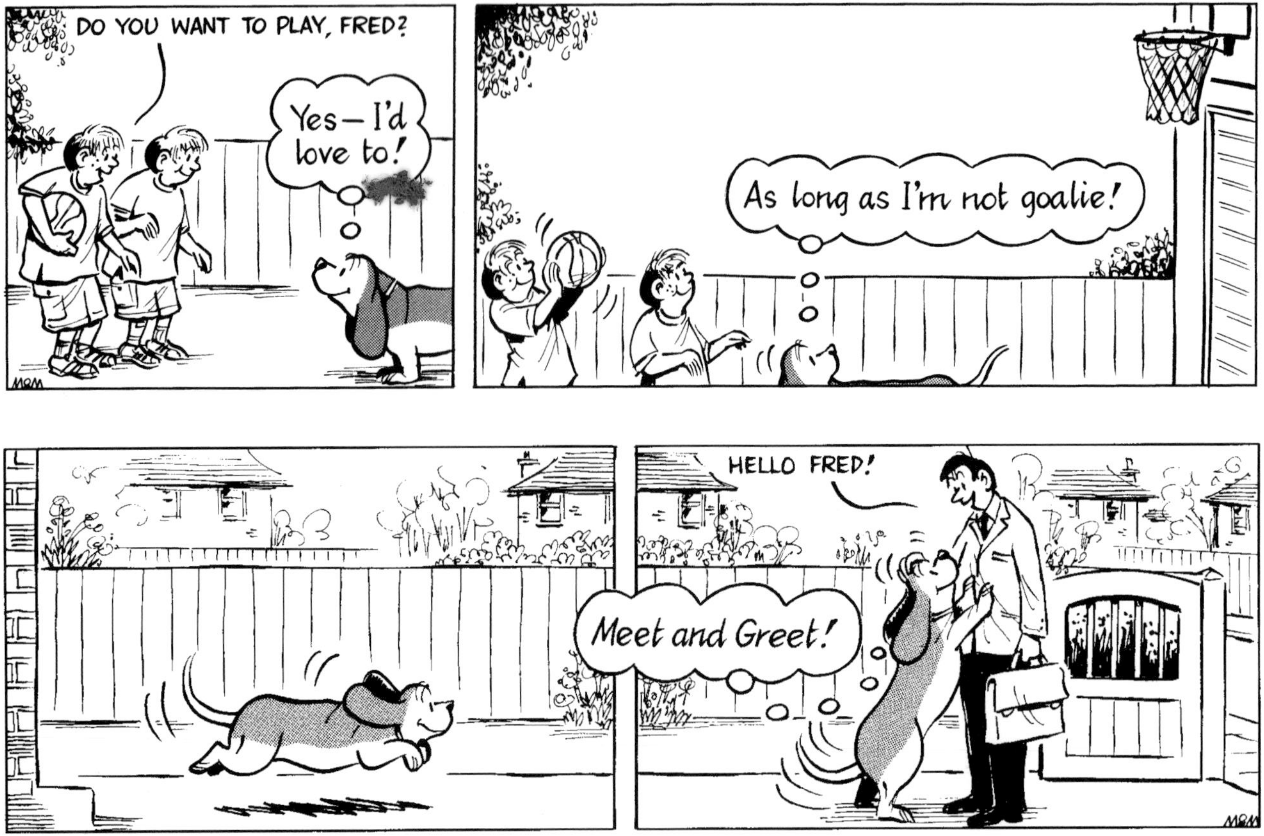
DO YOU WANT TO PLAY, FRED?
Yes — I'd love to!
As long as I'm not goalie!
HELLO FRED!
Meet and Greet!

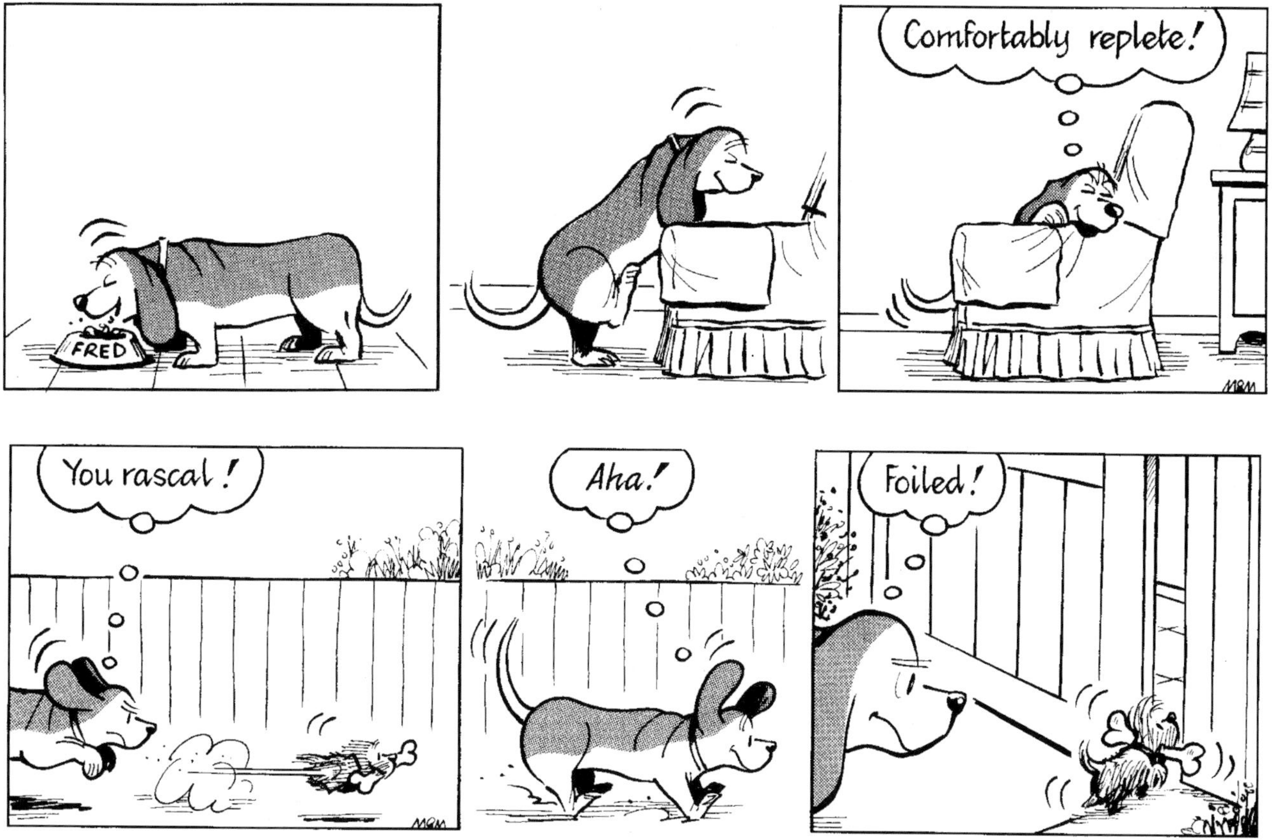
FRED
Comfortably replete!
MGM
You rascal!
MGM
Aha!
Foiled!

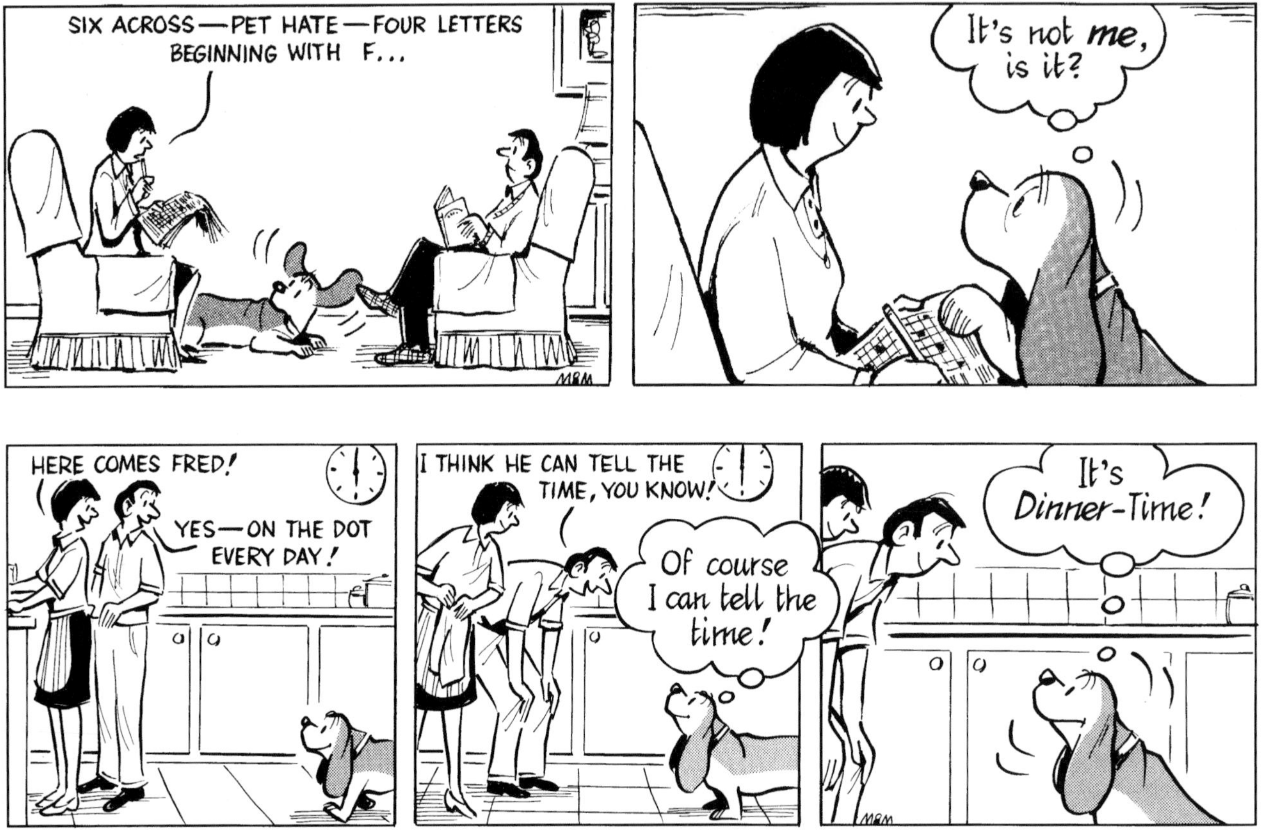
SIX ACROSS—PET HATE—FOUR LETTERS BEGINNING WITH F...
MBM
It's not *me*, is it?
HERE COMES FRED!
YES—ON THE DOT EVERY DAY!
I THINK HE CAN TELL THE TIME, YOU KNOW!
Of course I can tell the time!
It's Dinner-Time!
MBM

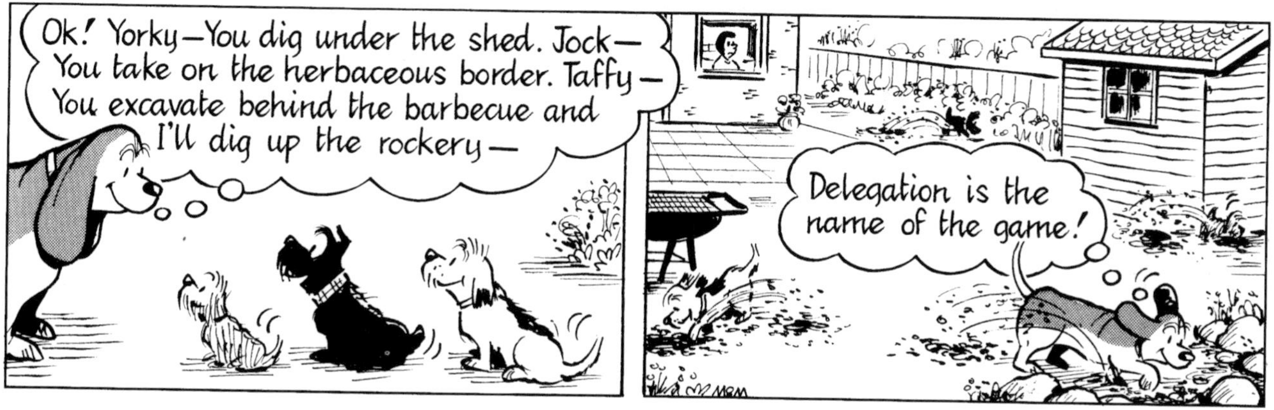
Ok! Yorky—You dig under the shed. Jock—You take on the herbaceous border. Taffy—You excavate behind the barbecue and I'll dig up the rockery—
Delegation is the name of the game!

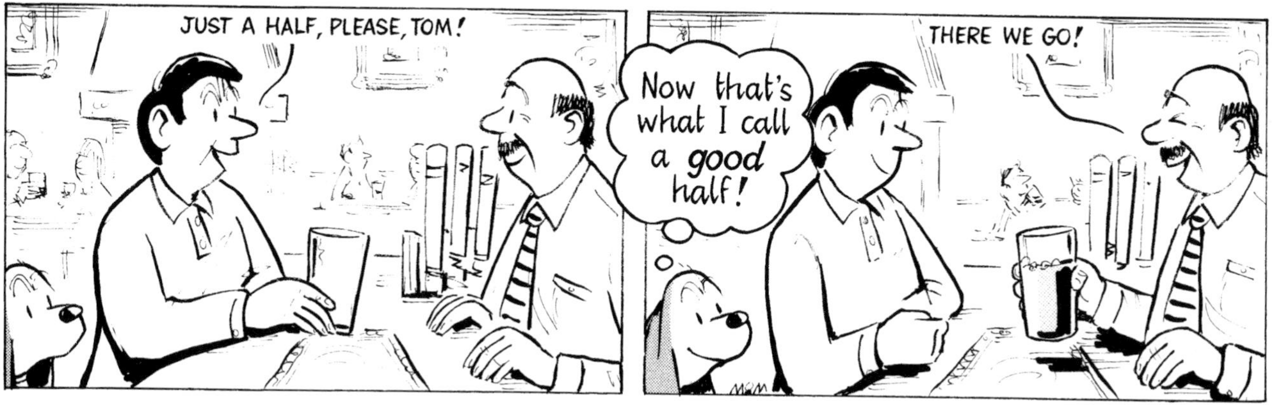
JUST A HALF, PLEASE, TOM!
THERE WE GO!
Now that's what I call a **good** half!

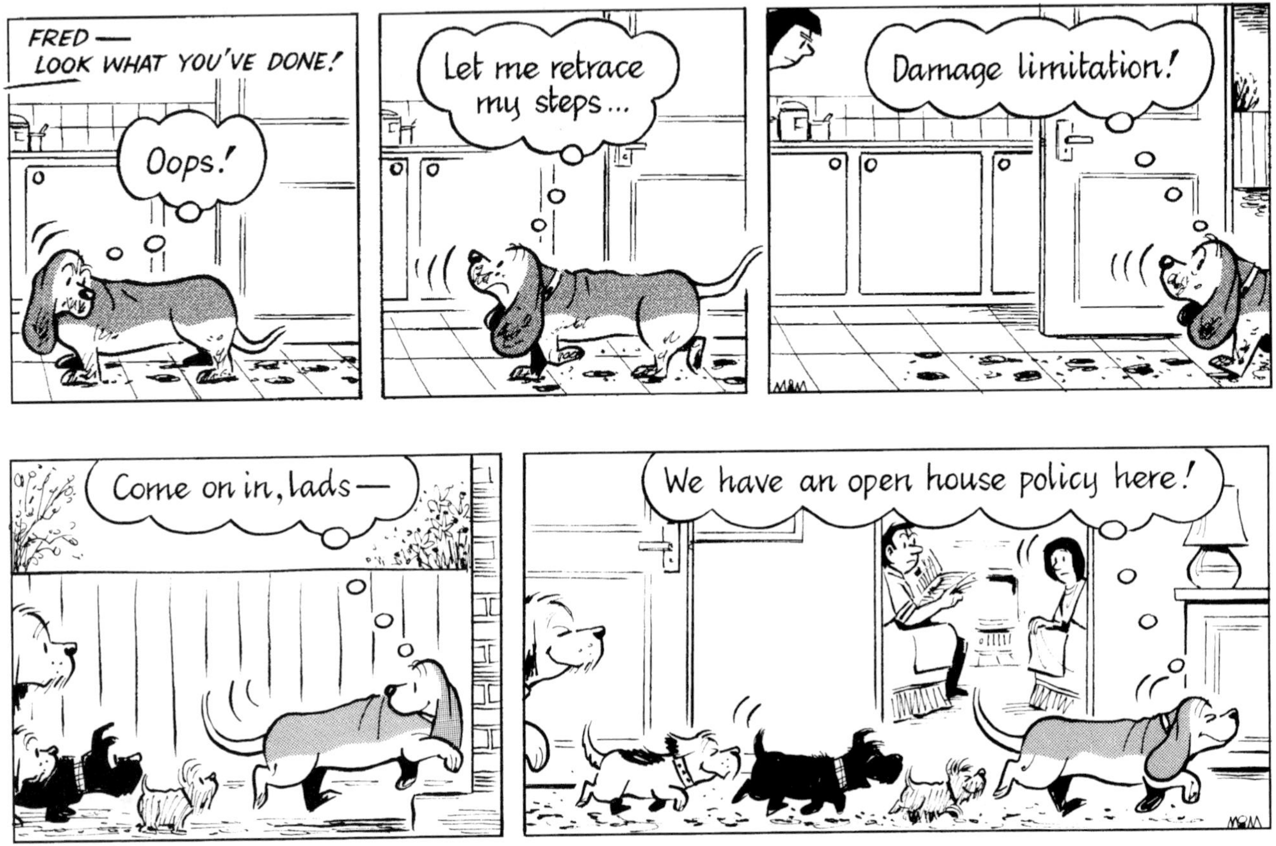
FRED —
LOOK WHAT YOU'VE DONE!
Oops!
Let me retrace my steps...
Damage limitation!
M&M
Come on in, lads —
We have an open house policy here!
M&M

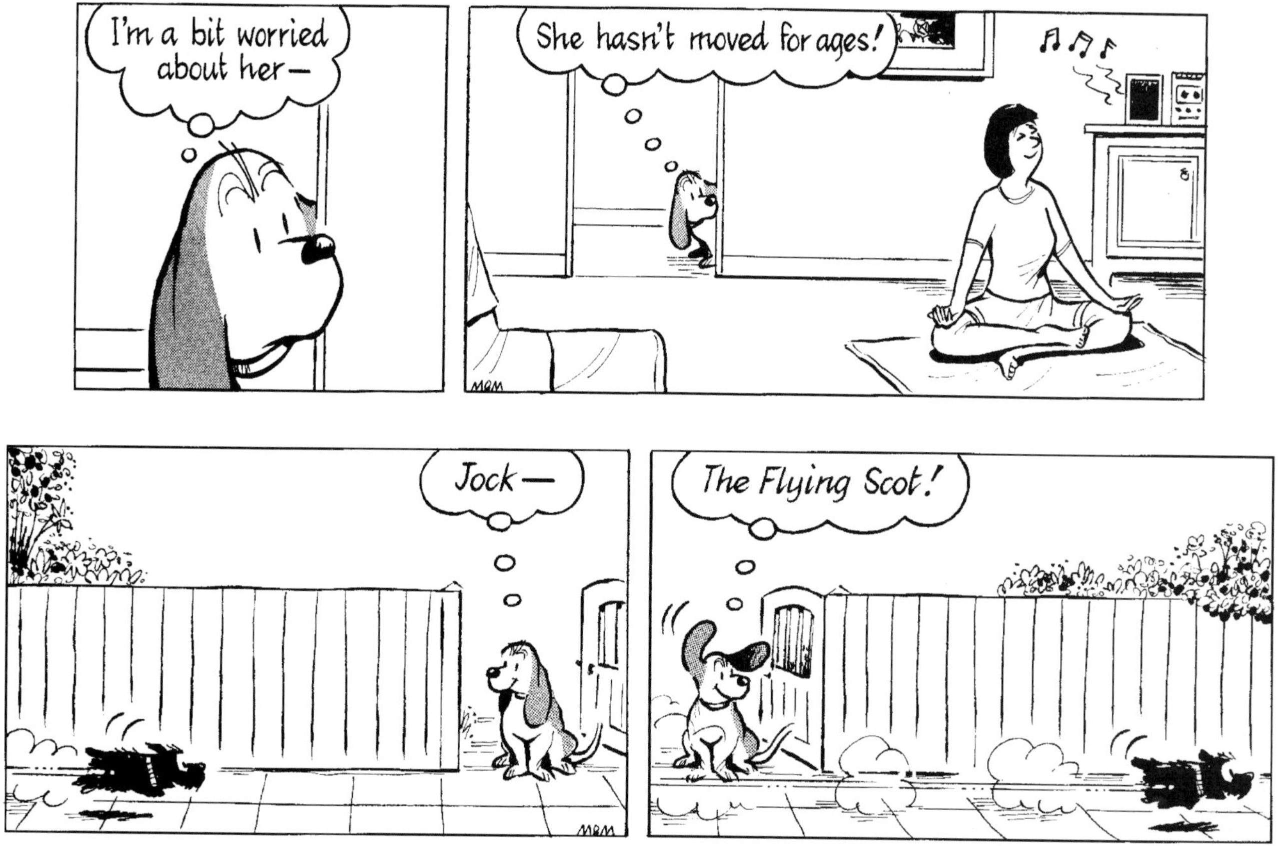

I'm a bit worried about her—
She hasn't moved for ages!
Jock—
The Flying Scot!

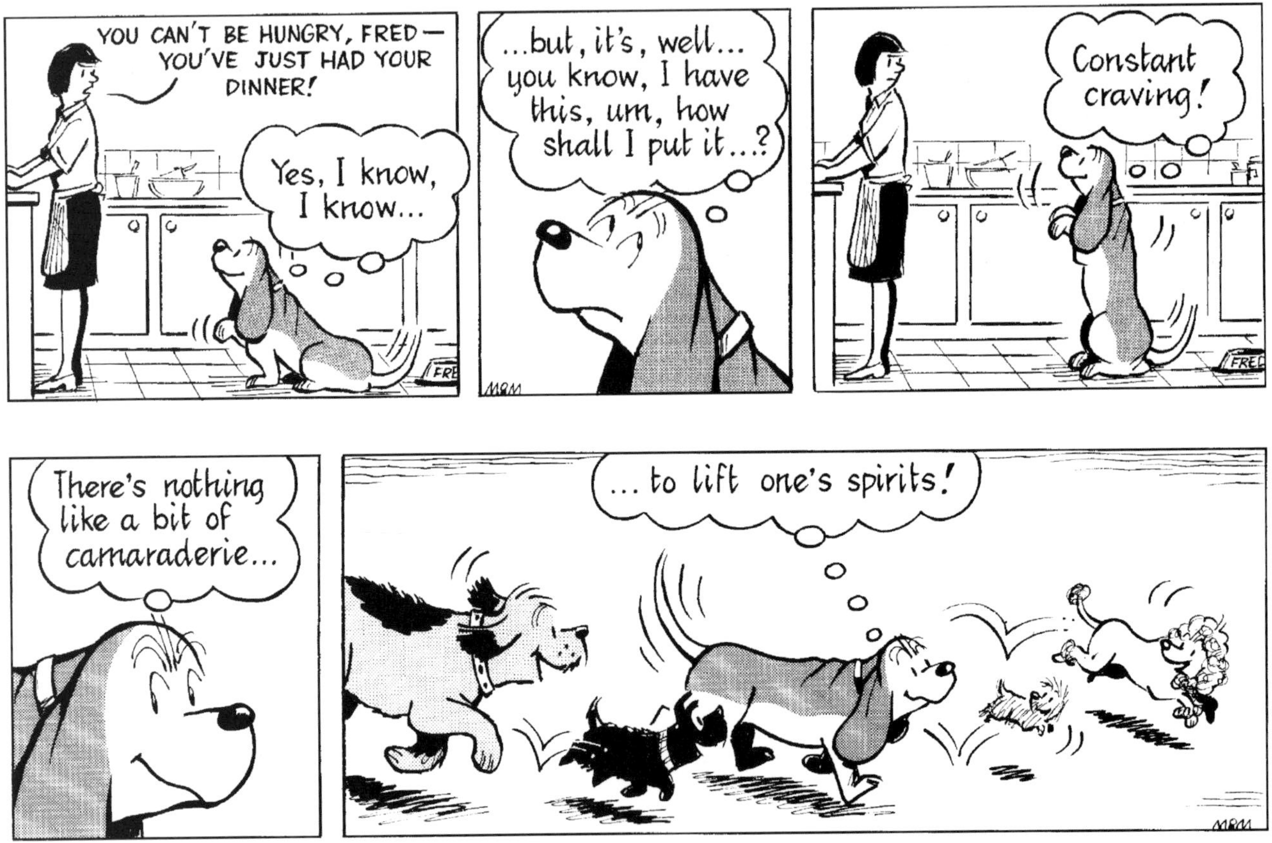
YOU CAN'T BE HUNGRY, FRED— YOU'VE JUST HAD YOUR DINNER!
Yes, I know, I know...
FRED
...but, it's, well... you know, I have this, um, how shall I put it...?
MSM
Constant craving!
FRED
There's nothing like a bit of camaraderie...
... to lift one's spirits!
MSM

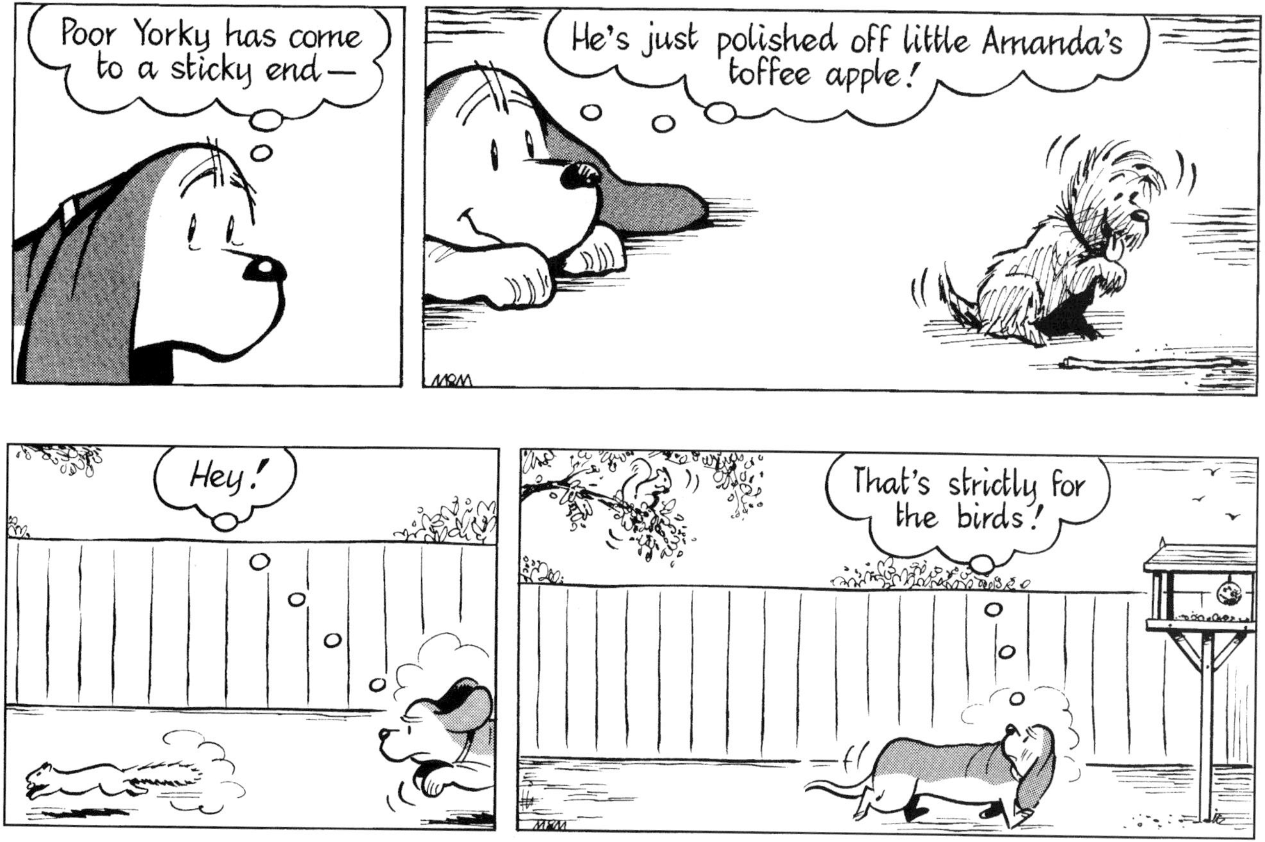
Poor Yorky has come to a sticky end—
He's just polished off little Amanda's toffee apple!
MRM
Hey!
That's strictly for the birds!
MRM

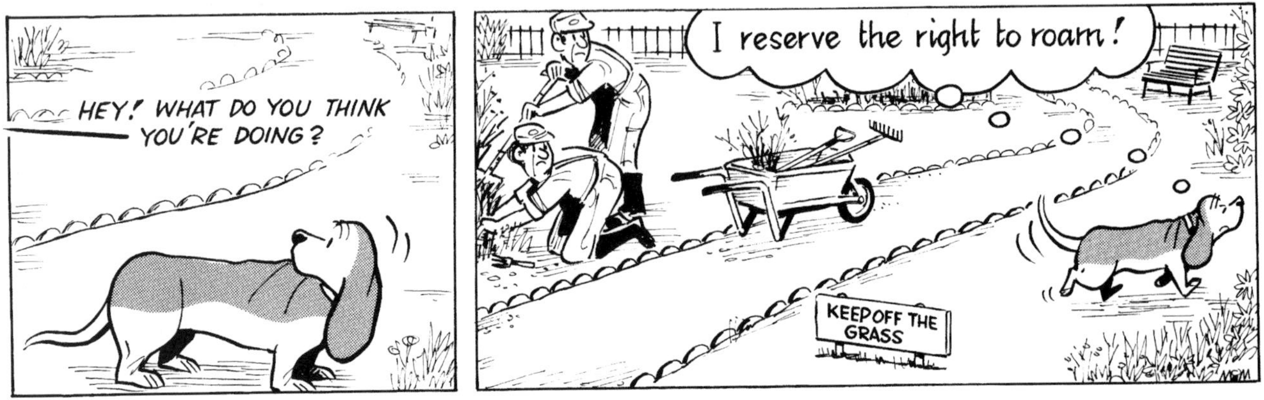
HEY! WHAT DO YOU THINK YOU'RE DOING?
I reserve the right to roam!
KEEP OFF THE GRASS

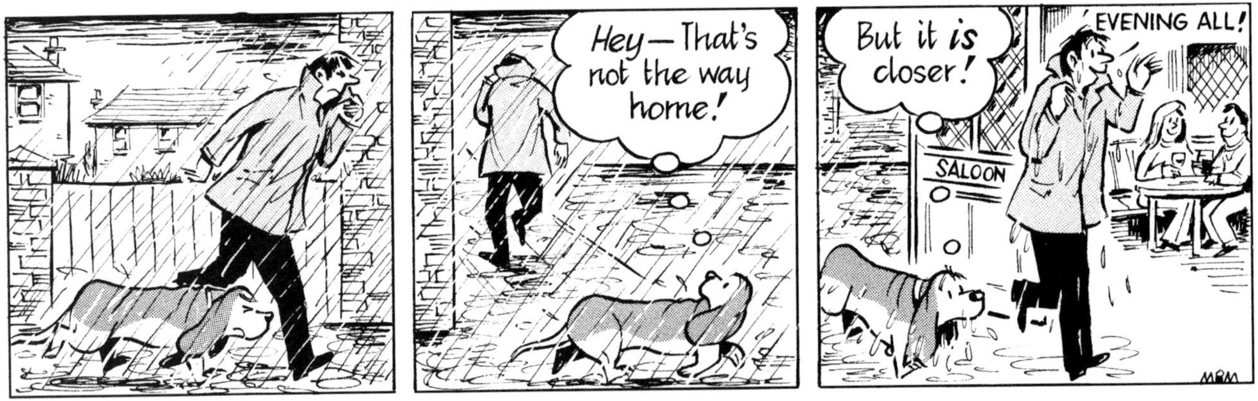
Hey—That's not the way home!
But it *is* closer!
SALOON
'EVENING ALL!

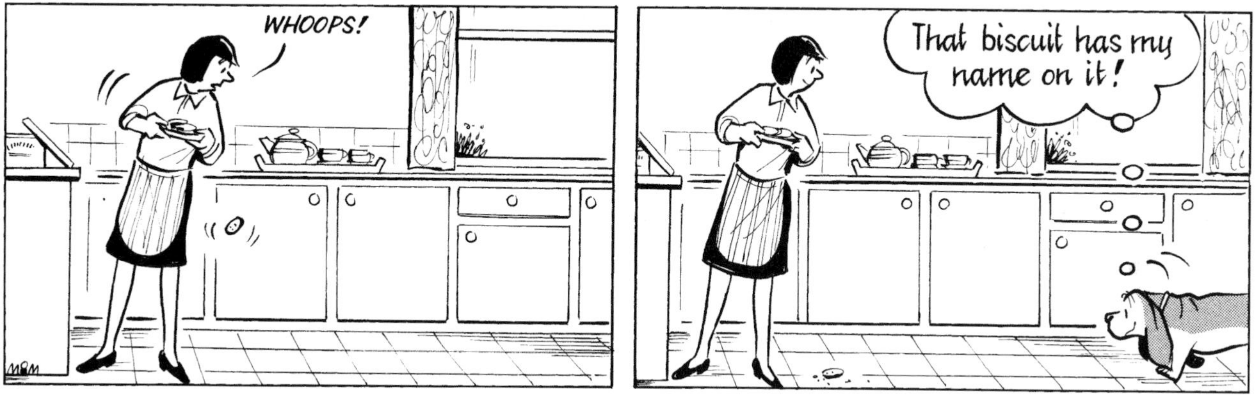
WHOOPS!
That biscuit has my name on it!

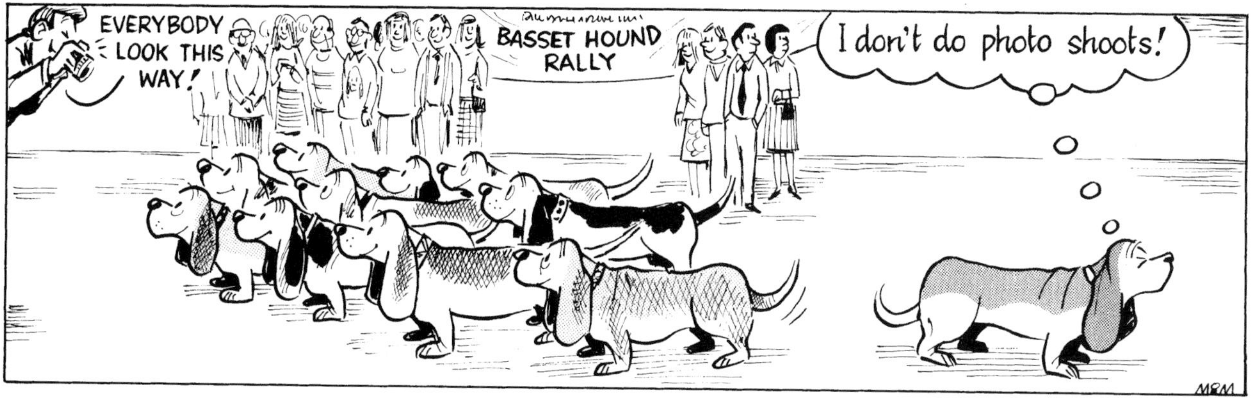
EVERYBODY LOOK THIS WAY!
BASSET HOUND RALLY
I don't do photo shoots!

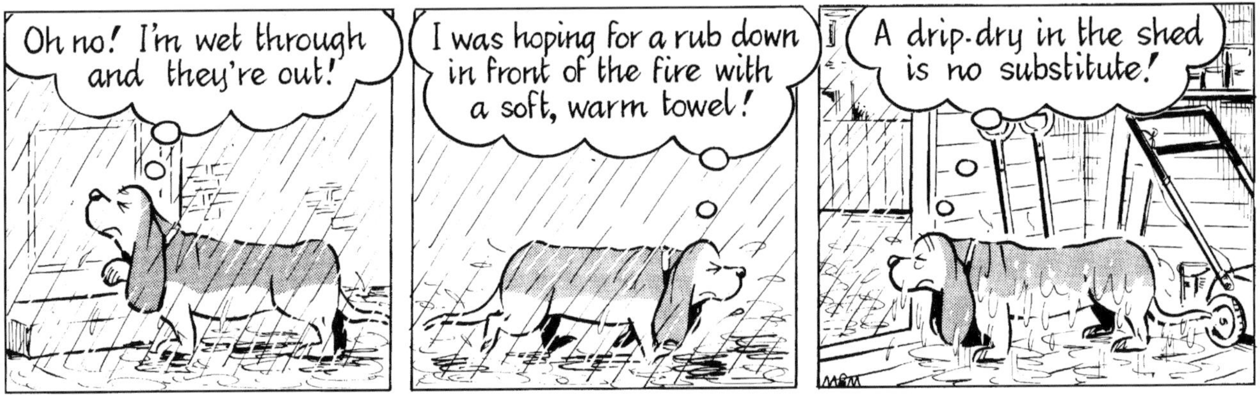
Oh no! I'm wet through and they're out!
I was hoping for a rub down in front of the fire with a soft, warm towel!
A drip-dry in the shed is no substitute!
M&M

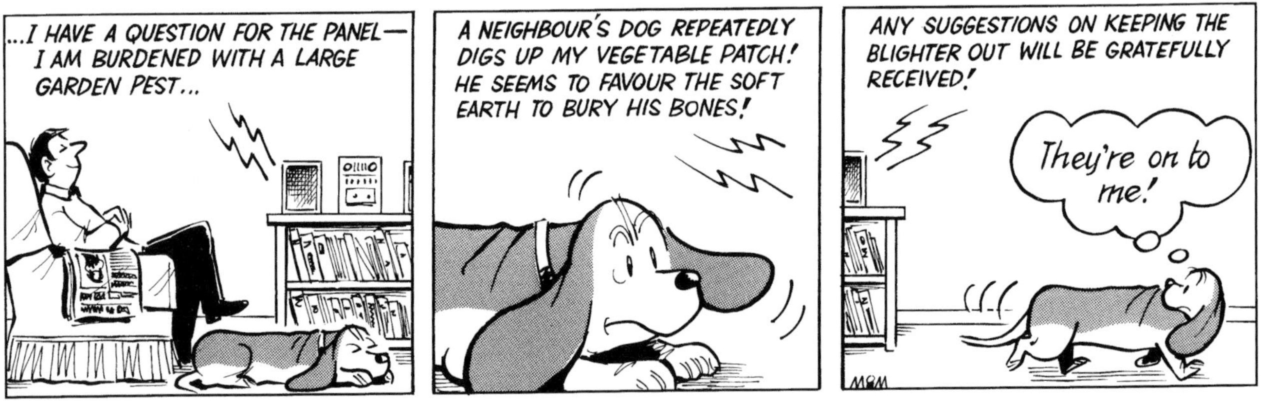
...I HAVE A QUESTION FOR THE PANEL— I AM BURDENED WITH A LARGE GARDEN PEST...
A NEIGHBOUR'S DOG REPEATEDLY DIGS UP MY VEGETABLE PATCH! HE SEEMS TO FAVOUR THE SOFT EARTH TO BURY HIS BONES!
ANY SUGGESTIONS ON KEEPING THE BLIGHTER OUT WILL BE GRATEFULLY RECEIVED!
They're on to me!
M&M

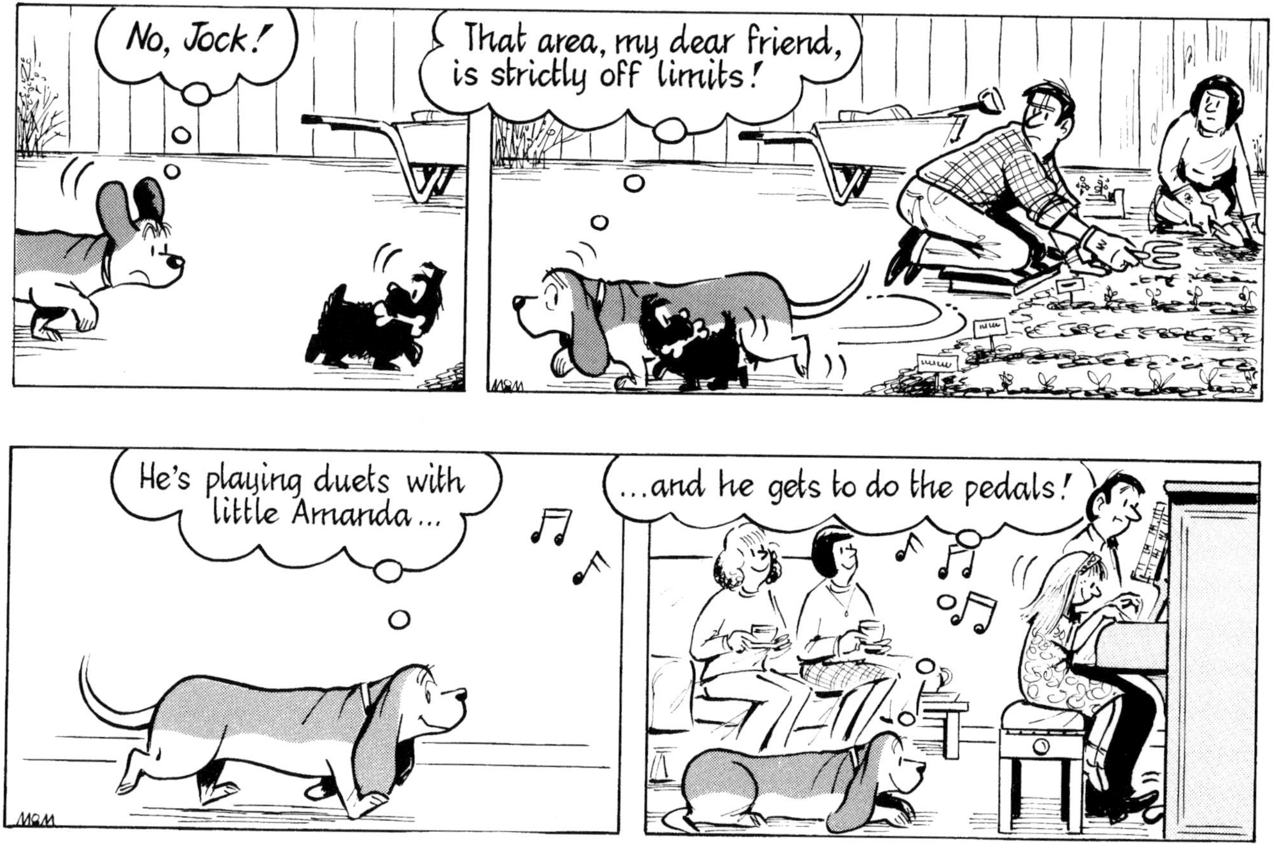
No, Jock!
That area, my dear friend, is strictly off limits!
He's playing duets with little Amanda...
...and he gets to do the pedals!

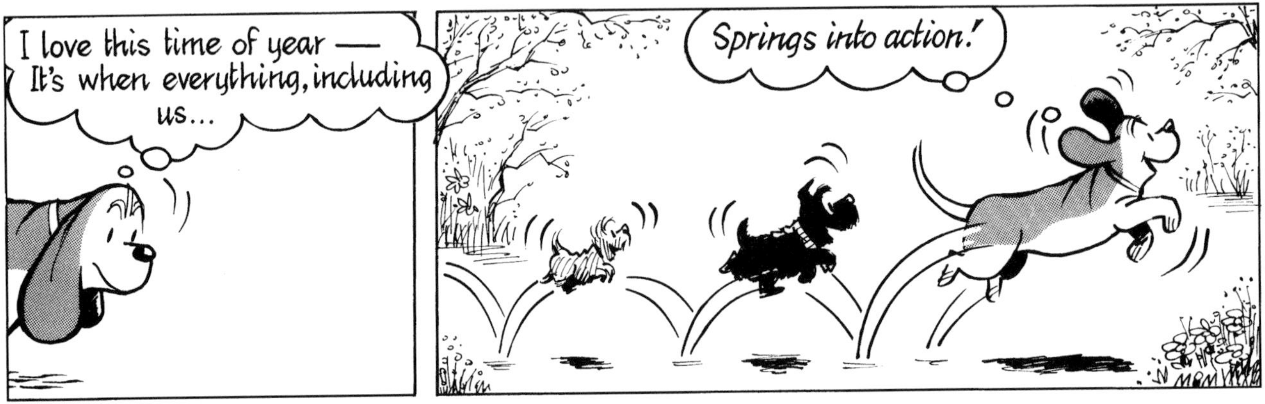
I love this time of year — It's when everything, including us...
Springs into action!

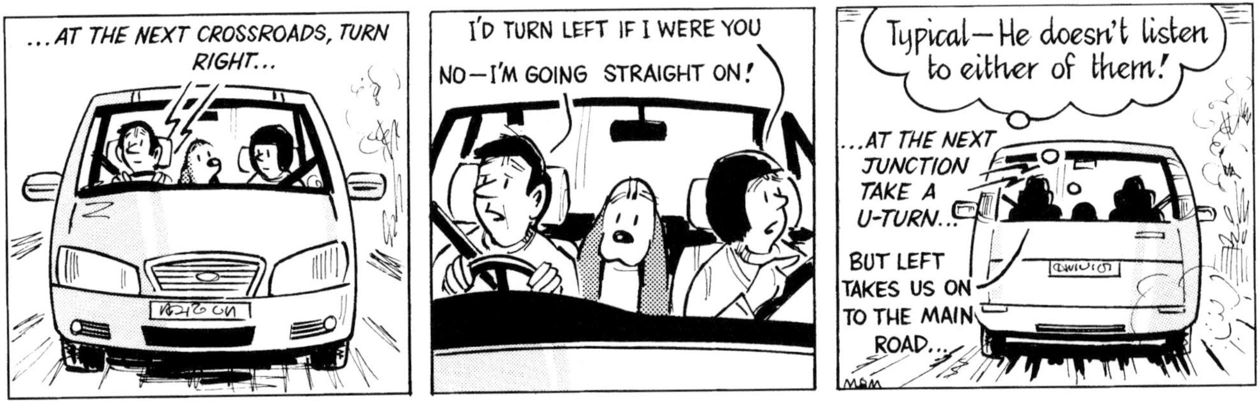
...AT THE NEXT CROSSROADS, TURN RIGHT...
I'D TURN LEFT IF I WERE YOU
NO—I'M GOING STRAIGHT ON!
Typical—He doesn't listen to either of them!
...AT THE NEXT JUNCTION TAKE A U-TURN...
BUT LEFT TAKES US ON TO THE MAIN ROAD...

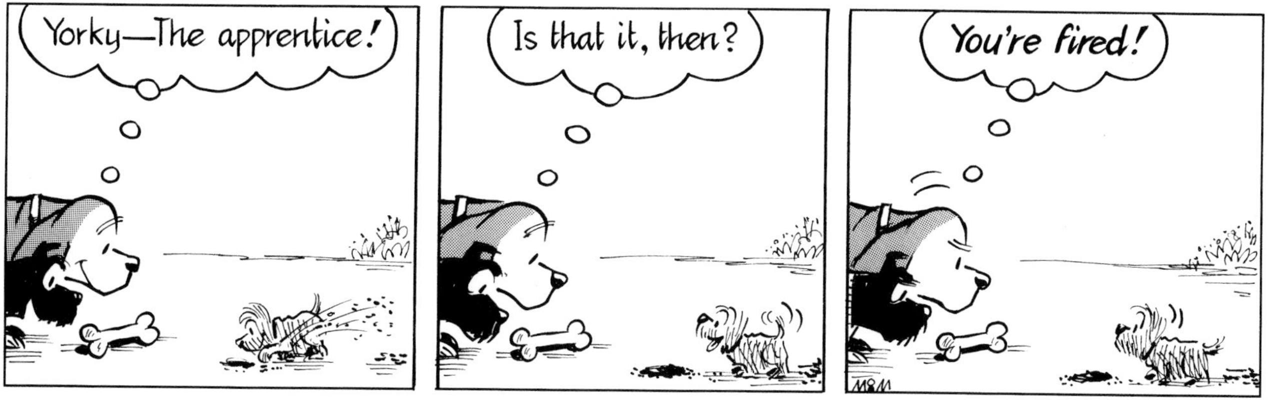
Yorky—The apprentice!
Is that it, then?
You're fired!
M&M

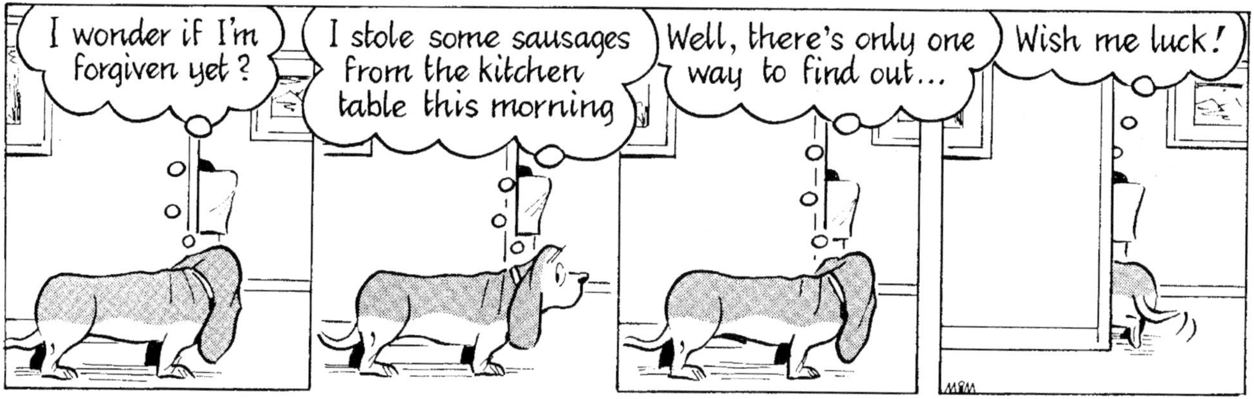
I wonder if I'm forgiven yet?
I stole some sausages from the kitchen table this morning
Well, there's only one way to find out...
Wish me luck!
M&M

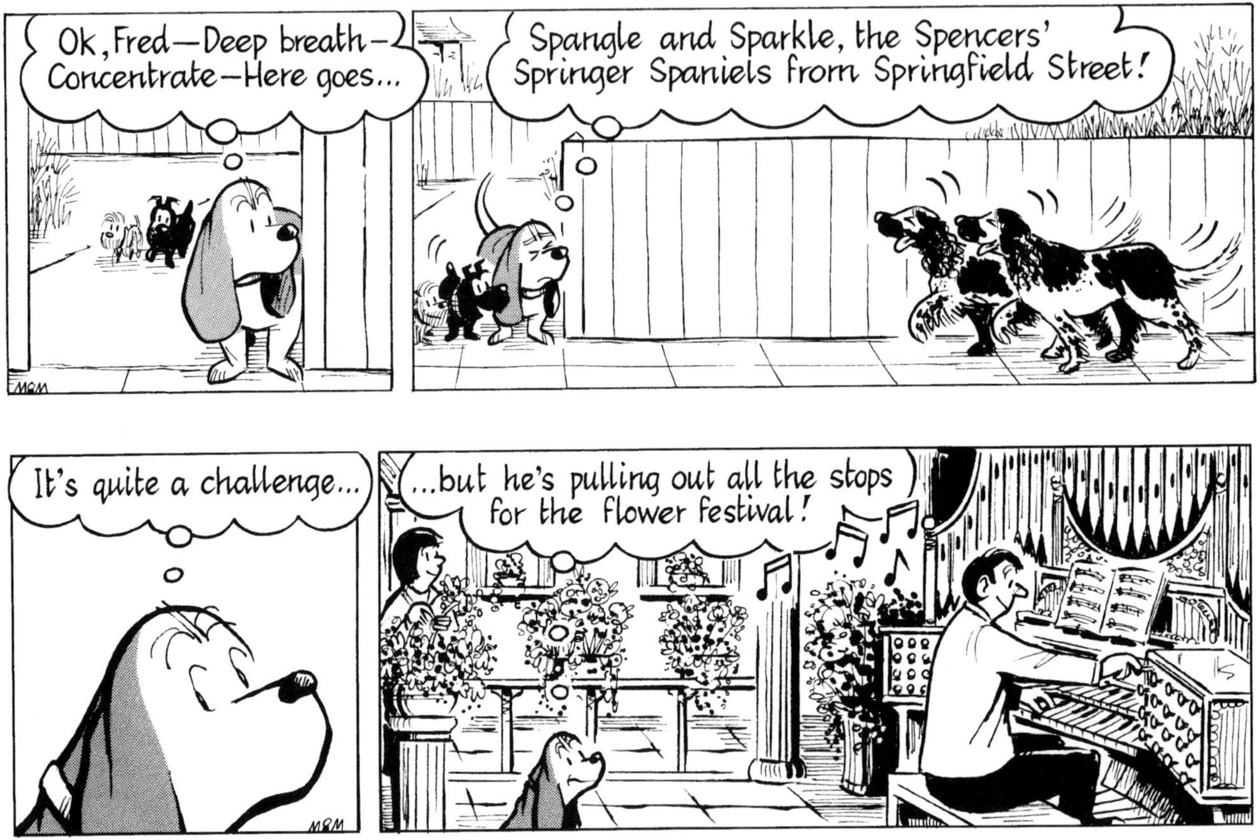
Ok, Fred—Deep breath—
Concentrate—Here goes...
Spangle and Sparkle, the Spencers' Springer Spaniels from Springfield Street!
It's quite a challenge...
...but he's pulling out all the stops for the flower festival!

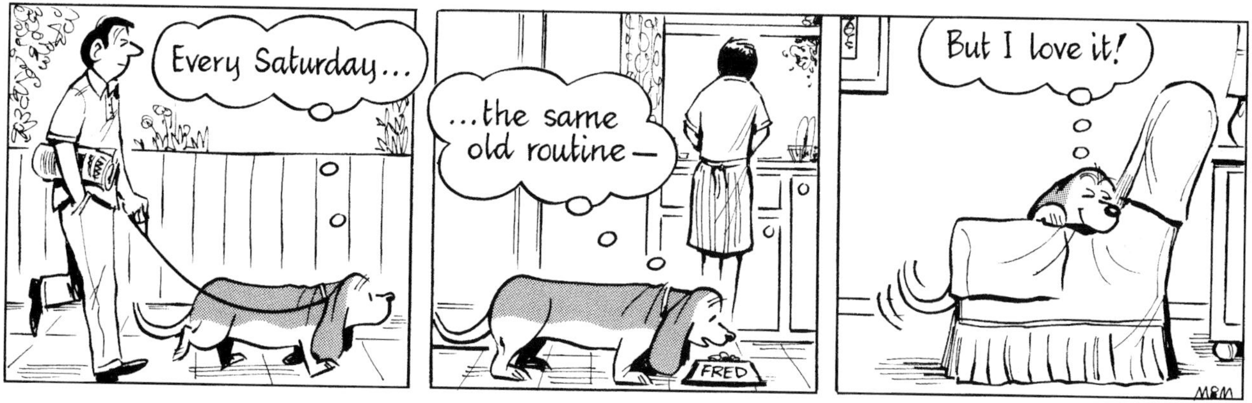
Every Saturday...
...the same old routine—
FRED
But I love it!

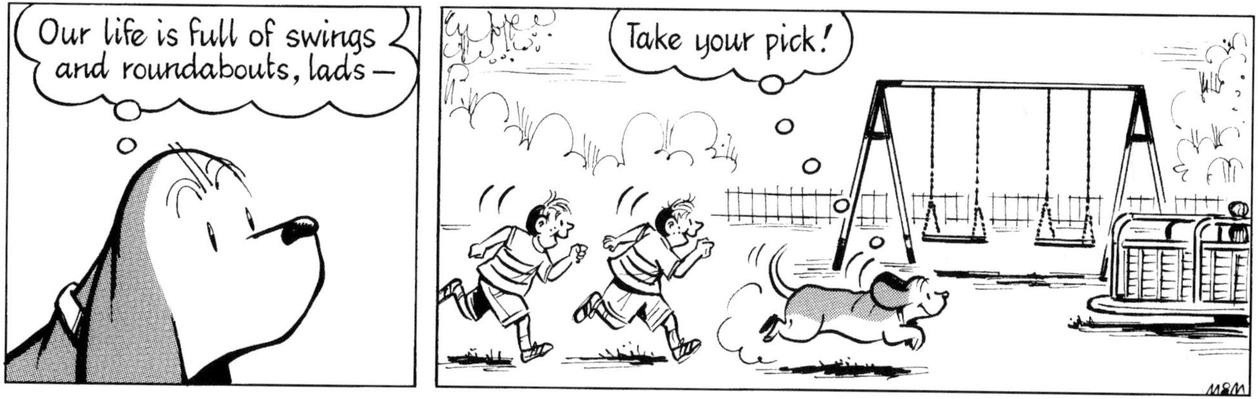
Our life is full of swings and roundabouts, lads—
Take your pick!

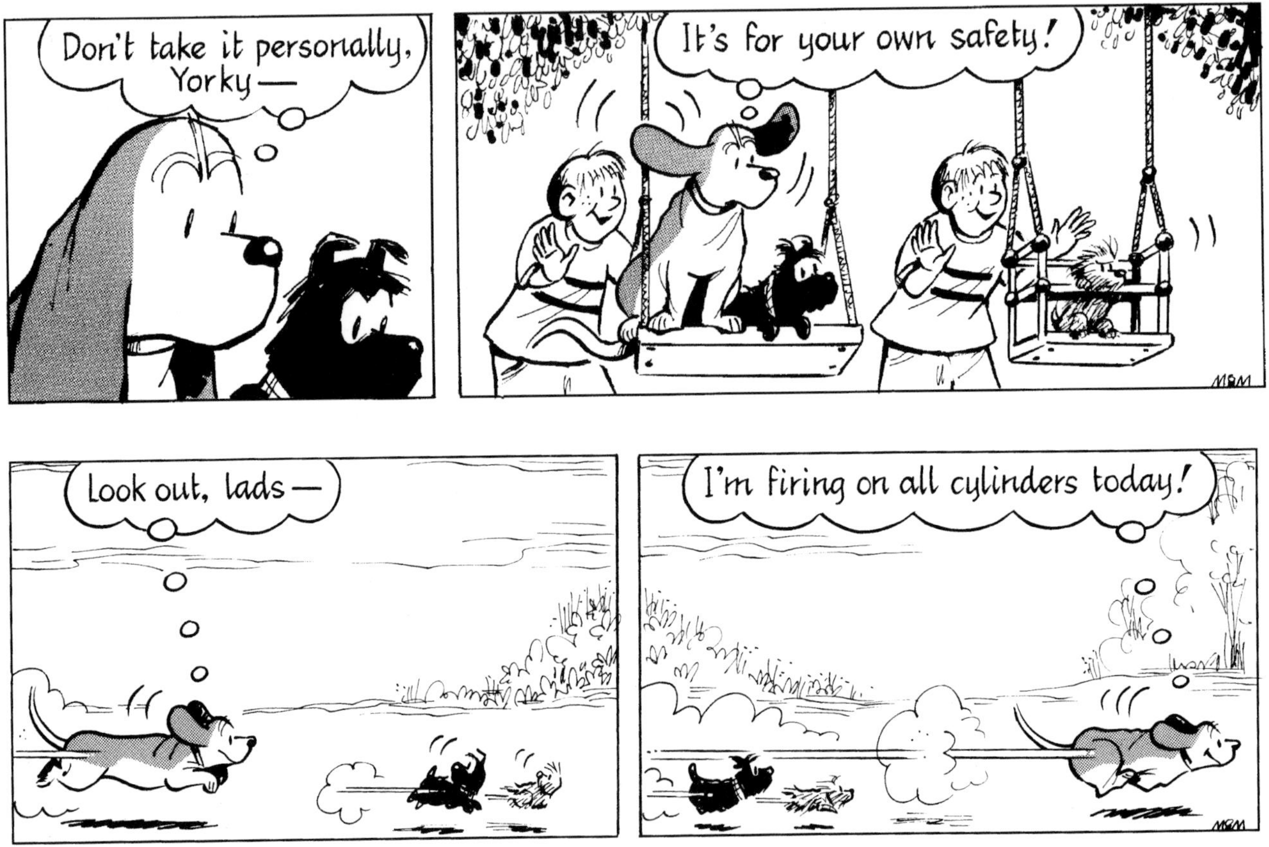
Don't take it personally, Yorky—
It's for your own safety!
Look out, lads—
I'm firing on all cylinders today!

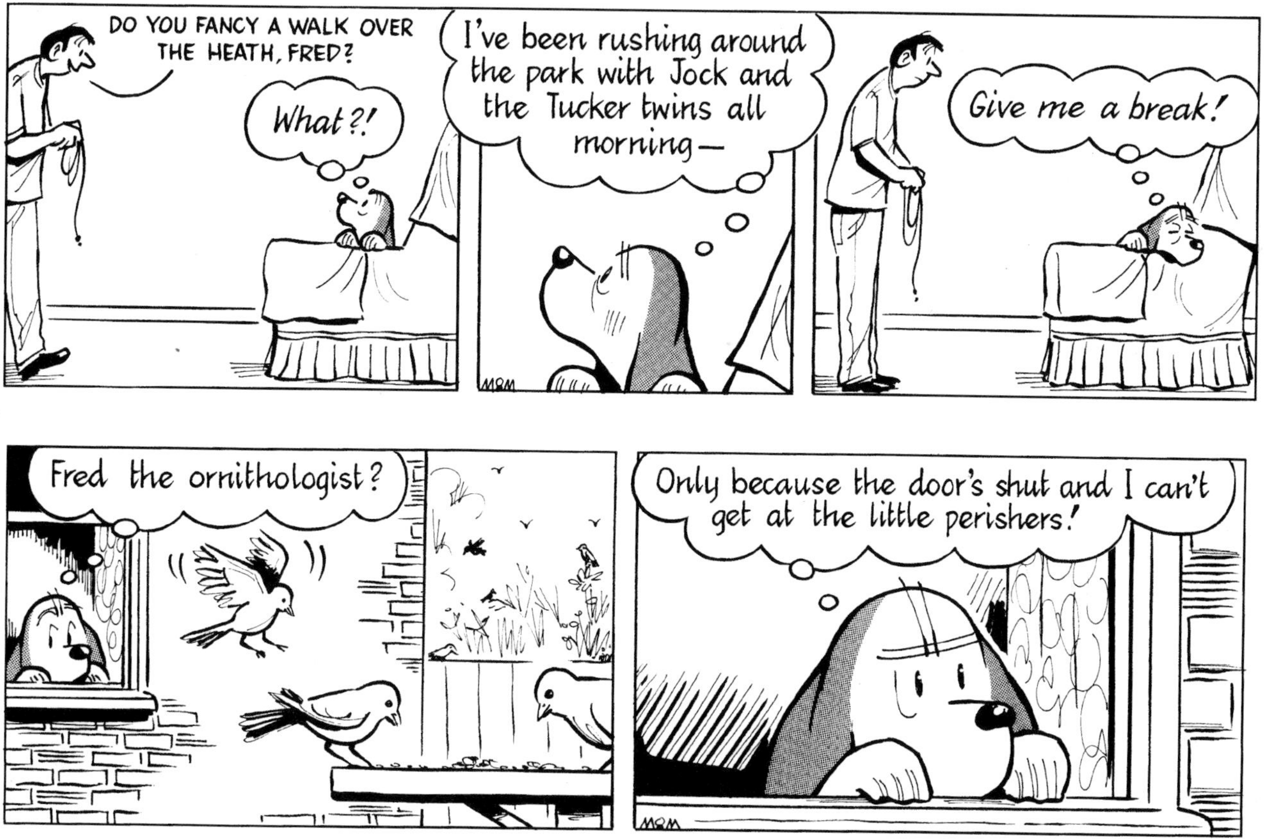
DO YOU FANCY A WALK OVER THE HEATH, FRED?
What?!
I've been rushing around the park with Jock and the Tucker twins all morning—
Give me a break!
Fred the ornithologist?
Only because the door's shut and I can't get at the little perishers!
M&M
M&M

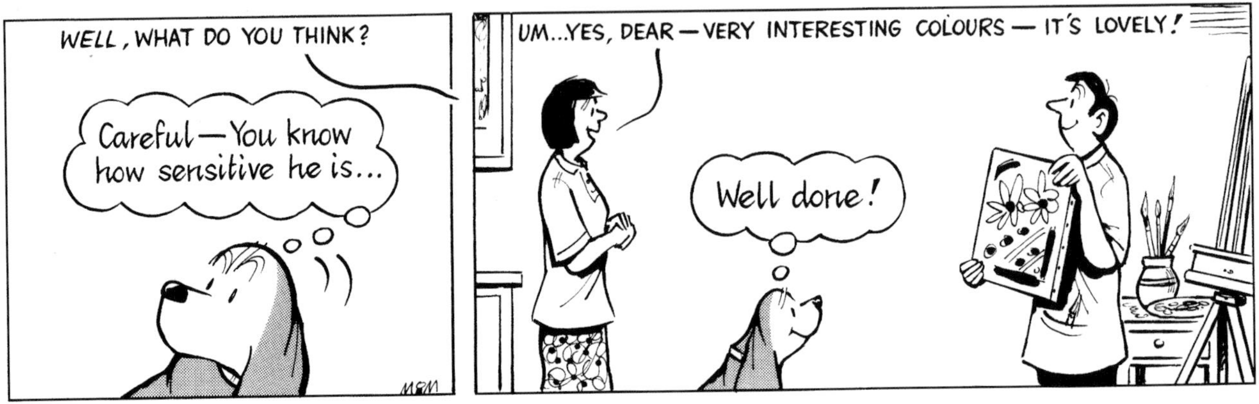
WELL, WHAT DO YOU THINK?
Careful — You know how sensitive he is...
UM... YES, DEAR — VERY INTERESTING COLOURS — IT'S LOVELY!
Well done!

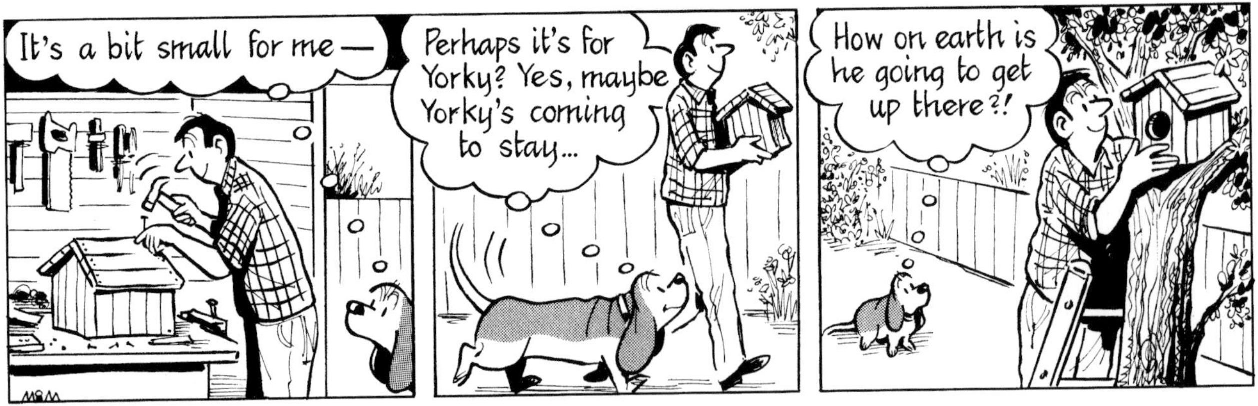
It's a bit small for me —
Perhaps it's for Yorky? Yes, maybe Yorky's coming to stay...
How on earth is he going to get up there?!

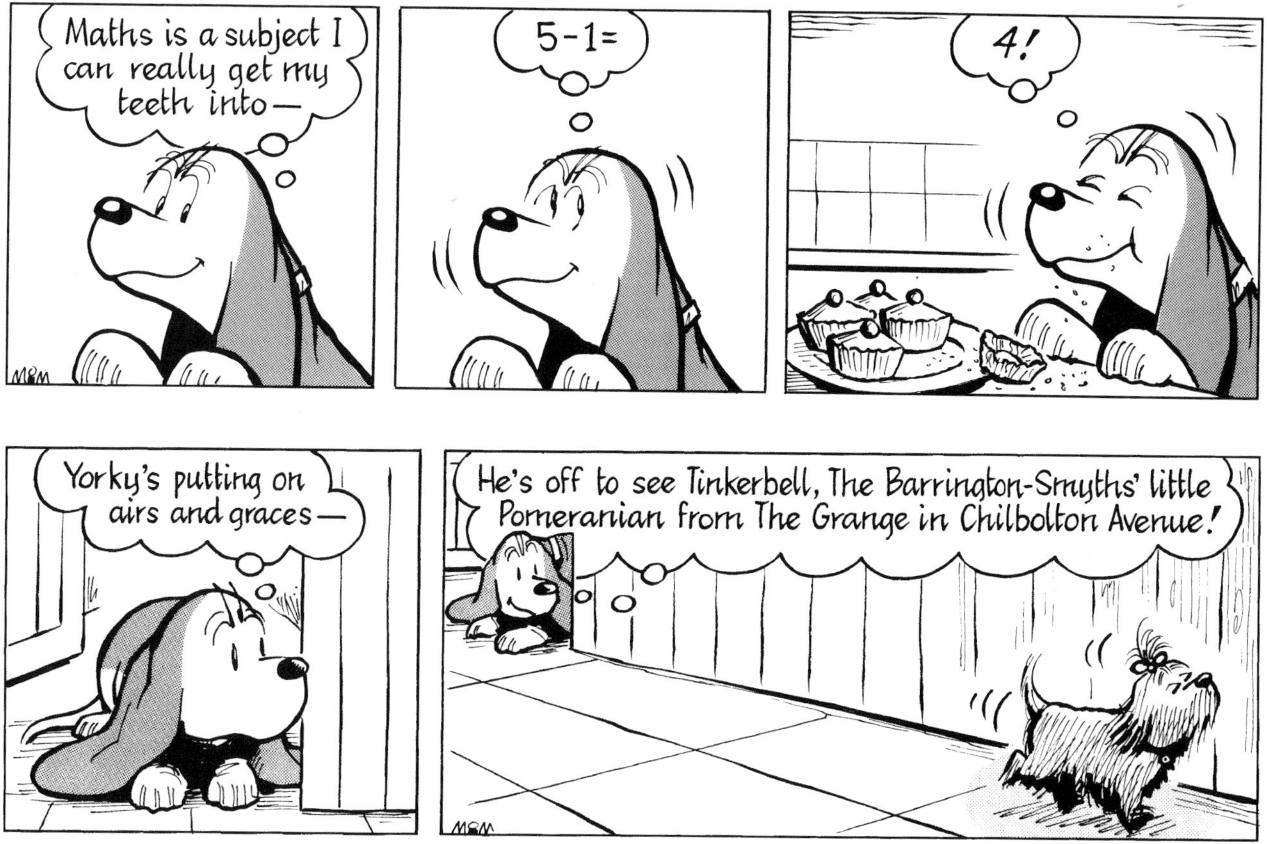

Maths is a subject I can really get my teeth into—
5-1=
4!
Yorky's putting on airs and graces—
He's off to see Tinkerbell, The Barrington-Smyths' little Pomeranian from The Grange in Chilbolton Avenue!
M&M
M&M

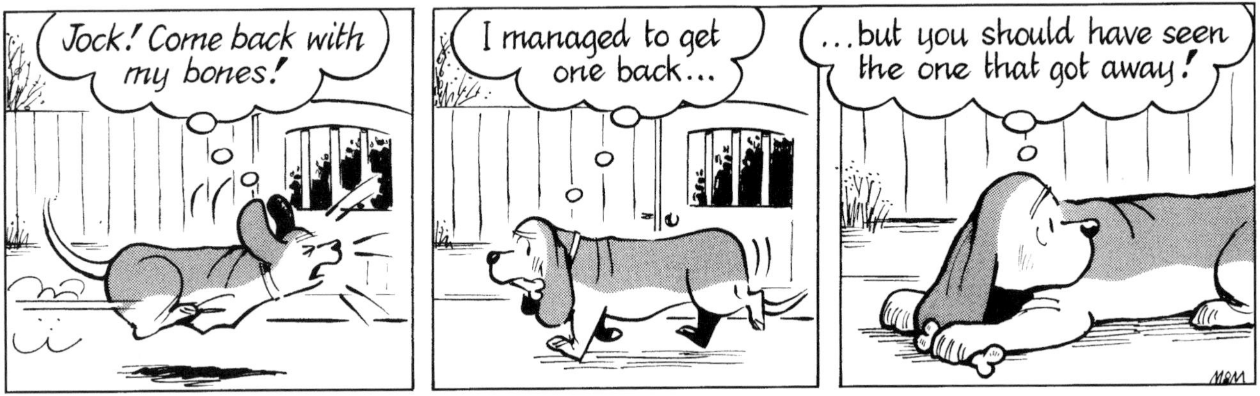
Jock! Come back with my bones!
I managed to get one back...
...but you should have seen the one that got away!

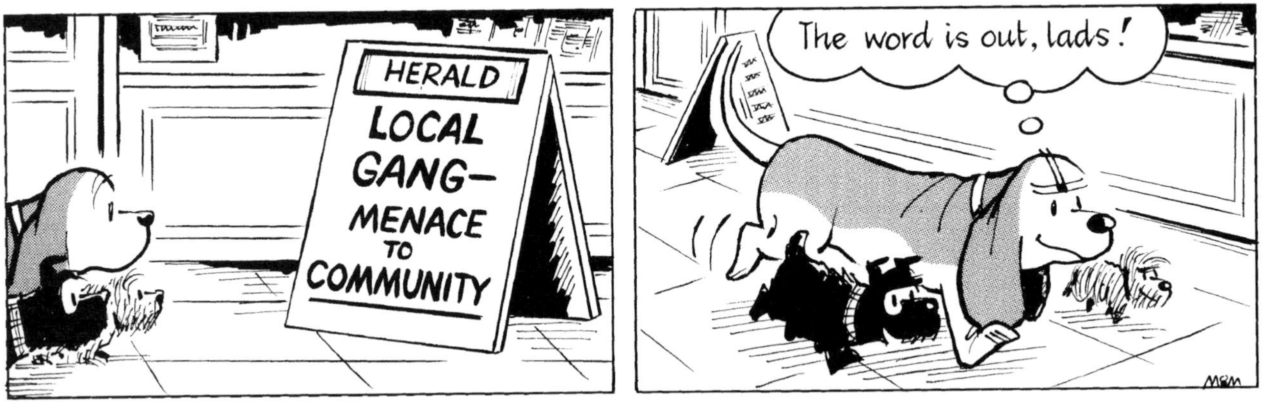
HERALD
LOCAL GANG—
MENACE TO COMMUNITY
The word is out, lads!

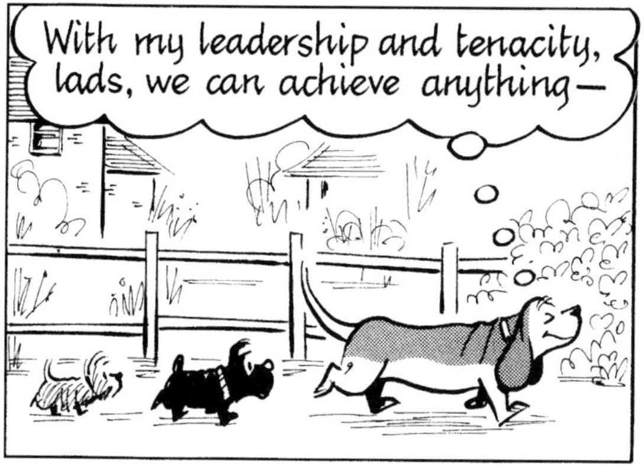
With my leadership and tenacity, lads, we can achieve anything—
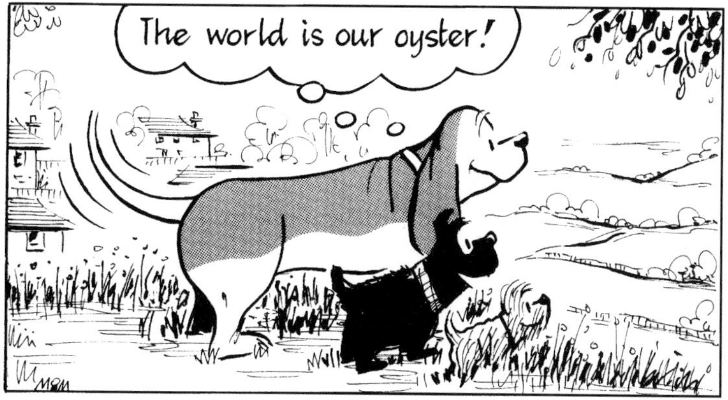
The world is our oyster!
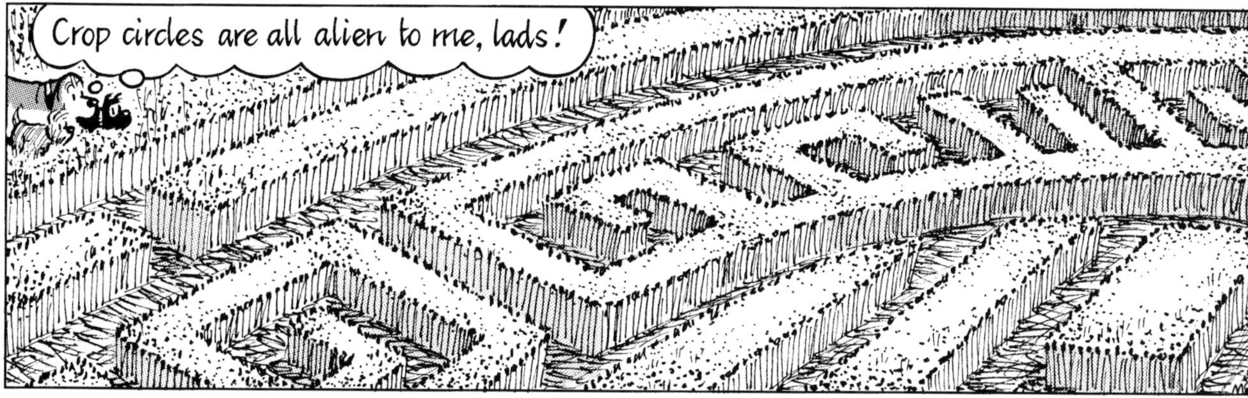
Crop circles are all alien to me, lads!

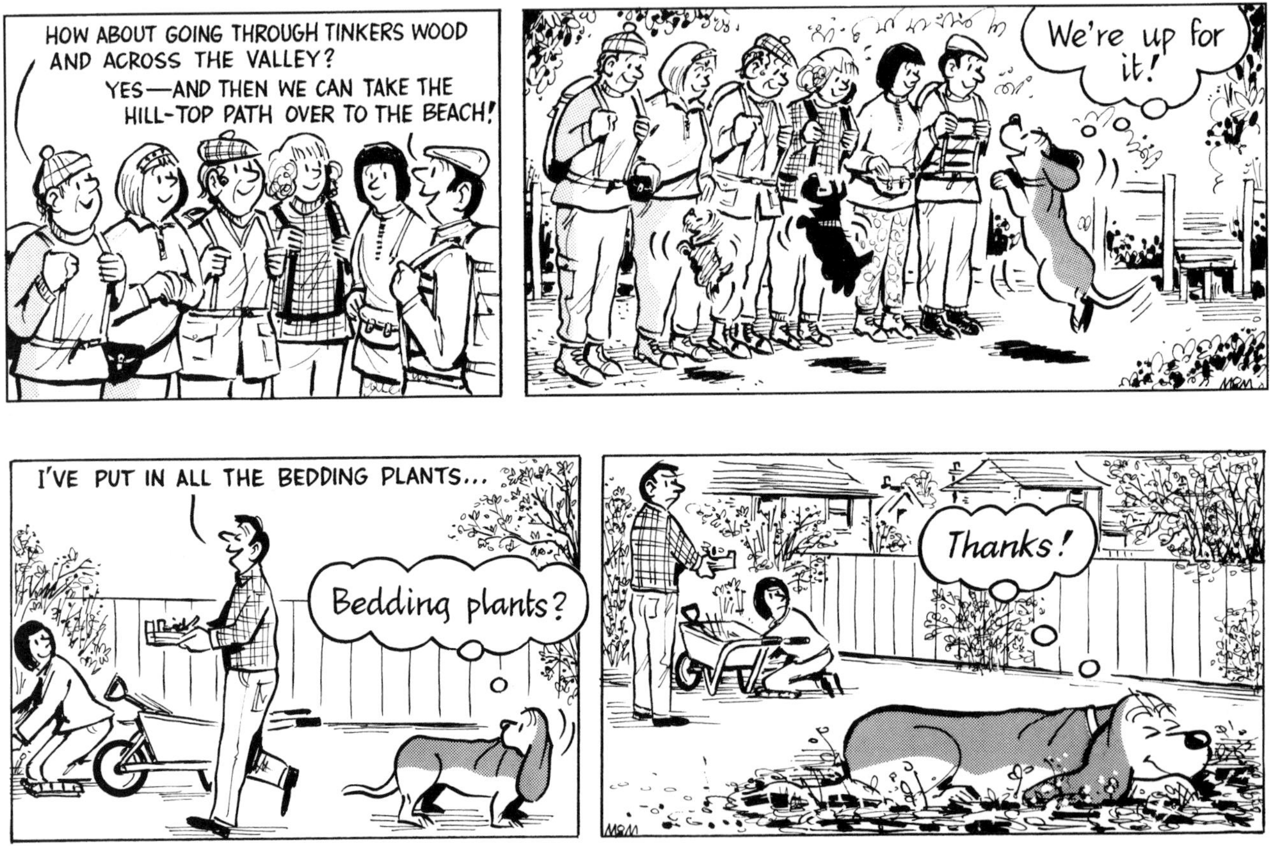
HOW ABOUT GOING THROUGH TINKERS WOOD AND ACROSS THE VALLEY?
YES—AND THEN WE CAN TAKE THE HILL-TOP PATH OVER TO THE BEACH!
We're up for it!
I'VE PUT IN ALL THE BEDDING PLANTS...
Bedding plants?
Thanks!

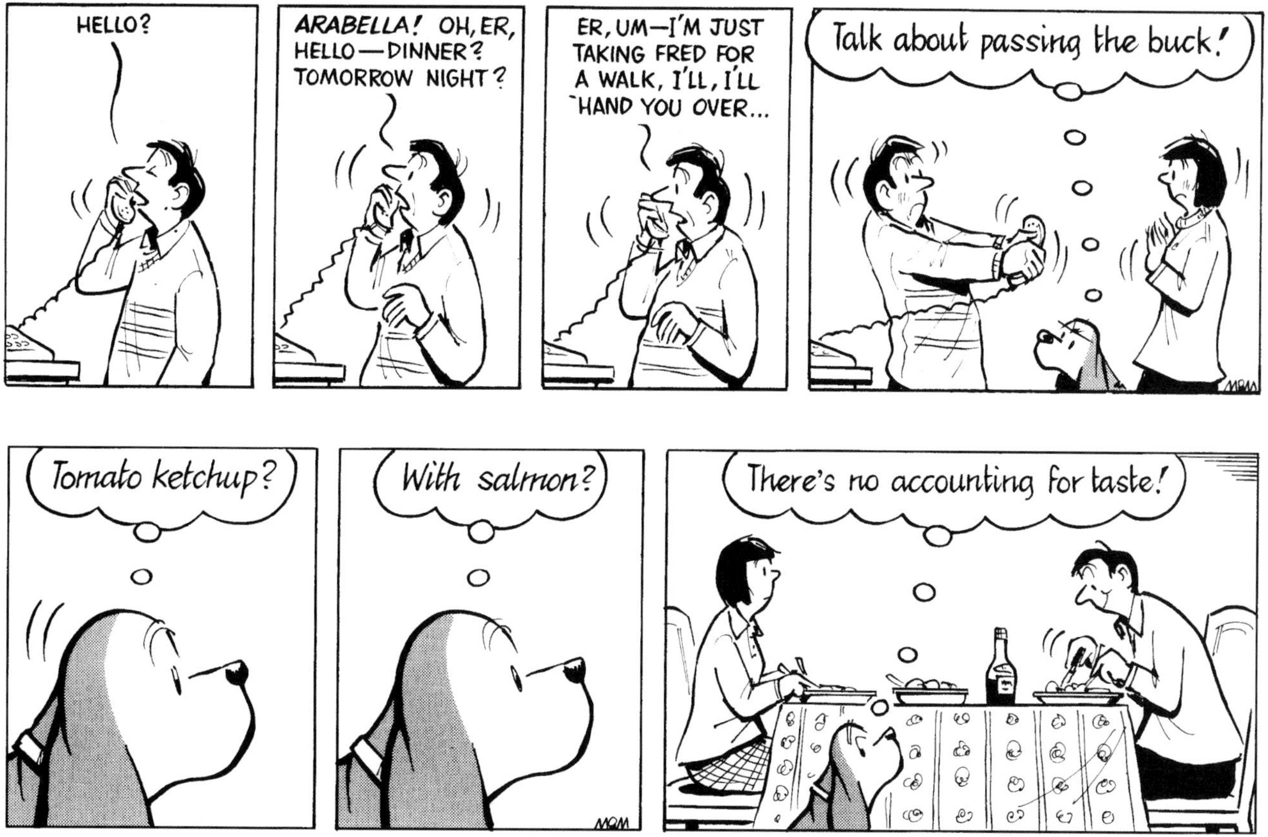
HELLO?
ARABELLA! OH, ER, HELLO—DINNER? TOMORROW NIGHT?
ER, UM—I'M JUST TAKING FRED FOR A WALK, I'LL, I'LL HAND YOU OVER...
Talk about passing the buck!
Tomato ketchup?
With salmon?
There's no accounting for taste!

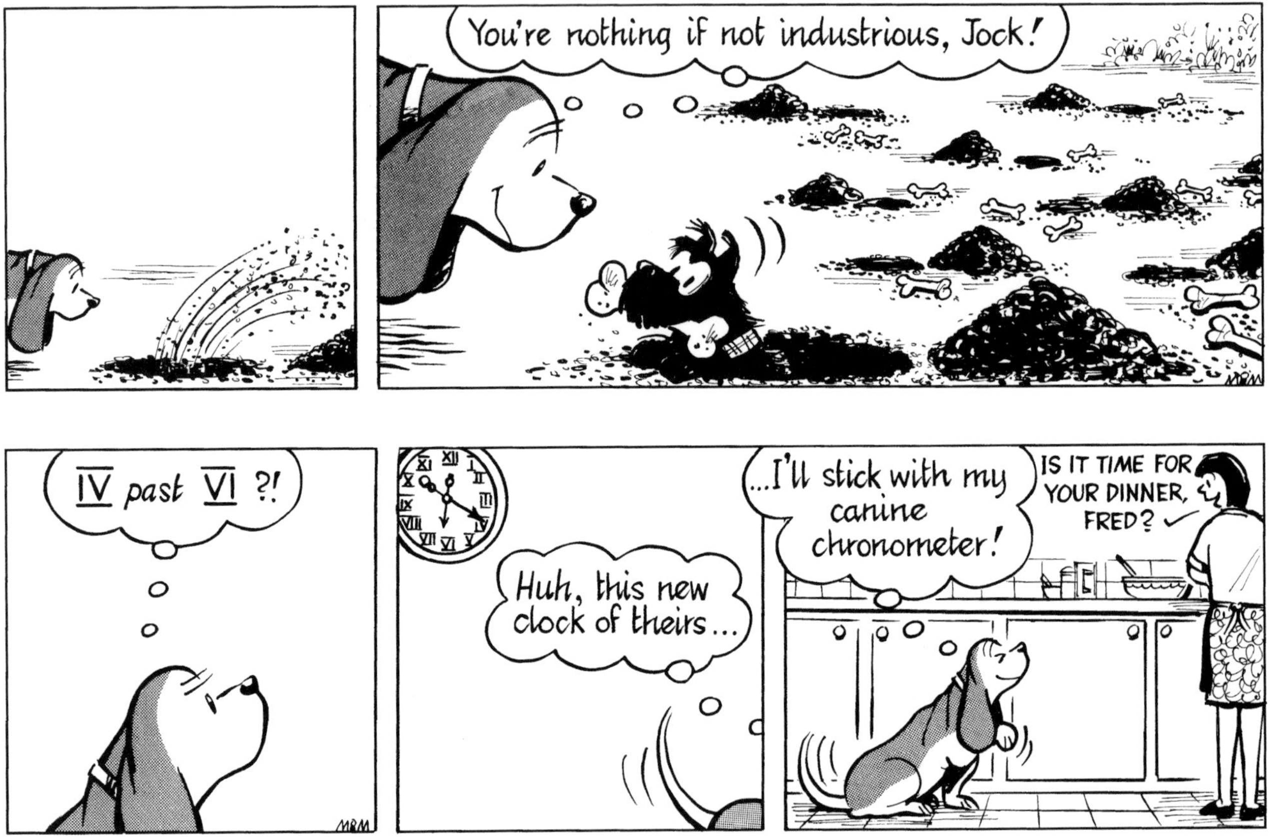
You're nothing if not industrious, Jock!
MRM
IV past VI ?!
MRM
Huh, this new clock of theirs...
...I'll stick with my canine chronometer!
IS IT TIME FOR YOUR DINNER, FRED?

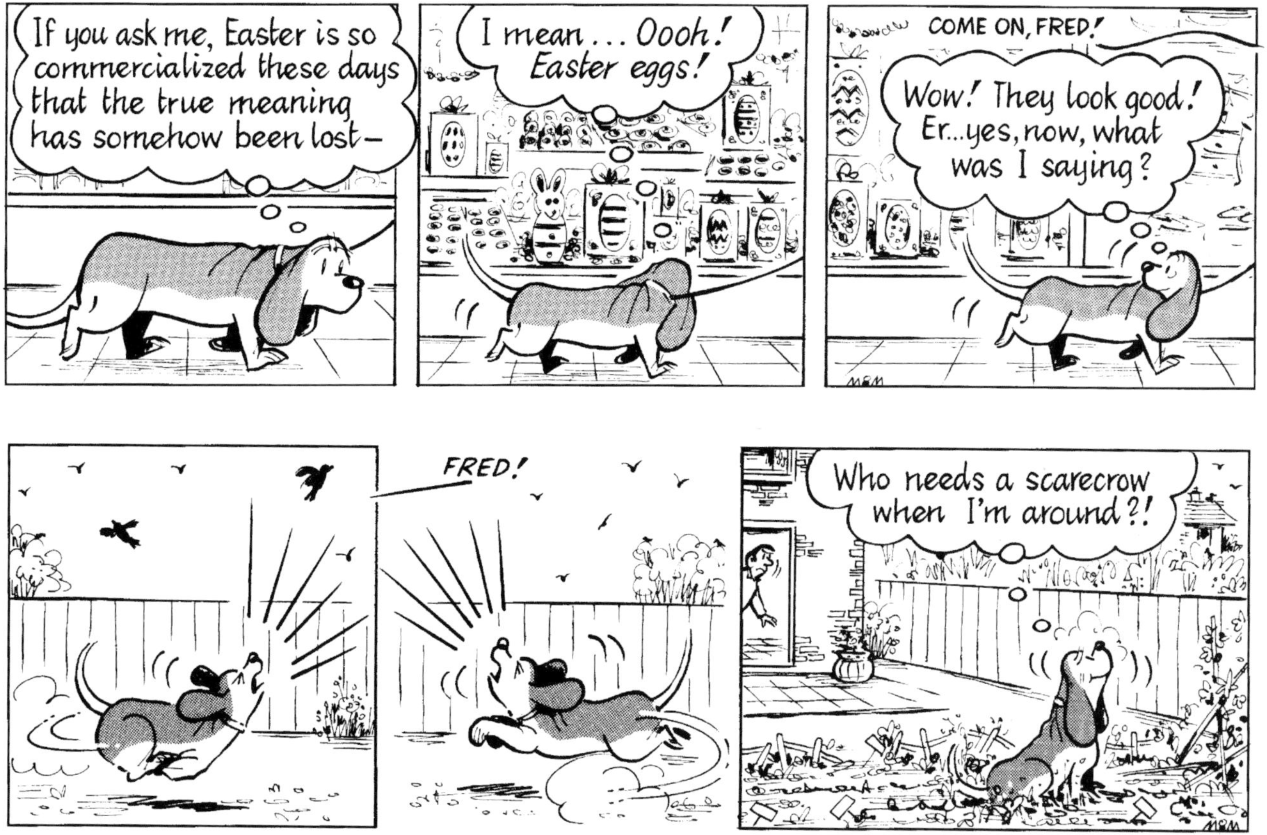

If you ask me, Easter is so commercialized these days that the true meaning has somehow been lost–
I mean ... Oooh! Easter eggs!
COME ON, FRED!
Wow! They look good! Er...yes, now, what was I saying?
FRED!
Who needs a scarecrow when I'm around?!

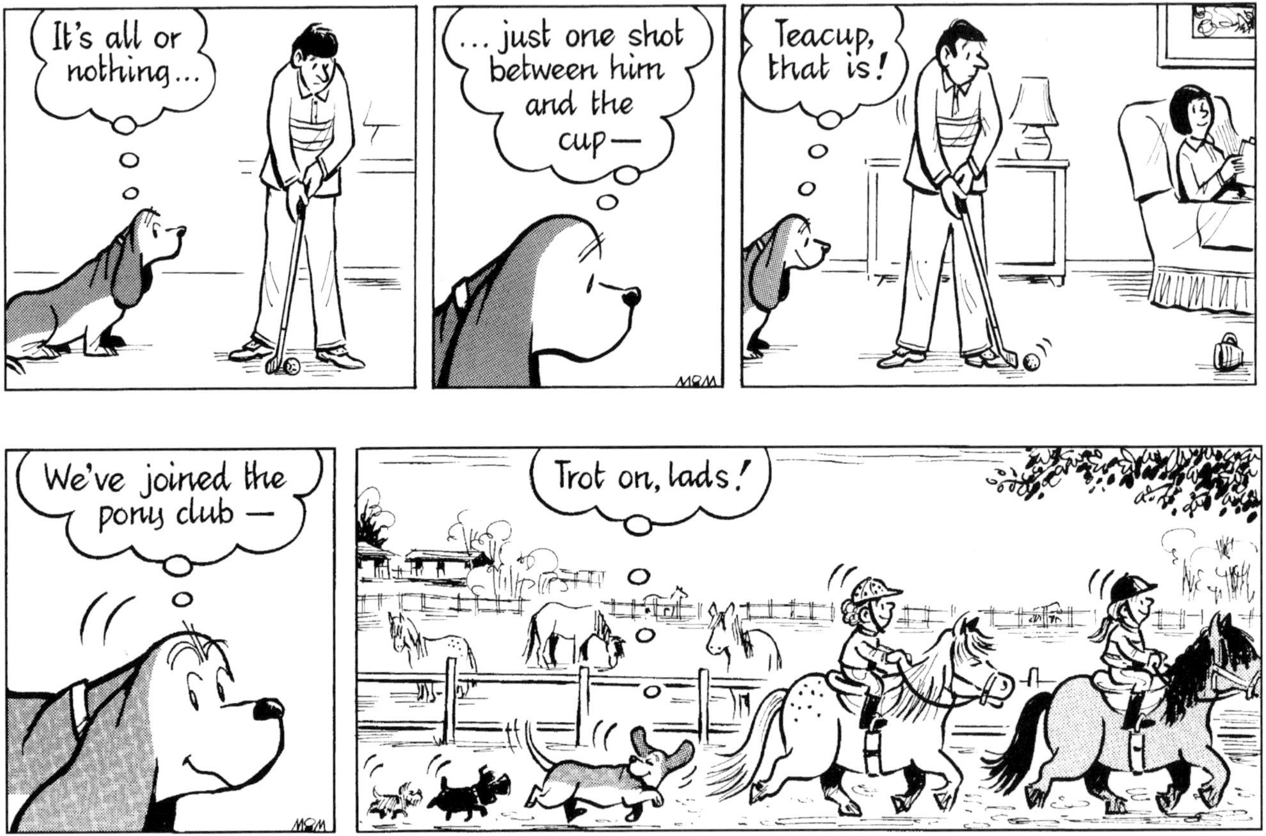
It's all or nothing...
... just one shot between him and the cup—
MGM
Teacup, that is!
We've joined the pony club —
MGM
Trot on, lads!

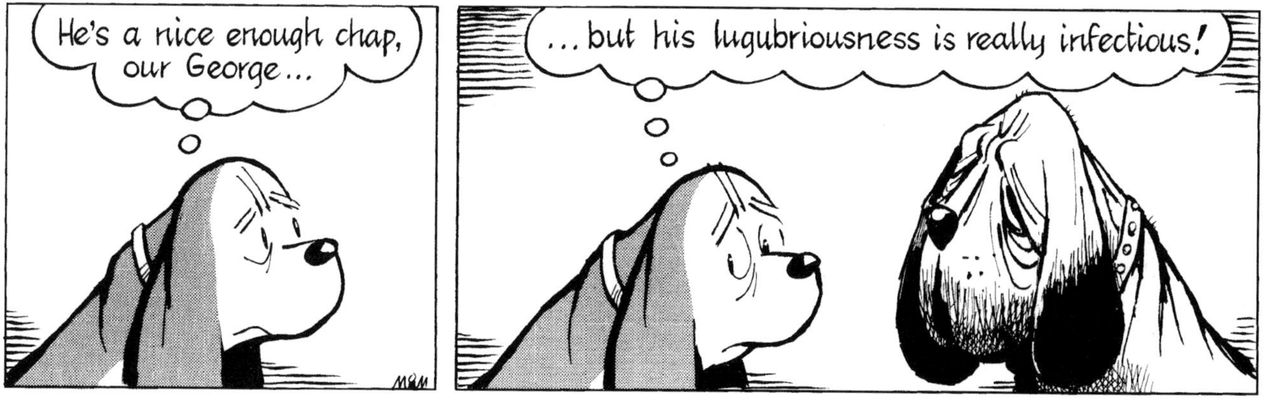
He's a nice enough chap, our George...
...but his lugubriousness is really infectious!
MGM

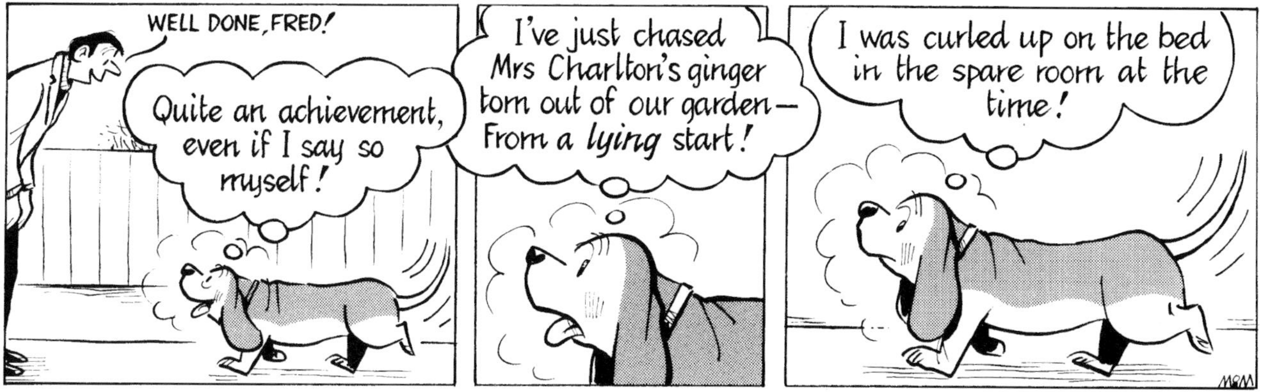
WELL DONE, FRED!
Quite an achievement, even if I say so myself!
I've just chased Mrs Charlton's ginger tom out of our garden – From a *lying* start!
I was curled up on the bed in the spare room at the time!
MGM

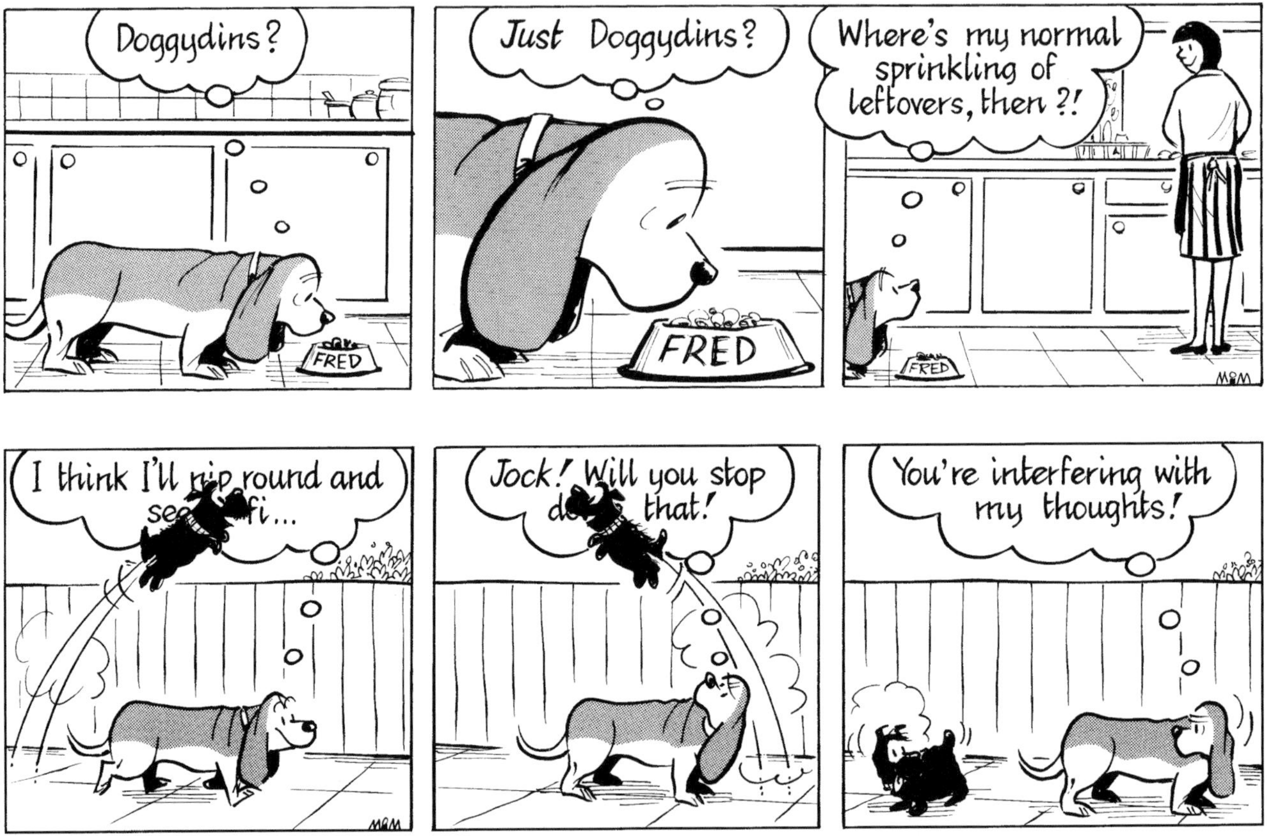
Doggydins?
Just Doggydins?
Where's my normal sprinkling of leftovers, then?!
FRED
I think I'll round and
fi...
Jock! Will you stop
that!
You're interfering with my thoughts!

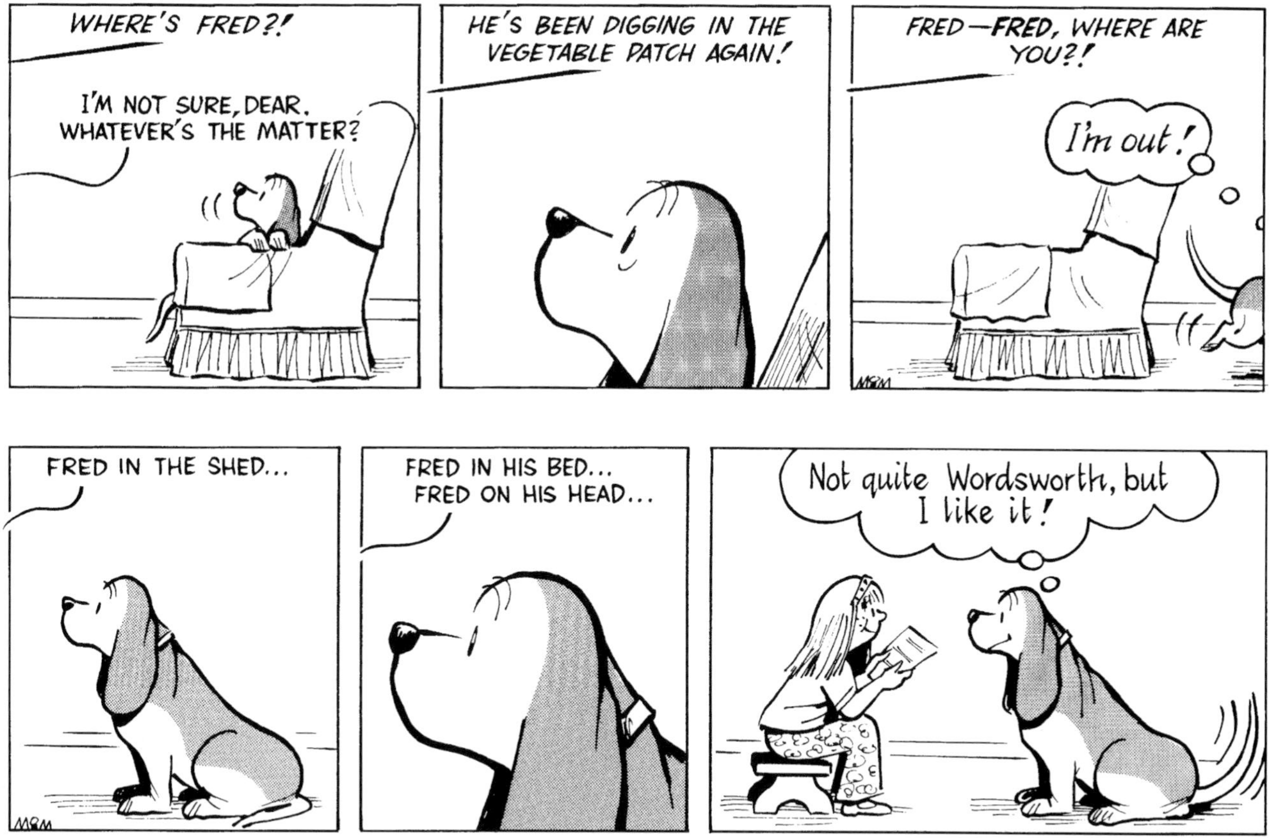
WHERE'S FRED?!
I'M NOT SURE, DEAR. WHATEVER'S THE MATTER?
HE'S BEEN DIGGING IN THE VEGETABLE PATCH AGAIN!
FRED—FRED, WHERE ARE YOU?!
I'm out!
FRED IN THE SHED...
FRED IN HIS BED... FRED ON HIS HEAD...
Not quite Wordsworth, but I like it!

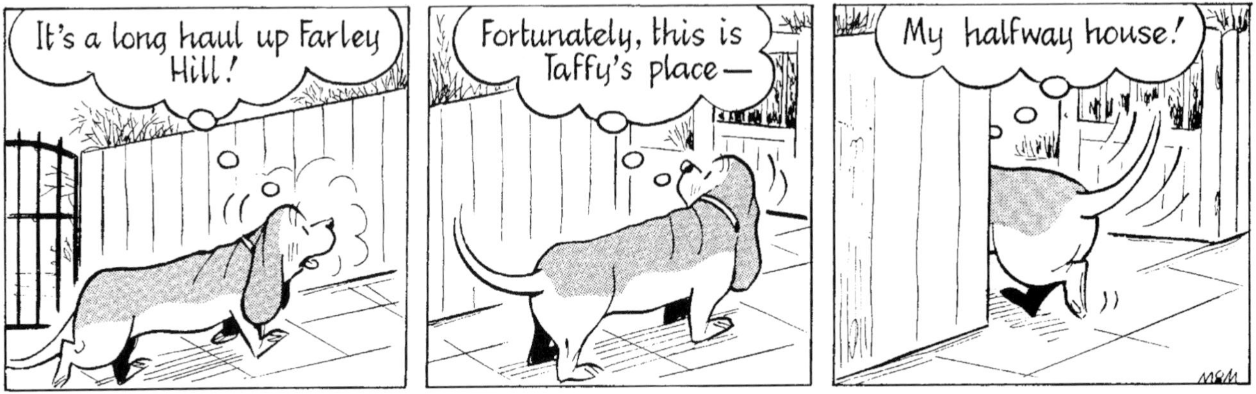
It's a long haul up Farley Hill!
Fortunately, this is Taffy's place—
My halfway house!

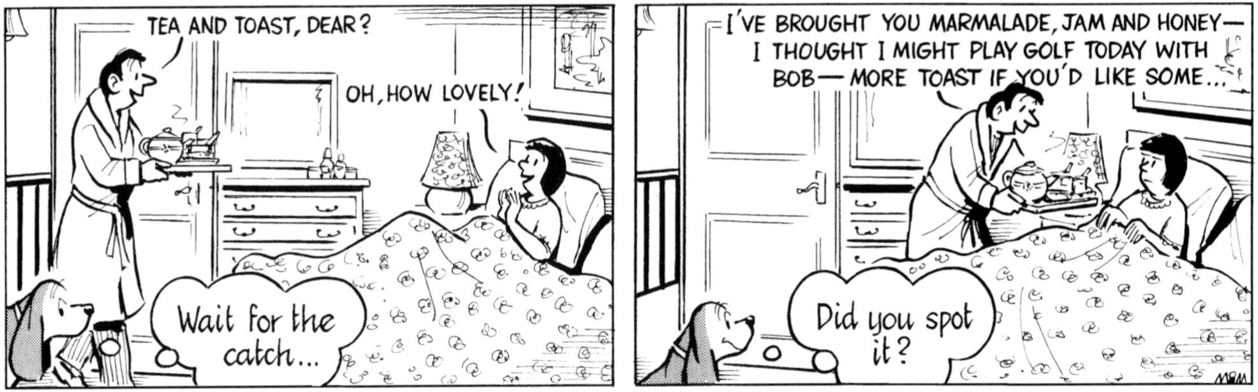
TEA AND TOAST, DEAR?
OH, HOW LOVELY!
Wait for the catch...
I'VE BROUGHT YOU MARMALADE, JAM AND HONEY— I THOUGHT I MIGHT PLAY GOLF TODAY WITH BOB— MORE TOAST IF YOU'D LIKE SOME...
Did you spot it?

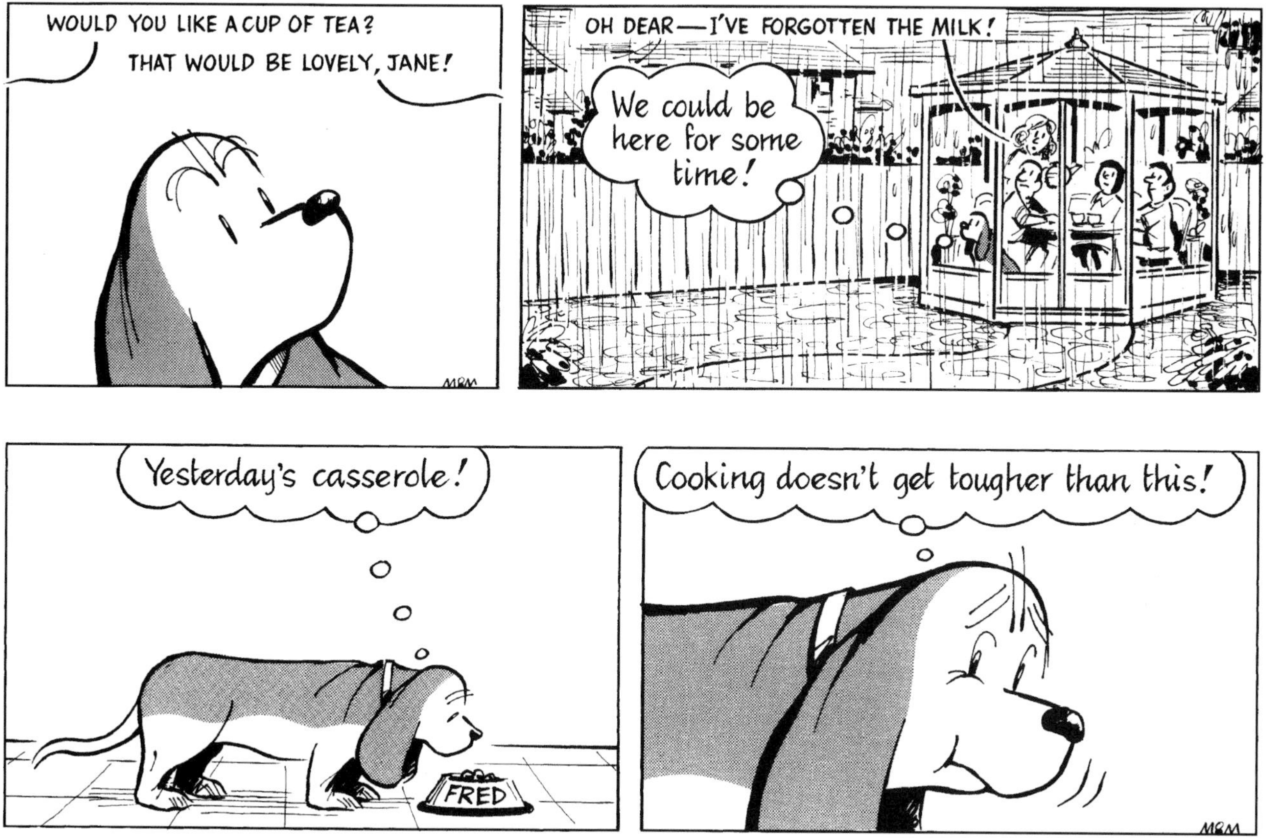
WOULD YOU LIKE A CUP OF TEA?
THAT WOULD BE LOVELY, JANE!
OH DEAR—I'VE FORGOTTEN THE MILK!
We could be here for some time!
Yesterday's casserole!
FRED
Cooking doesn't get tougher than this!

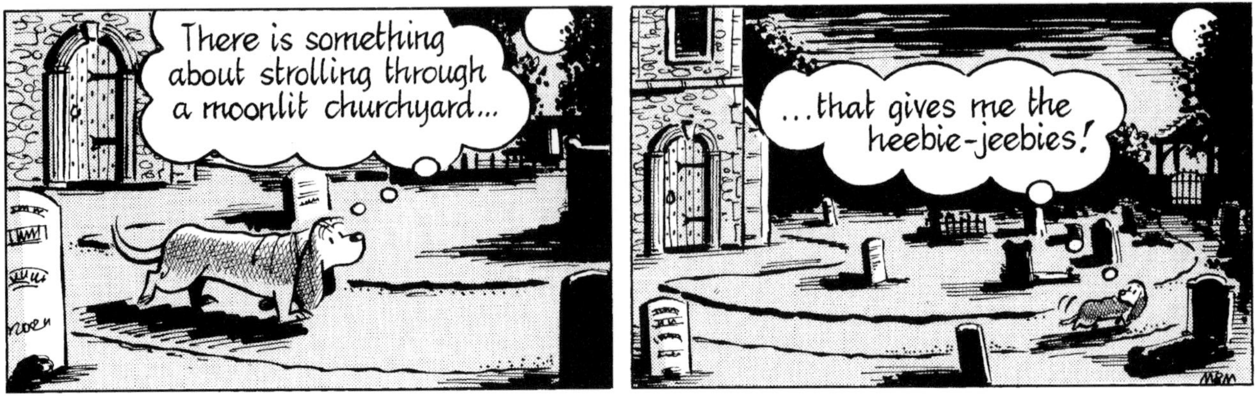
There is something about strolling through a moonlit churchyard...
...that gives me the heebie-jeebies!
MRM

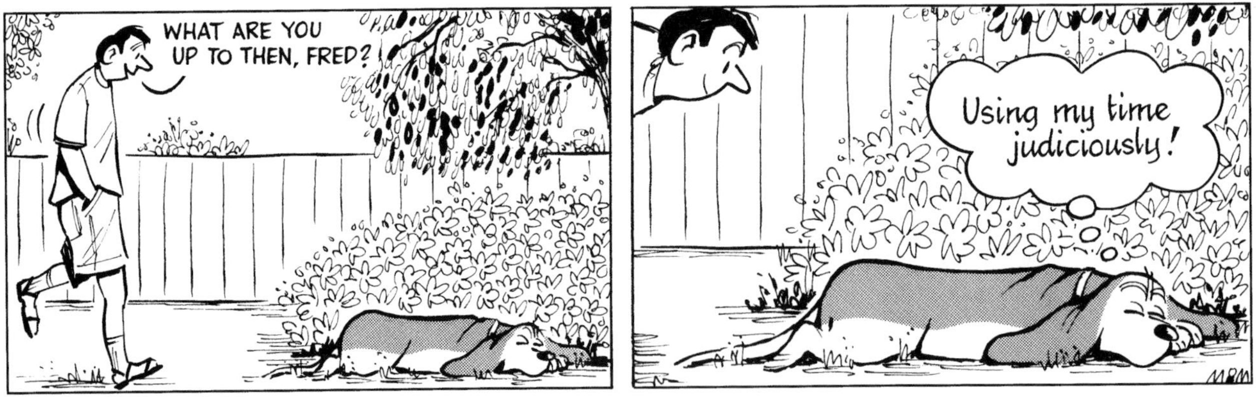
WHAT ARE YOU UP TO THEN, FRED?
Using my time judiciously!
MRM

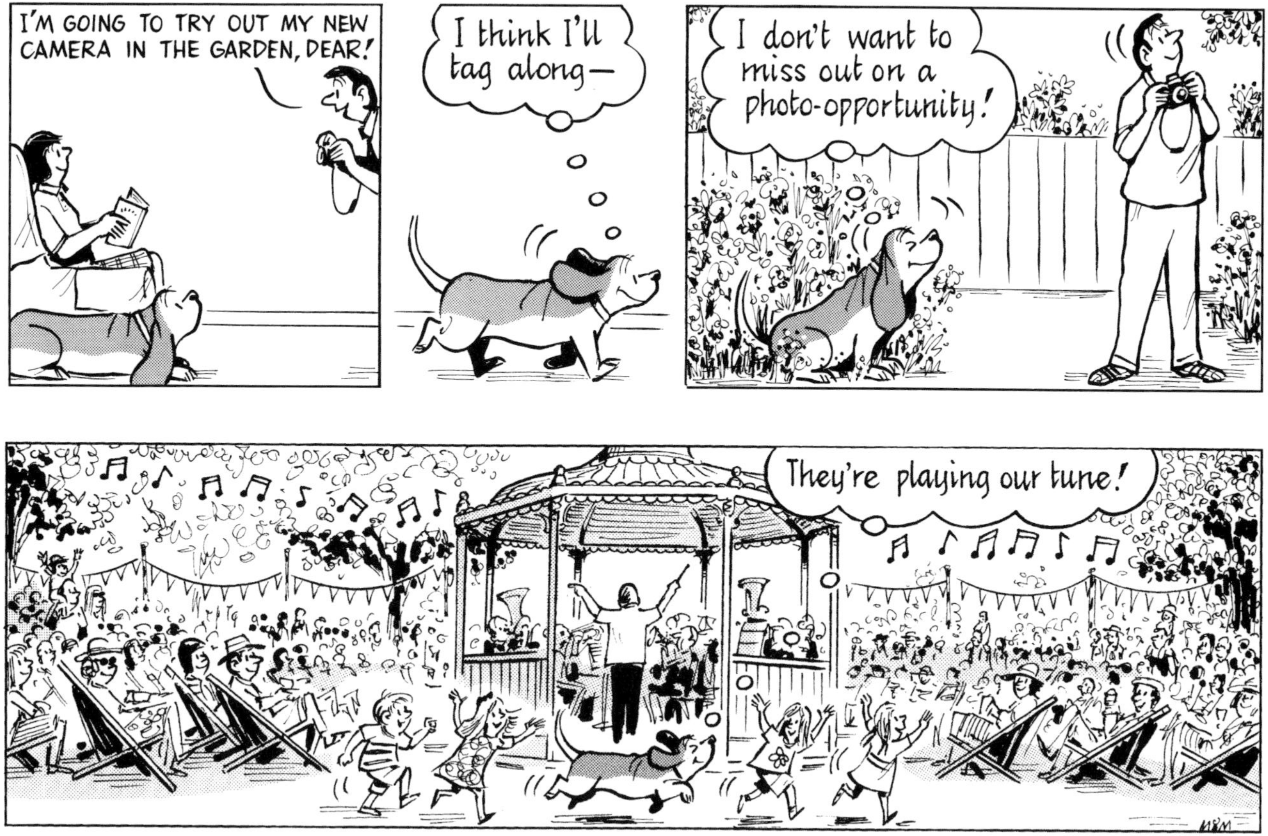
I'M GOING TO TRY OUT MY NEW CAMERA IN THE GARDEN, DEAR!
I think I'll tag along—
I don't want to miss out on a photo-opportunity!
They're playing our tune!

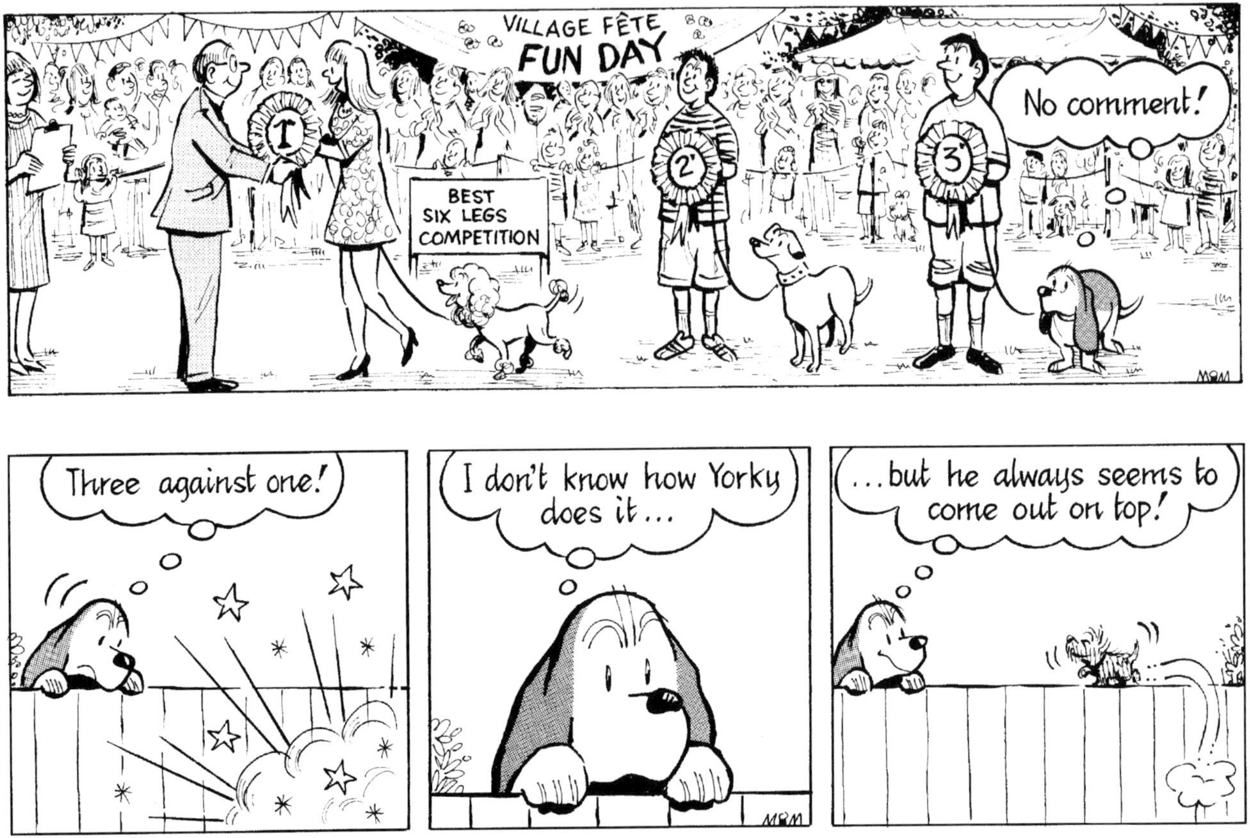
VILLAGE FÊTE
FUN DAY
BEST SIX LEGS COMPETITION
No comment!
Three against one!
I don't know how Yorky does it...
...but he always seems to come out on top!

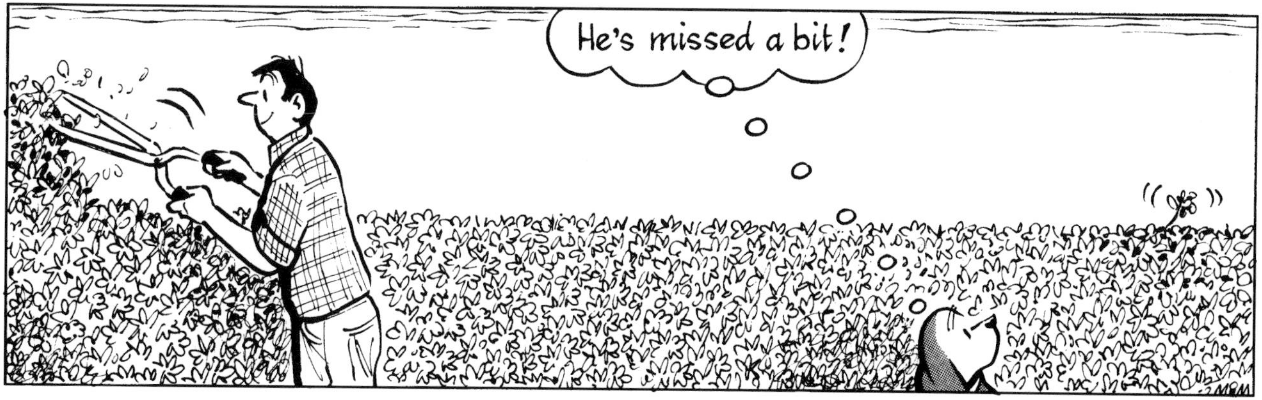
He's missed a bit!
MBM

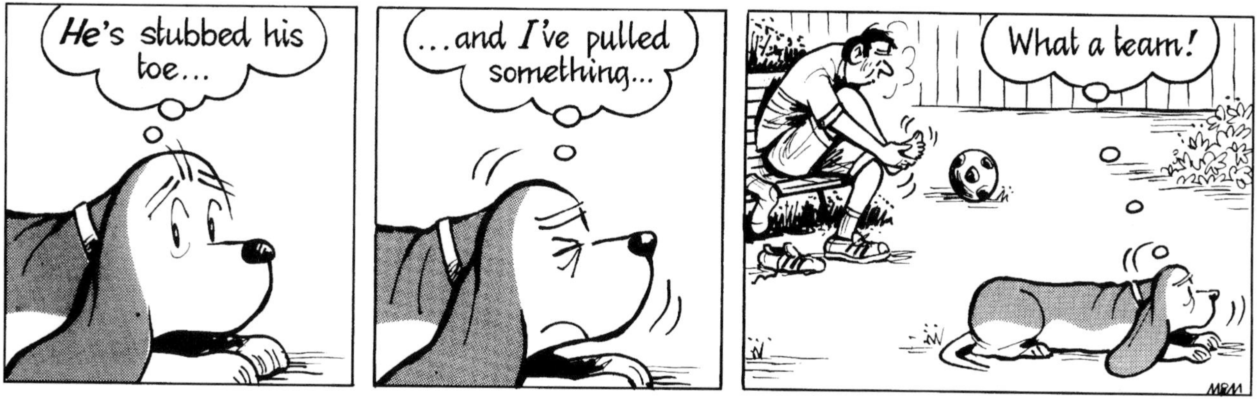
He's stubbed his toe...
...and I've pulled something...
What a team!
MBM

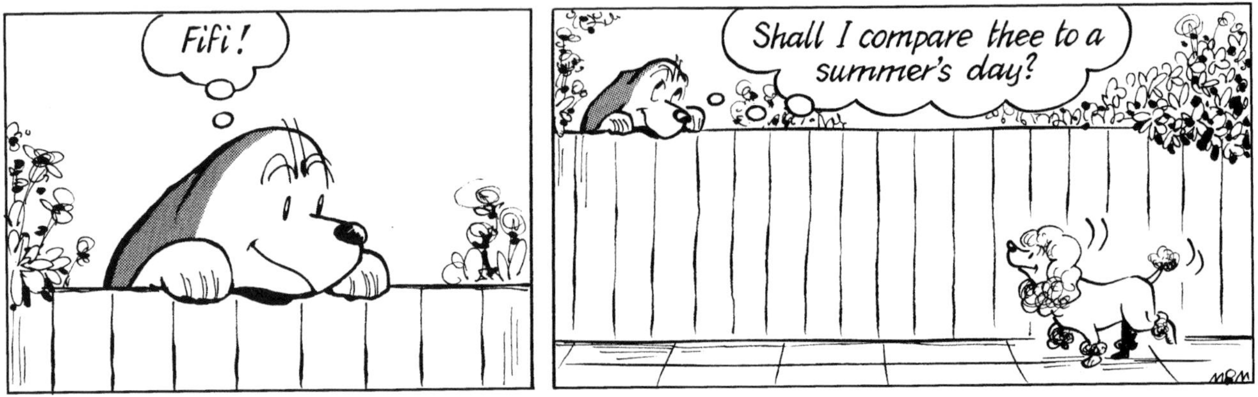

Fifi!
Shall I compare thee to a summer's day?

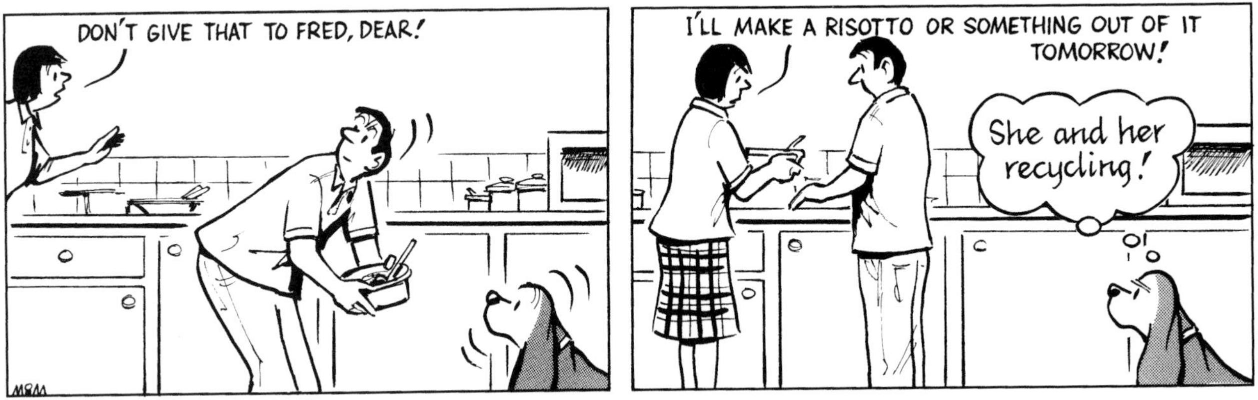

DON'T GIVE THAT TO FRED, DEAR!
I'LL MAKE A RISOTTO OR SOMETHING OUT OF IT TOMORROW!
She and her recycling!

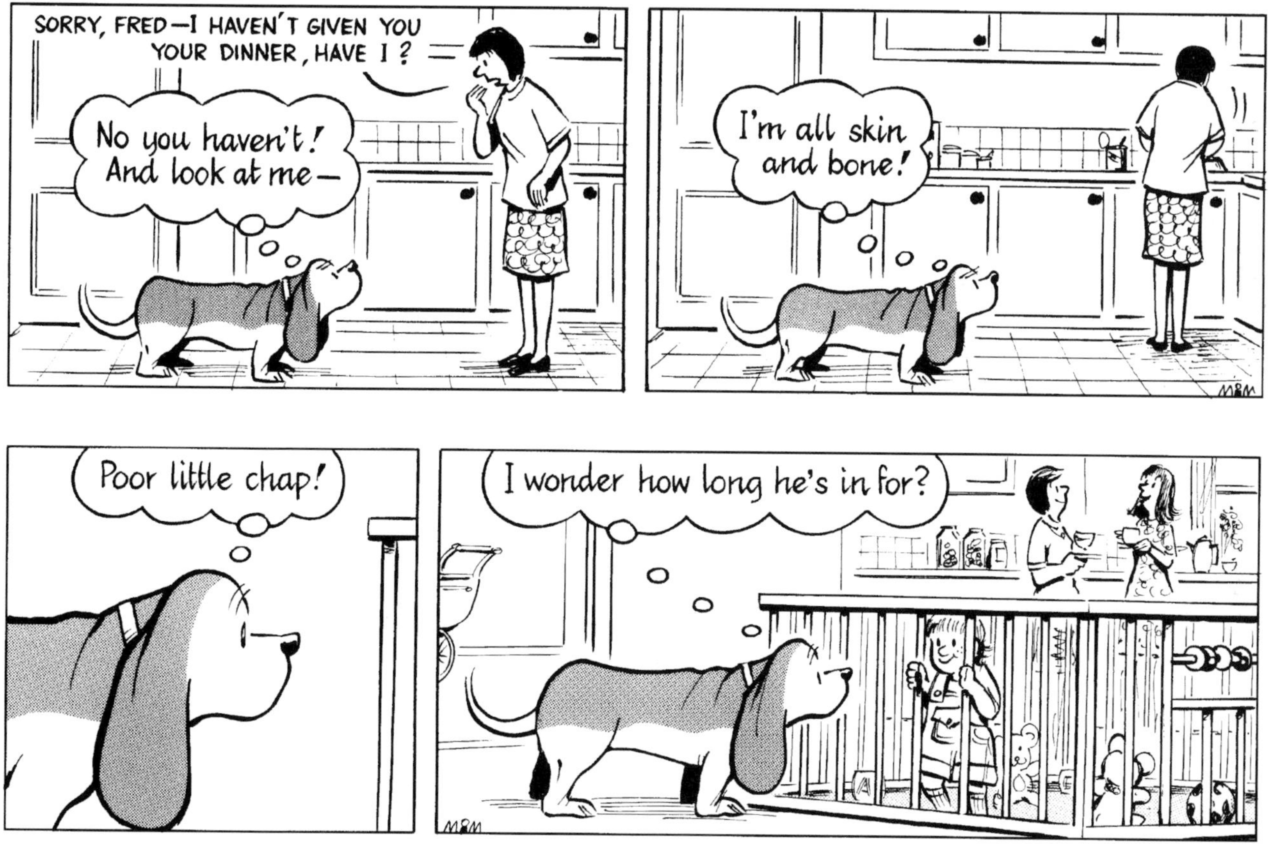
SORRY, FRED—I HAVEN'T GIVEN YOU YOUR DINNER, HAVE I?
No you haven't! And look at me—
I'm all skin and bone!
Poor little chap!
I wonder how long he's in for?
M&M
M&M

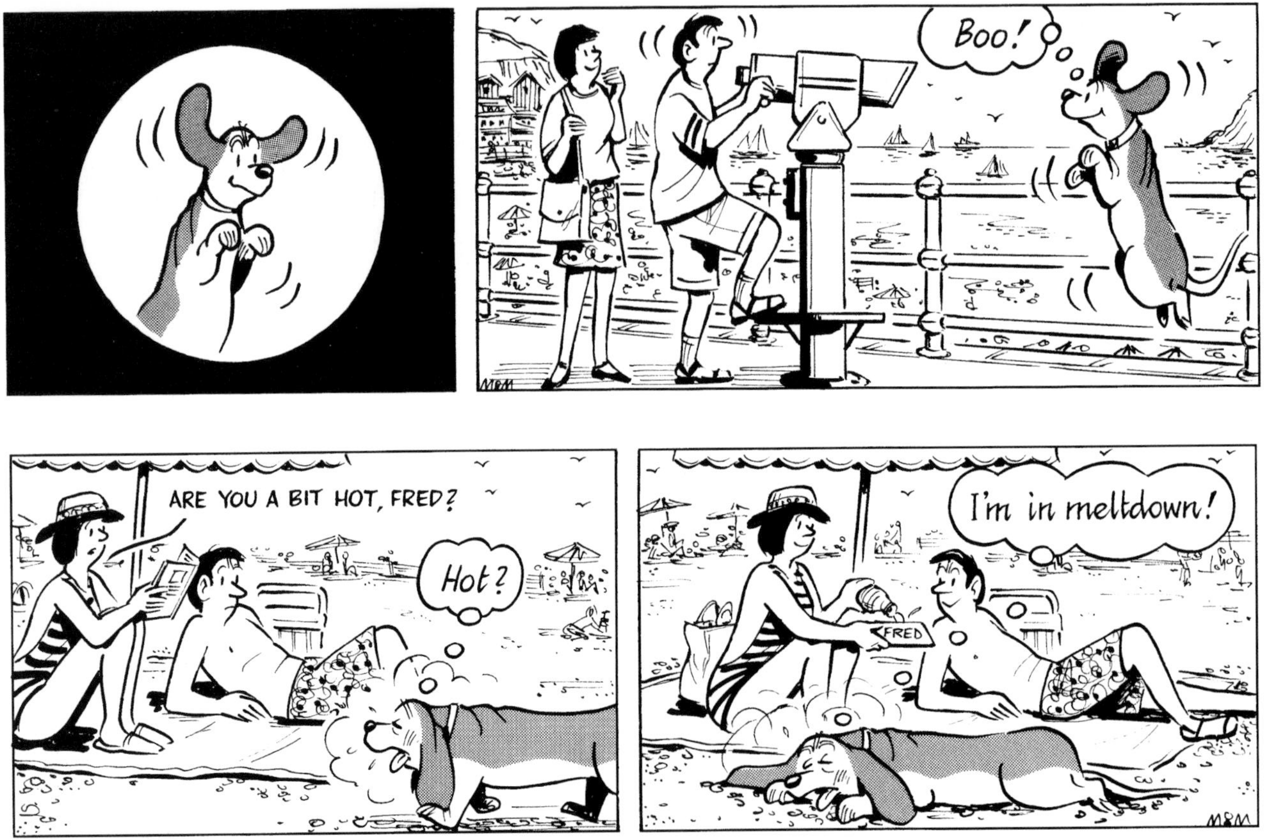
Boo!
ARE YOU A BIT HOT, FRED?
Hot?
FRED
I'm in meltdown!

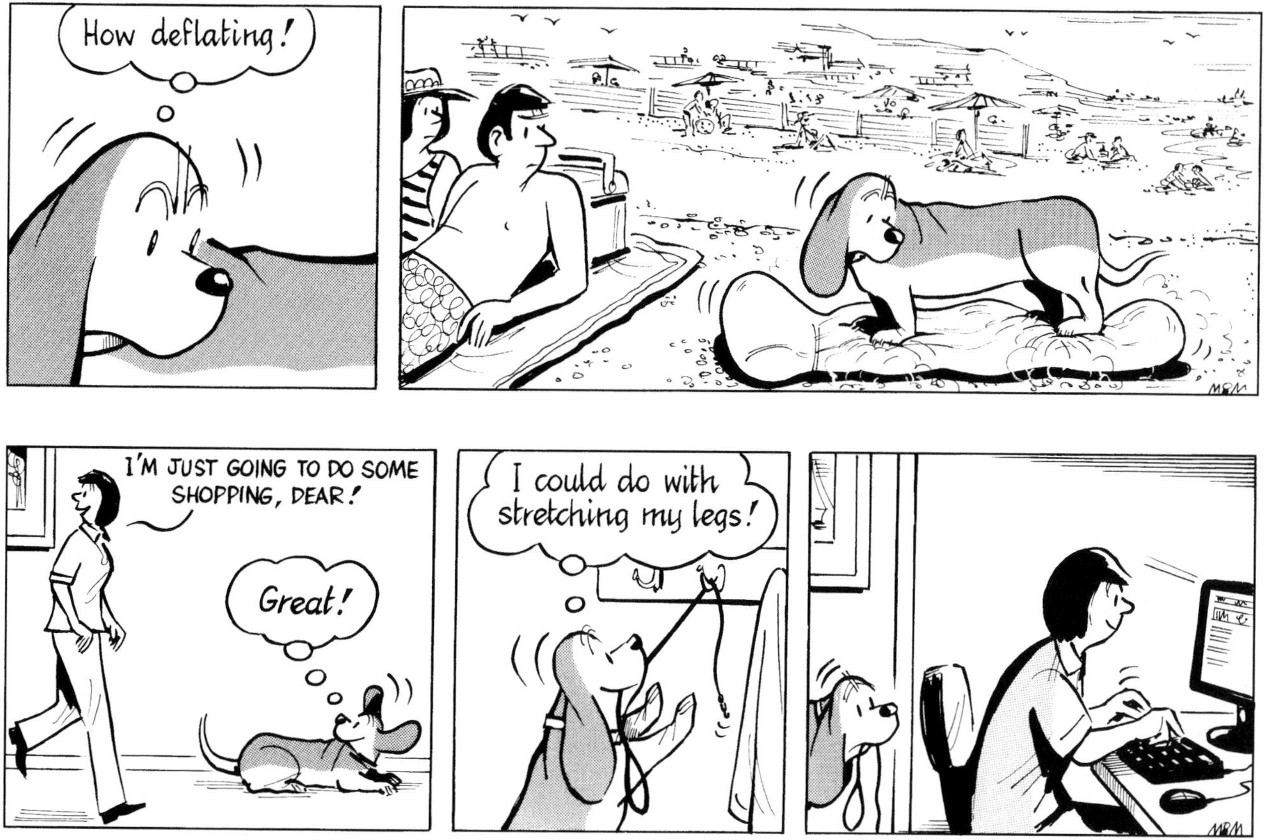
How deflating!
I'M JUST GOING TO DO SOME SHOPPING, DEAR!
Great!
I could do with stretching my legs!
MBM

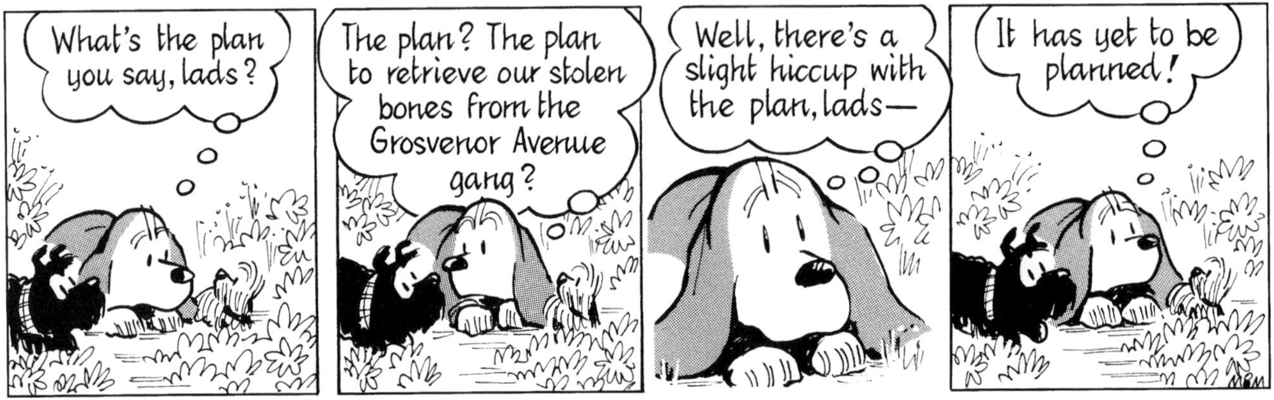
What's the plan you say, lads?
The plan? The plan to retrieve our stolen bones from the Grosvenor Avenue gang?
Well, there's a slight hiccup with the plan, lads—
It has yet to be planned!
MOM

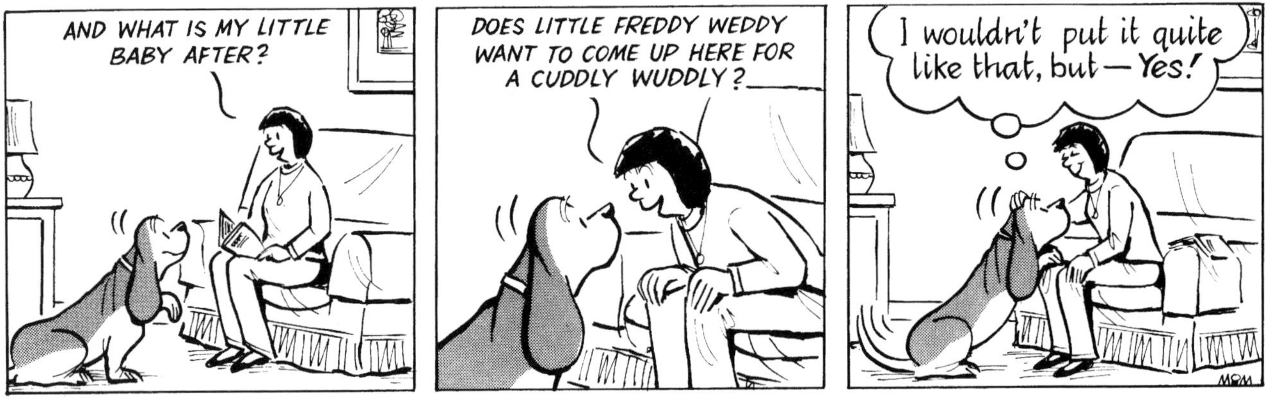
AND WHAT IS MY LITTLE BABY AFTER?
DOES LITTLE FREDDY WEDDY WANT TO COME UP HERE FOR A CUDDLY WUDDLY?
I wouldn't put it quite like that, but—Yes!
MOM

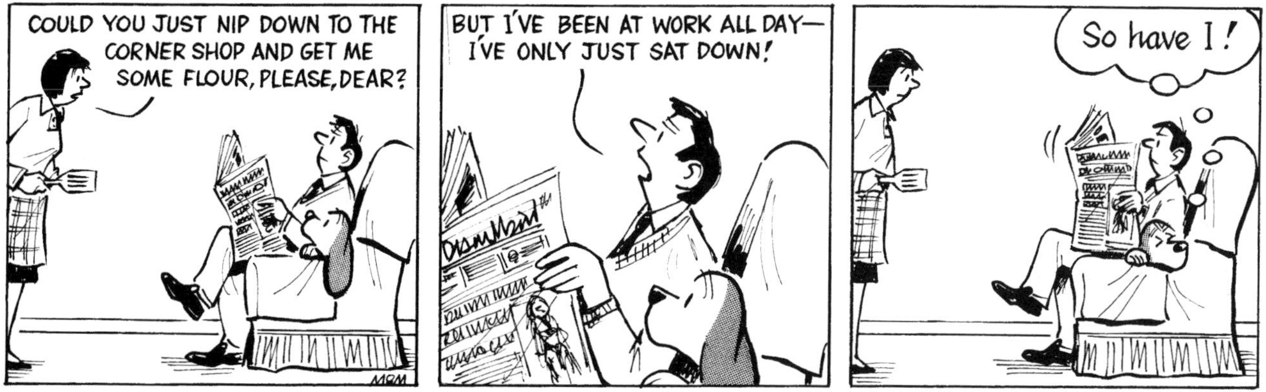
COULD YOU JUST NIP DOWN TO THE CORNER SHOP AND GET ME SOME FLOUR, PLEASE, DEAR?
BUT I'VE BEEN AT WORK ALL DAY—I'VE ONLY JUST SAT DOWN!
So have I!

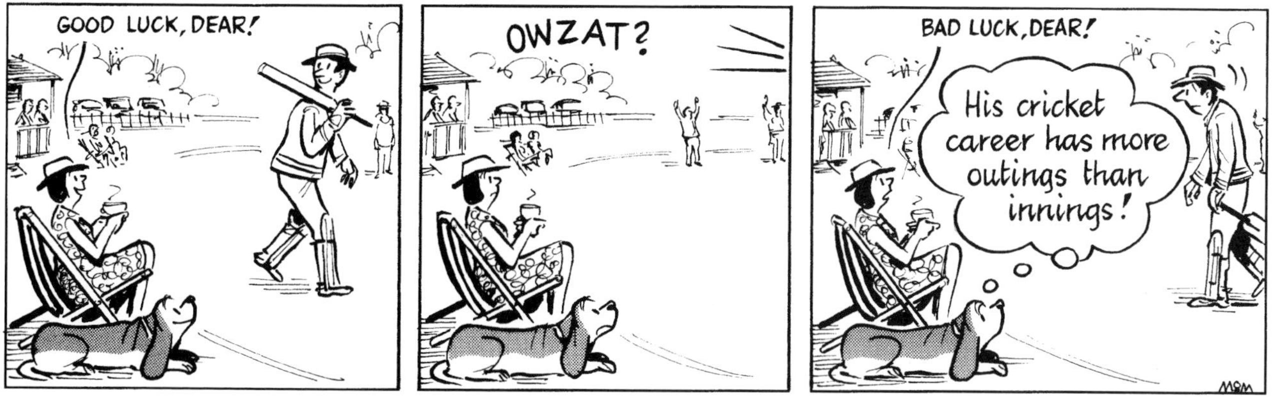
GOOD LUCK, DEAR!
OWZAT?
BAD LUCK, DEAR!
His cricket career has more outings than innings!

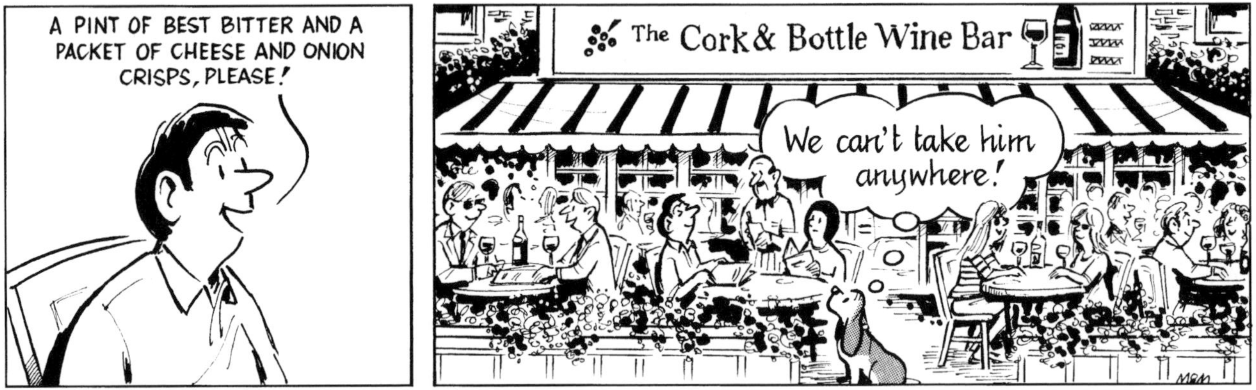
A PINT OF BEST BITTER AND A PACKET OF CHEESE AND ONION CRISPS, PLEASE!
The Cork & Bottle Wine Bar
We can't take him anywhere!
M&M

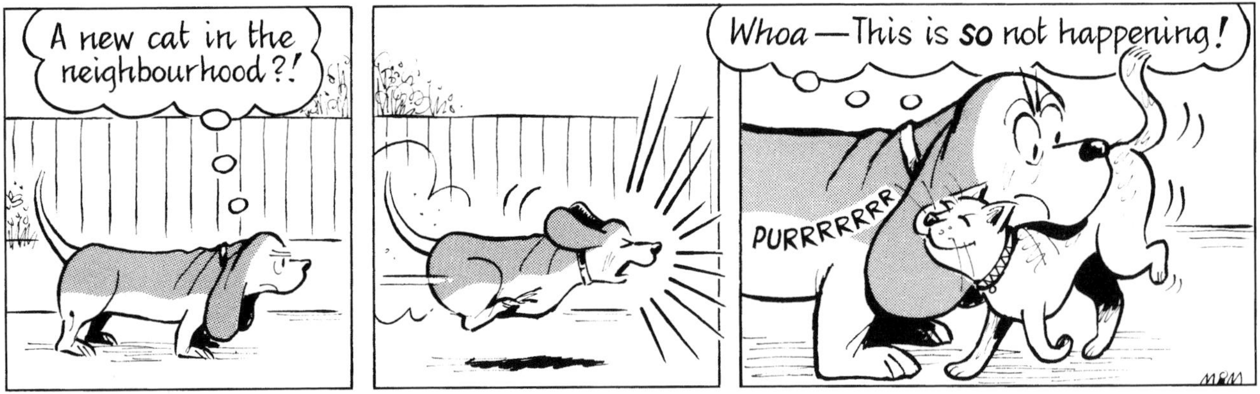
A new cat in the neighbourhood?!
Whoa—This is SO not happening!
PURRRRRRR
M&M

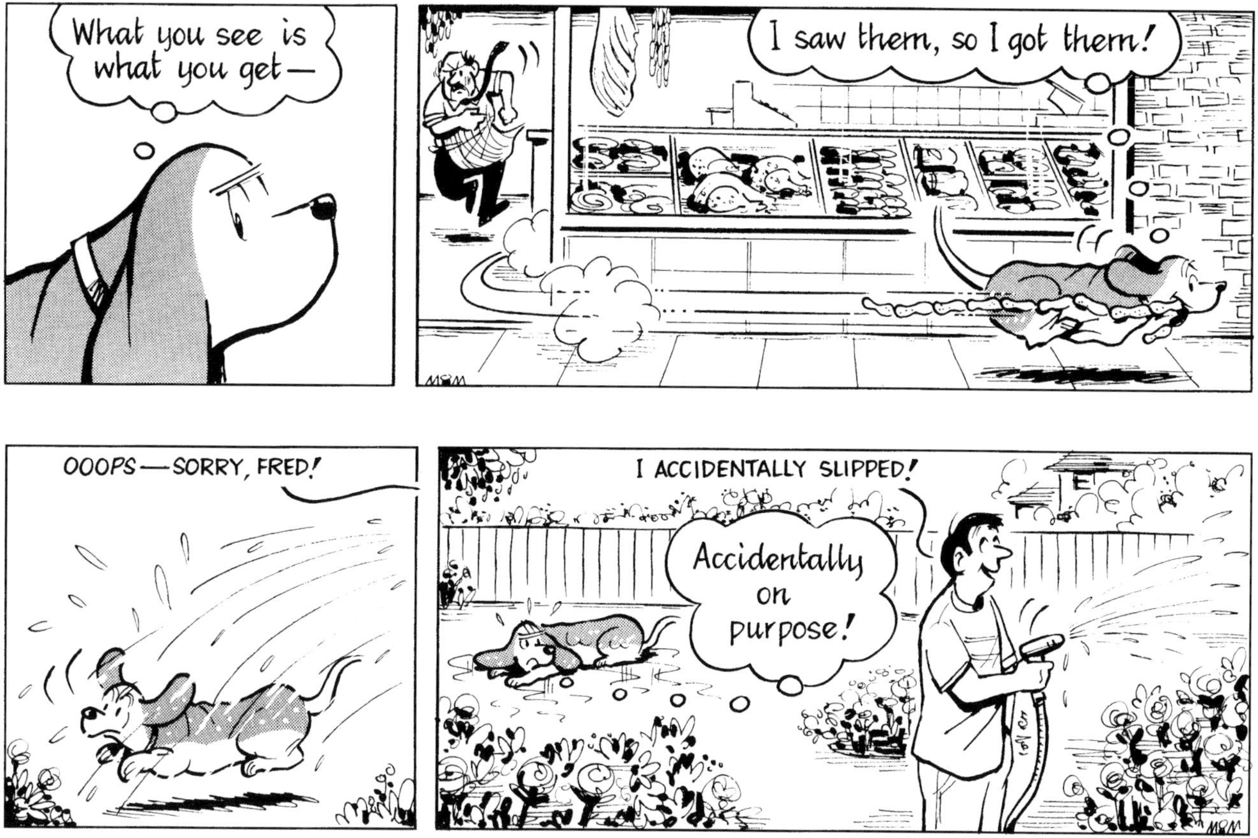
What you see is what you get—
I saw them, so I got them!
OOOPS—SORRY, FRED!
I ACCIDENTALLY SLIPPED!
Accidentally on purpose!

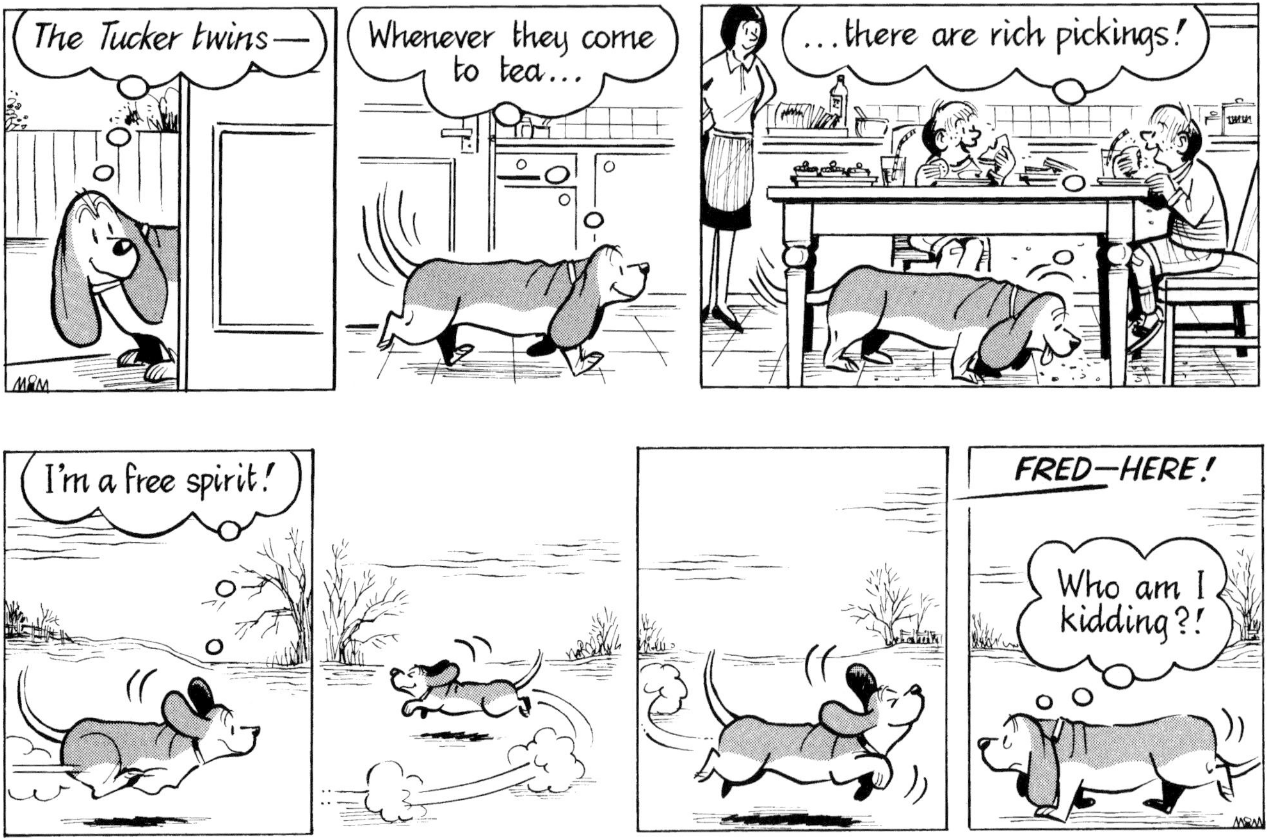
The Tucker twins—
Whenever they come to tea...
...there are rich pickings!
I'm a free spirit!
FRED—HERE!
Who am I kidding?!

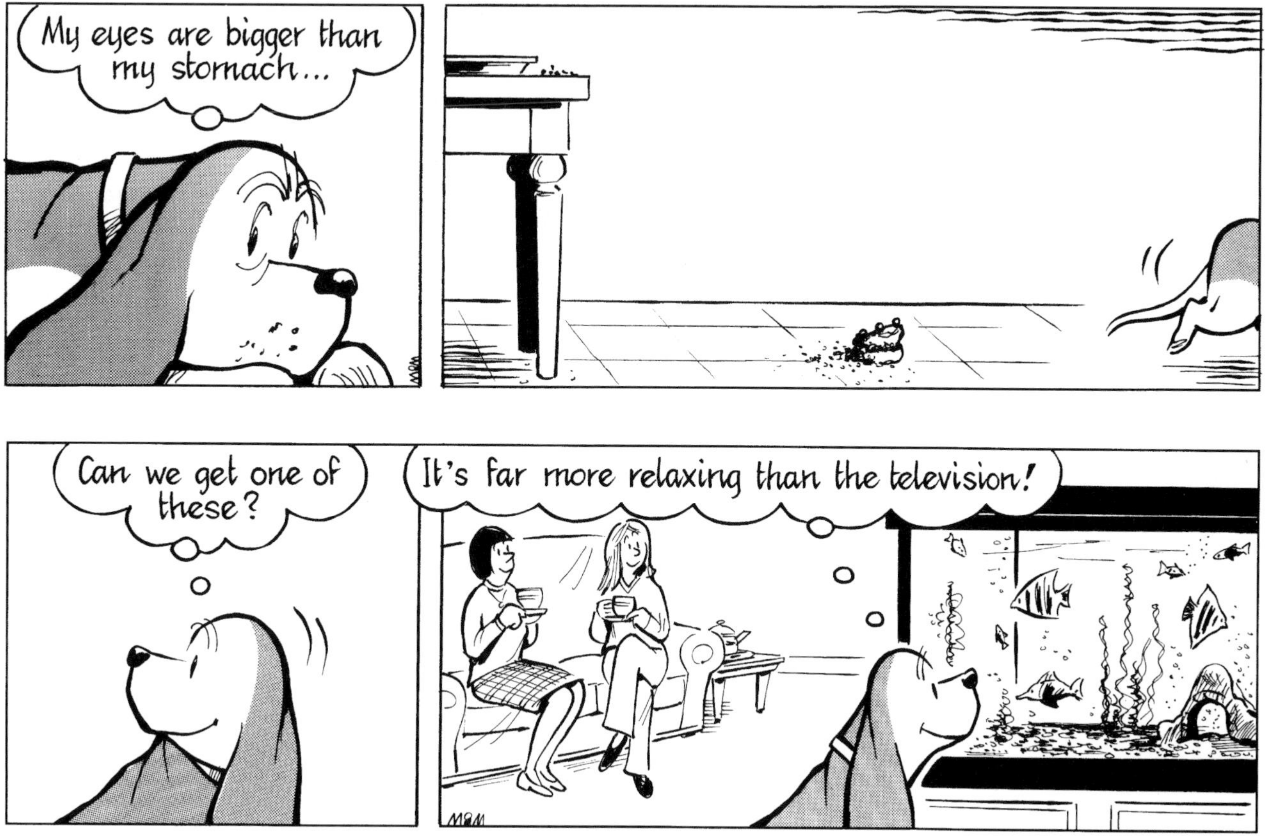
My eyes are bigger than my stomach...
Can we get one of these?
It's far more relaxing than the television!

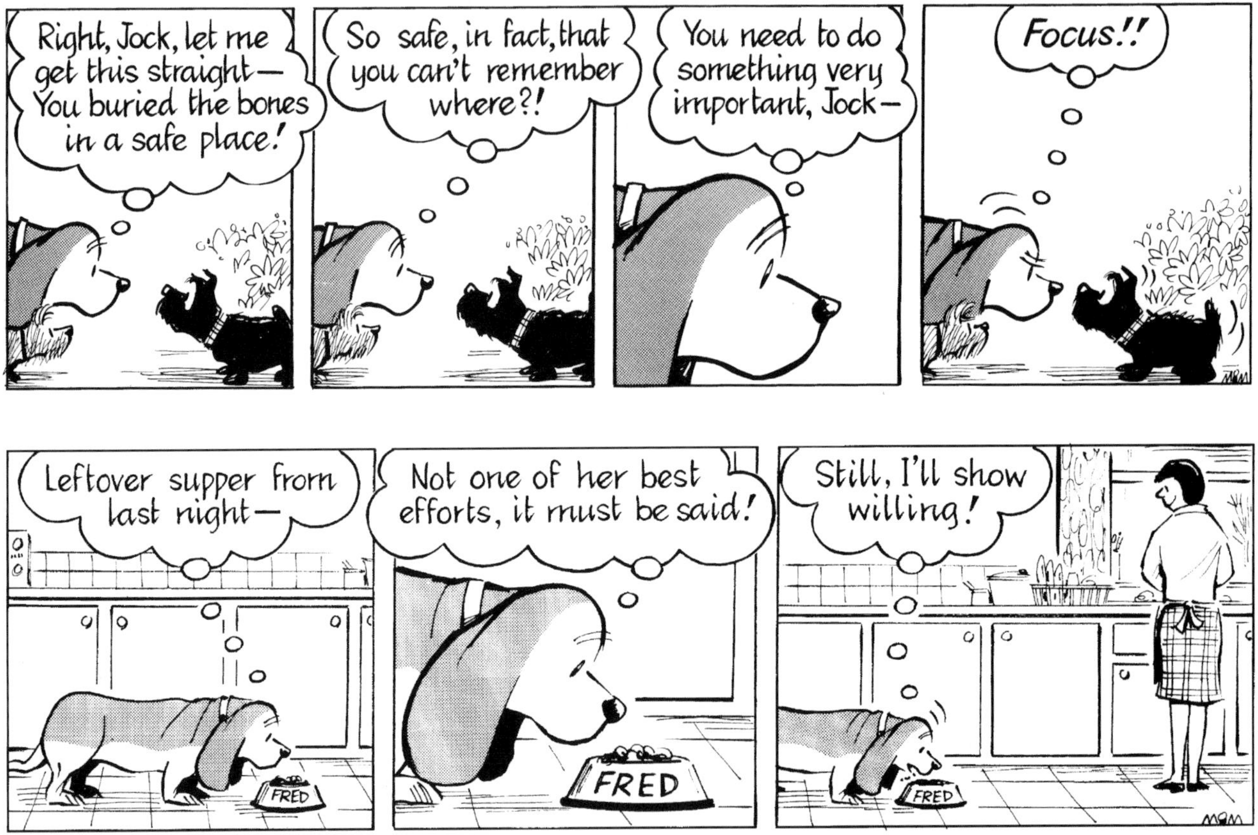

Right, Jock, let me get this straight— You buried the bones in a safe place!
So safe, in fact, that you can't remember where?!
You need to do something very important, Jock—
Focus!!
Leftover supper from last night—
Not one of her best efforts, it must be said!
FRED
Still, I'll show willing!
FRED
FRED

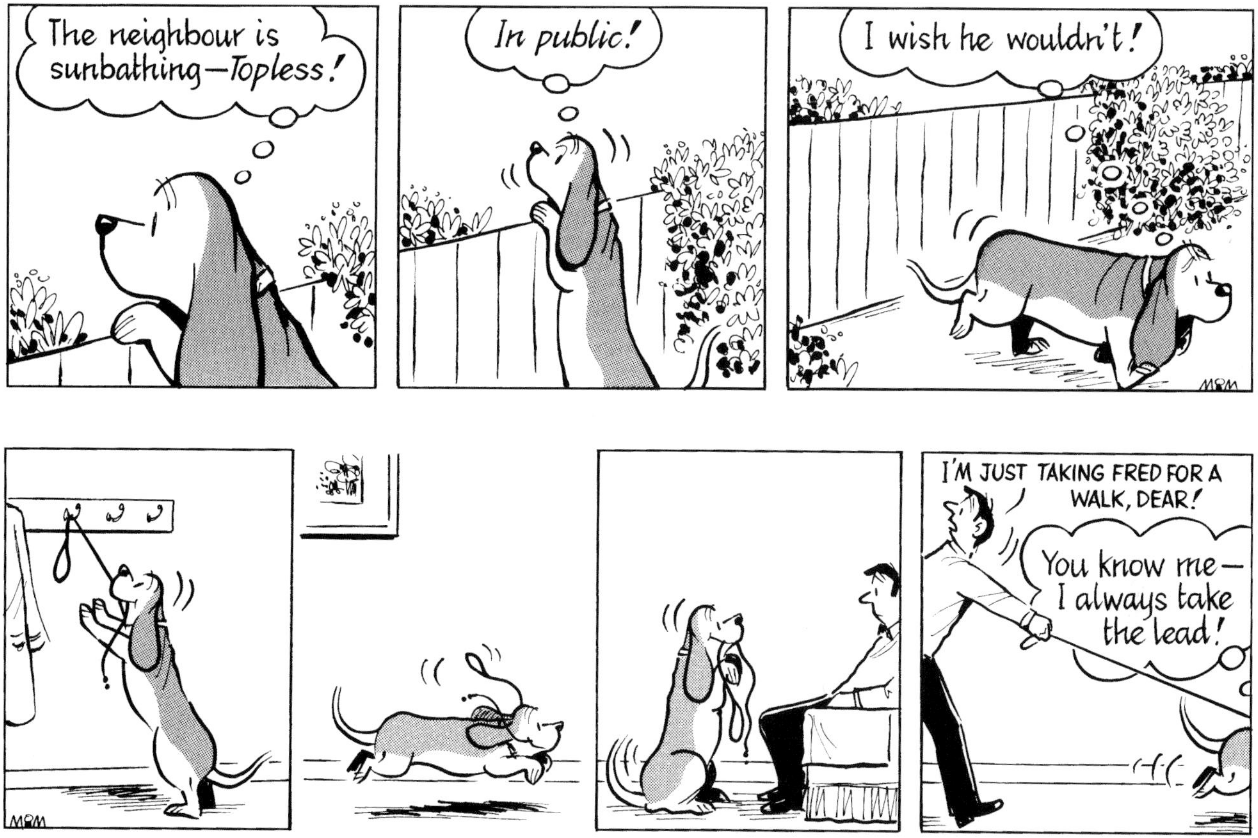

The neighbour is sunbathing—*Topless*!
In public!
I wish he wouldn't!
MGM
MGM
I'M JUST TAKING FRED FOR A WALK, DEAR!
You know me— I always take the lead!

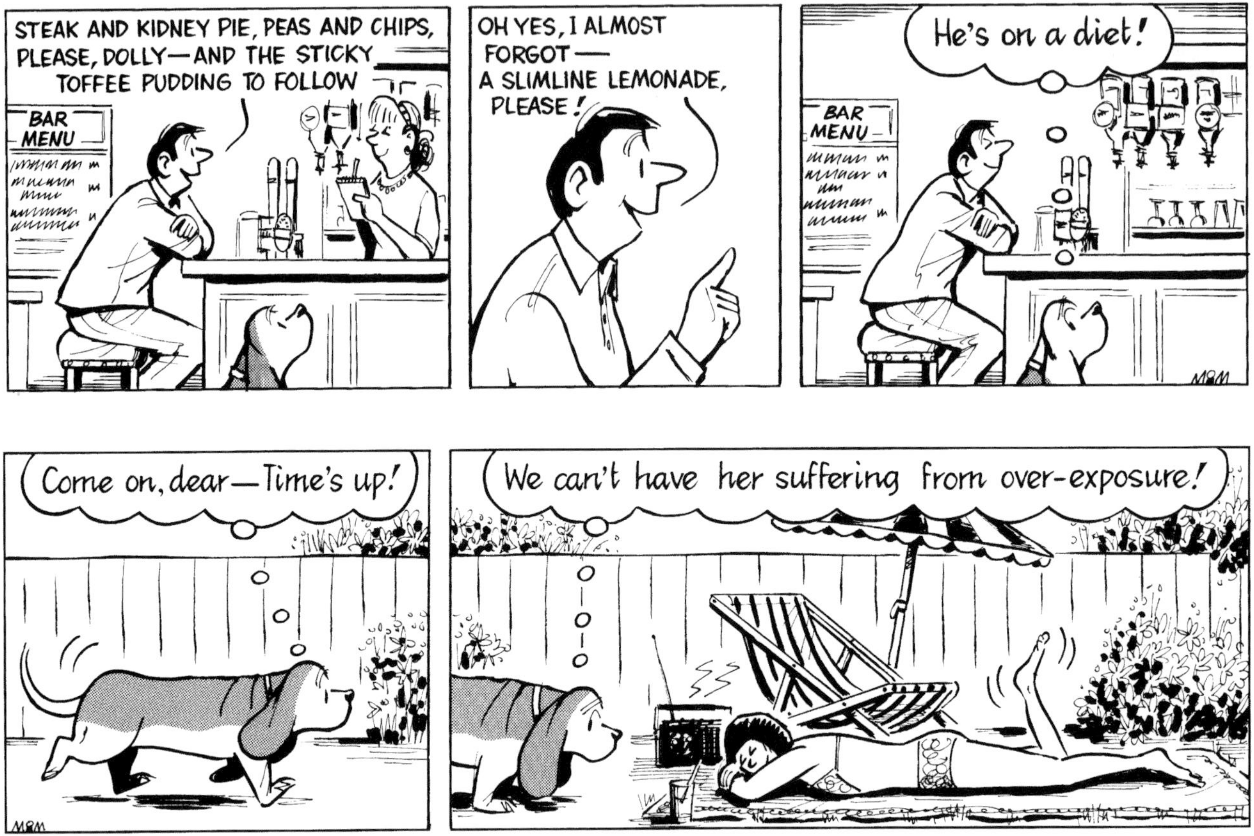
STEAK AND KIDNEY PIE, PEAS AND CHIPS, PLEASE, DOLLY—AND THE STICKY TOFFEE PUDDING TO FOLLOW
BAR MENU
OH YES, I ALMOST FORGOT— A SLIMLINE LEMONADE, PLEASE!
He's on a diet!
BAR MENU
Come on, dear—Time's up!
We can't have her suffering from over-exposure!

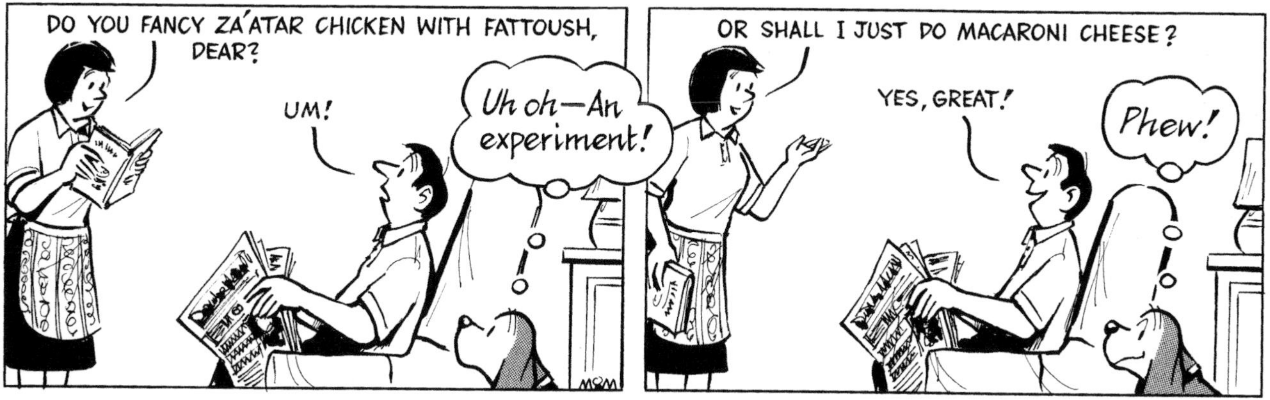
DO YOU FANCY ZA'ATAR CHICKEN WITH FATTOUSH, DEAR?
UM!
Uh oh—An experiment!
OR SHALL I JUST DO MACARONI CHEESE?
YES, GREAT!
Phew!

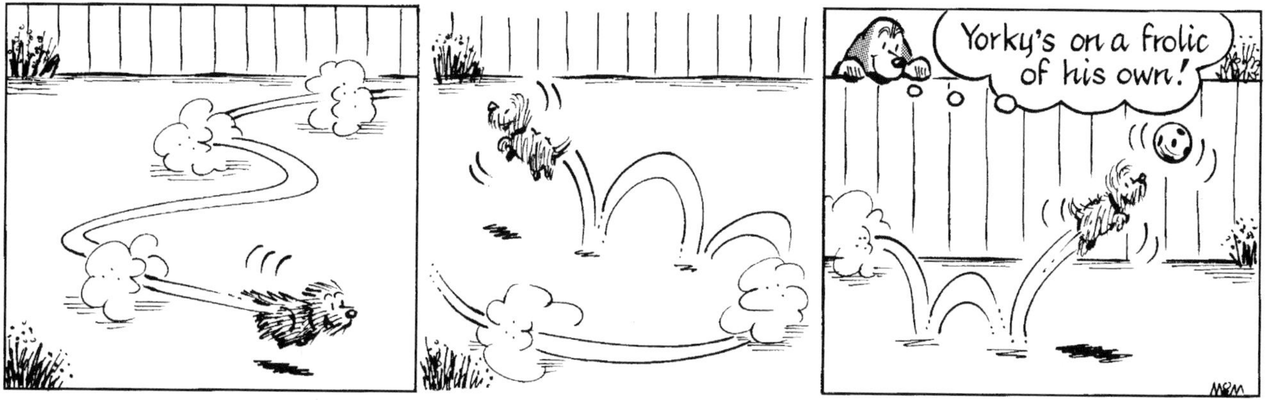
Yorky's on a frolic of his own!

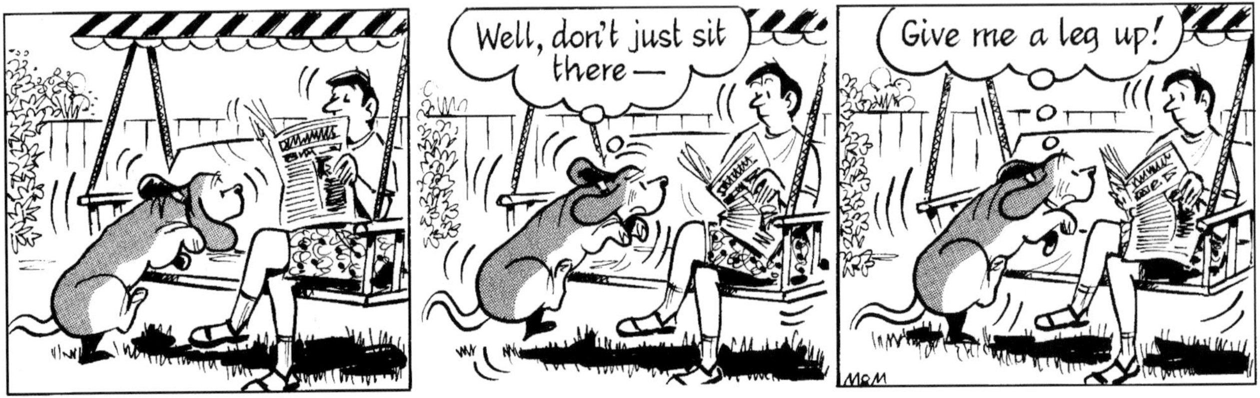
Well, don't just sit there—
Give me a leg up!
M&M

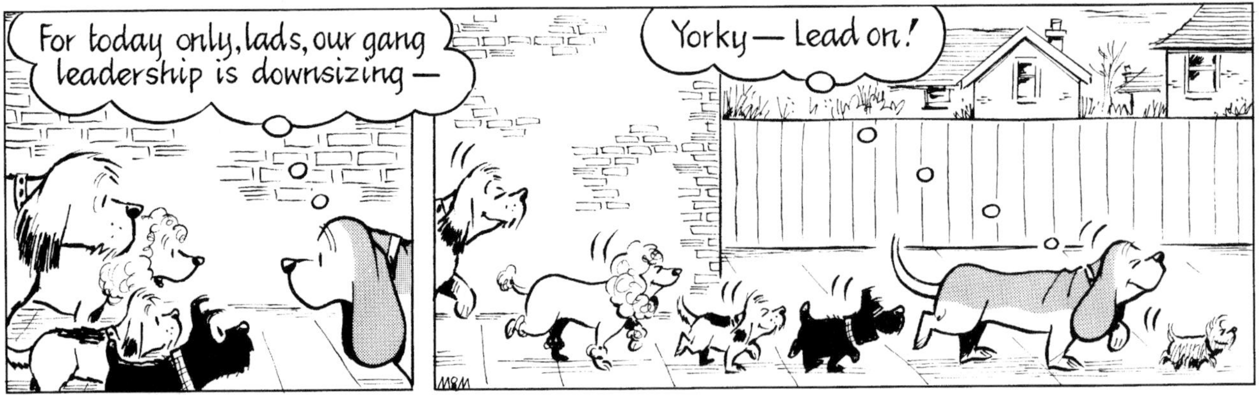
For today only, lads, our gang leadership is downsizing—
Yorky— Lead on!
M&M

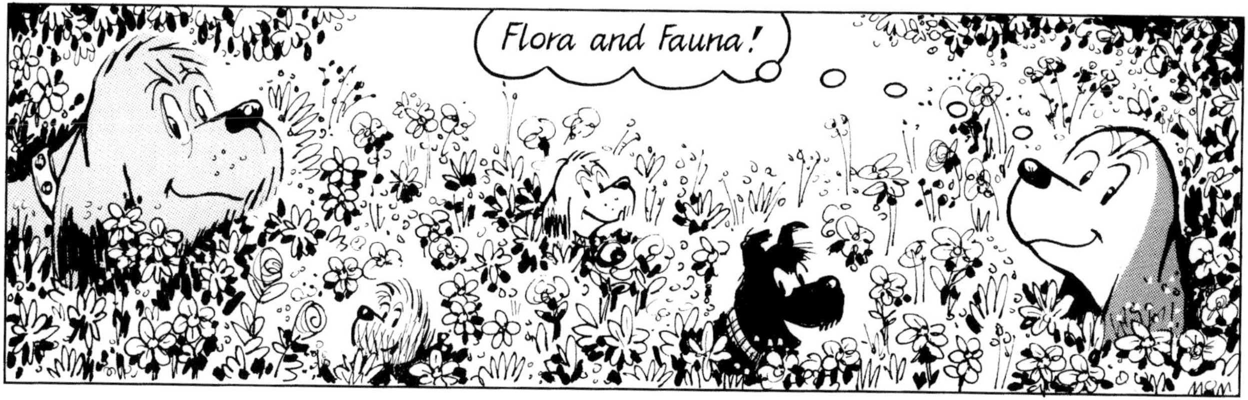
Flora and Fauna!

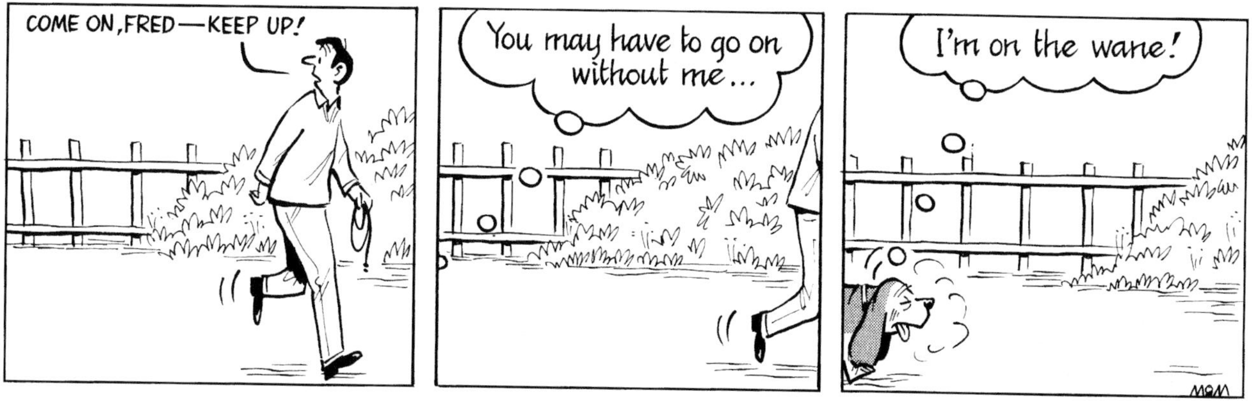
COME ON, FRED—KEEP UP!
You may have to go on without me...
I'm on the wane!

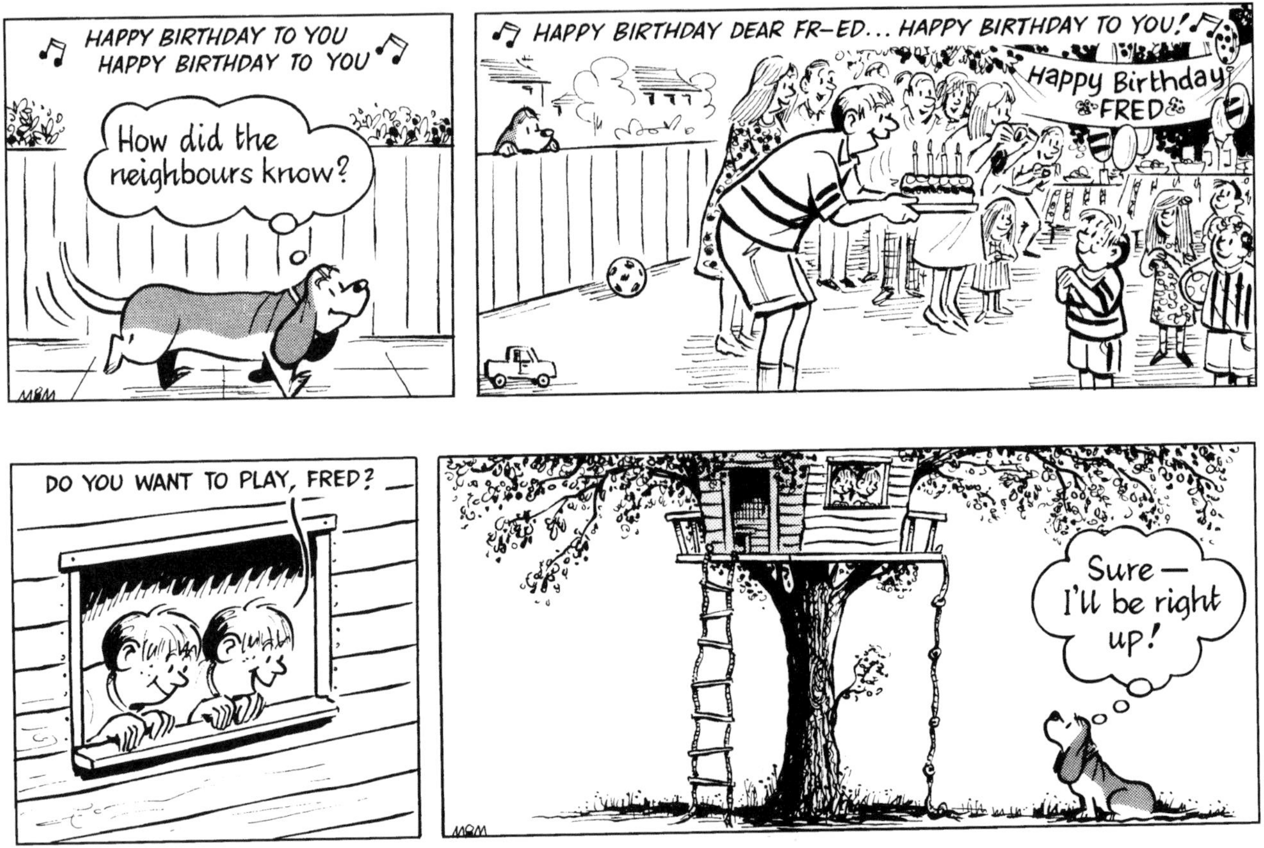
HAPPY BIRTHDAY TO YOU
HAPPY BIRTHDAY TO YOU
How did the neighbours know?
HAPPY BIRTHDAY DEAR FR—ED... HAPPY BIRTHDAY TO YOU!
Happy Birthday FRED
DO YOU WANT TO PLAY, FRED?
Sure — I'll be right up!

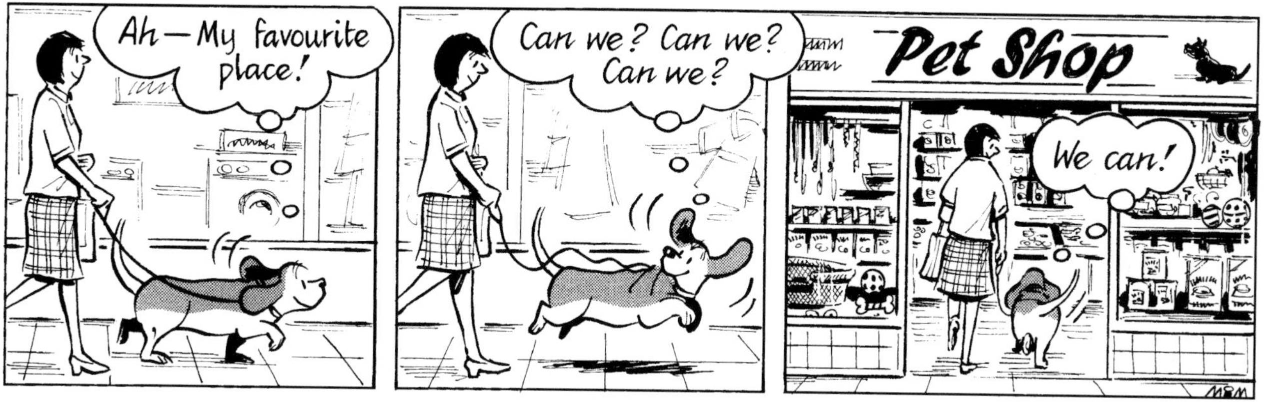
Ah—My favourite place!
Can we? Can we? Can we?
Pet Shop
We can!

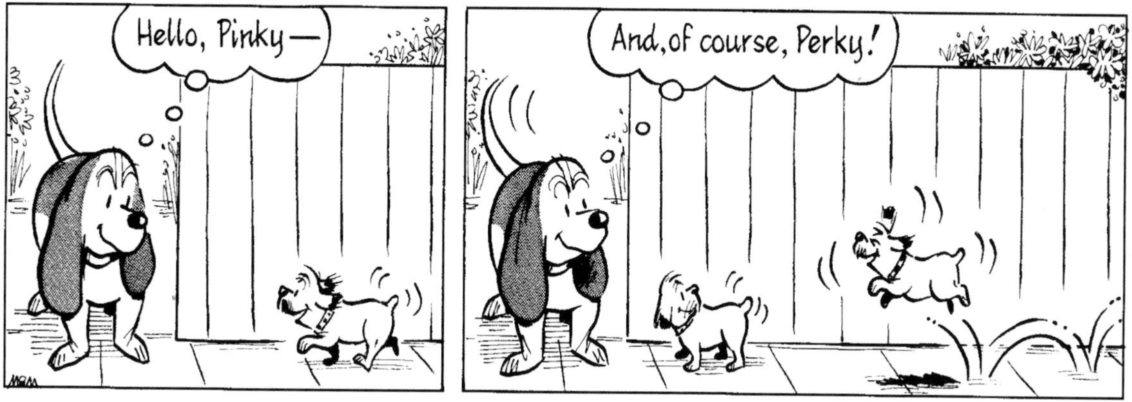
Hello, Pinky—
And, of course, Perky!

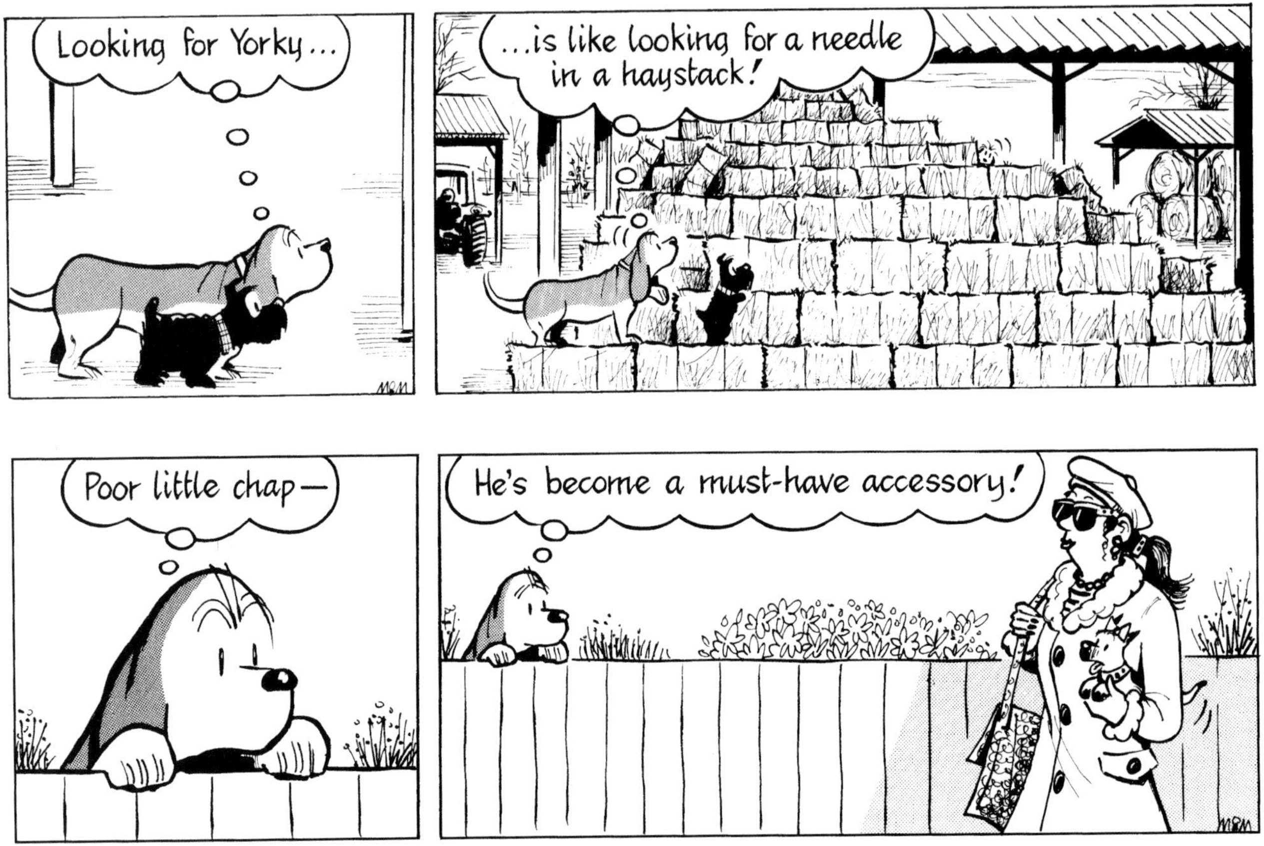
Looking for Yorky...
...is like looking for a needle in a haystack!
Poor little chap—
He's become a must-have accessory!

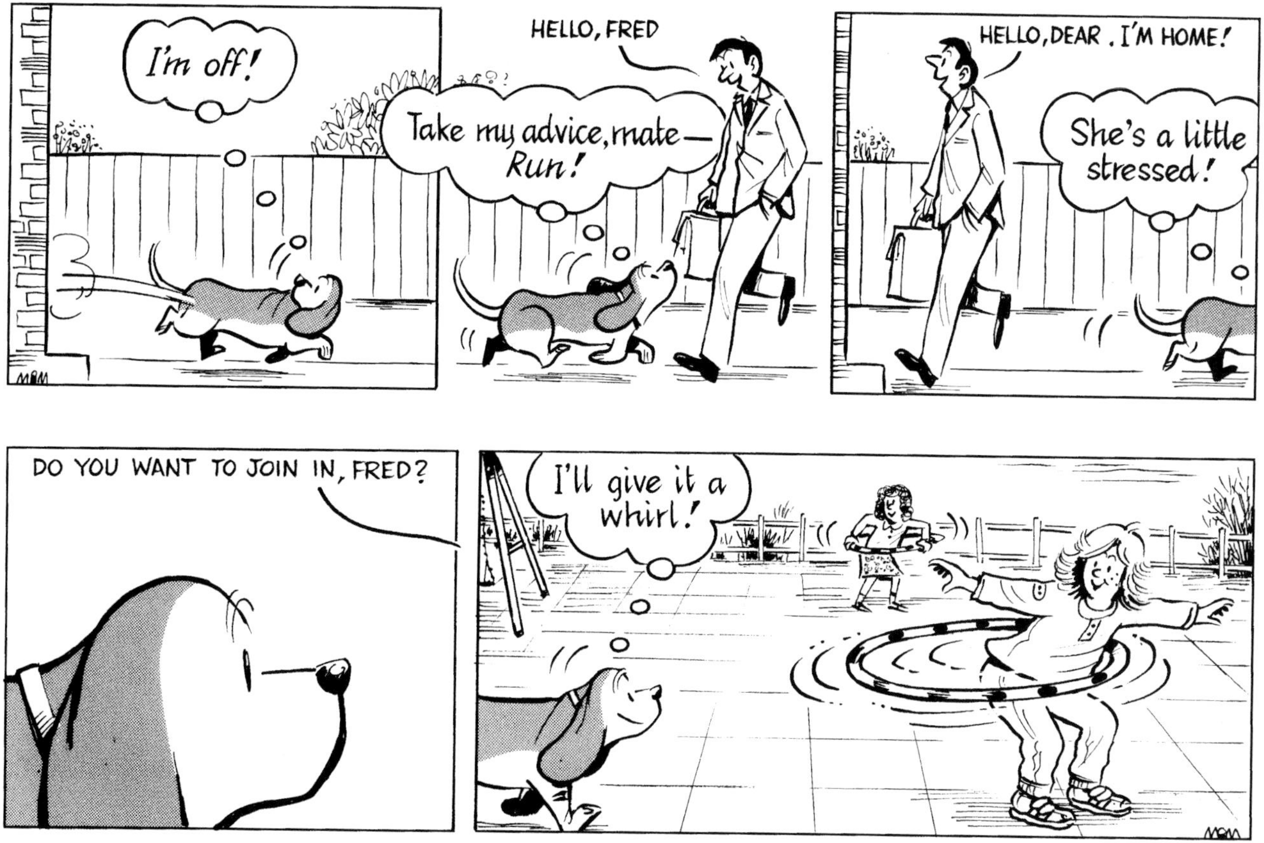
I'm off!
HELLO, FRED
Take my advice, mate — Run!
HELLO, DEAR. I'M HOME!
She's a little stressed!
DO YOU WANT TO JOIN IN, FRED?
I'll give it a whirl!

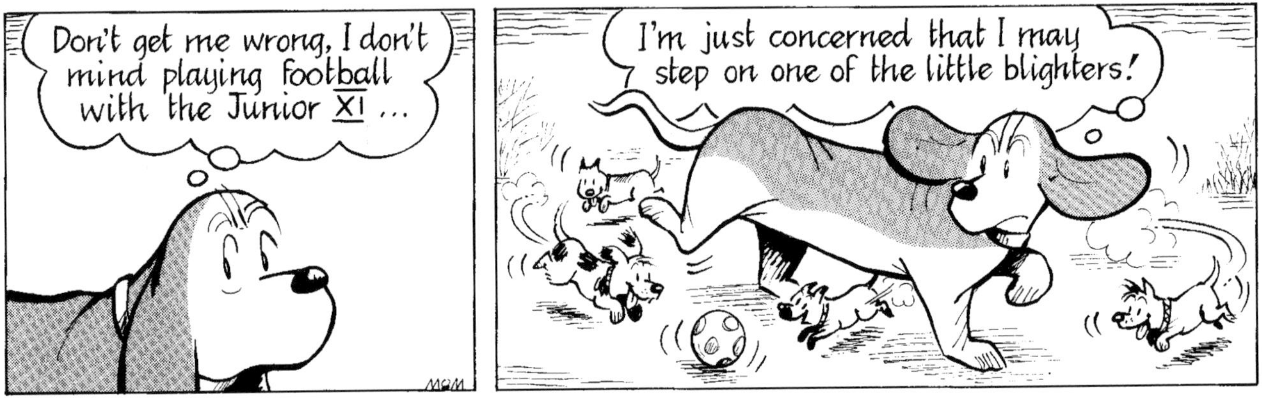
Don't get me wrong, I don't mind playing football with the Junior XI ...
I'm just concerned that I may step on one of the little blighters!

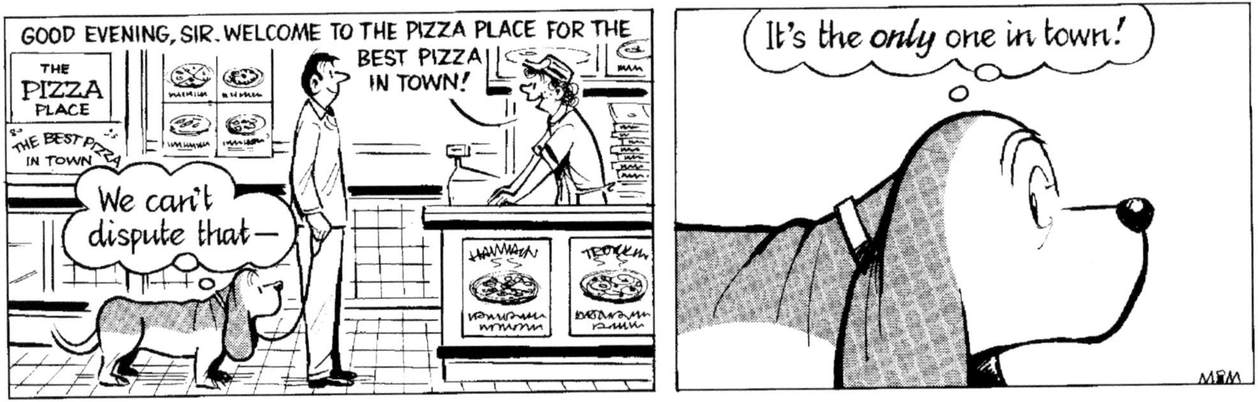
GOOD EVENING, SIR. WELCOME TO THE PIZZA PLACE FOR THE BEST PIZZA IN TOWN!
THE PIZZA PLACE
THE BEST PIZZA IN TOWN
We can't dispute that—
It's the *only* one in town!

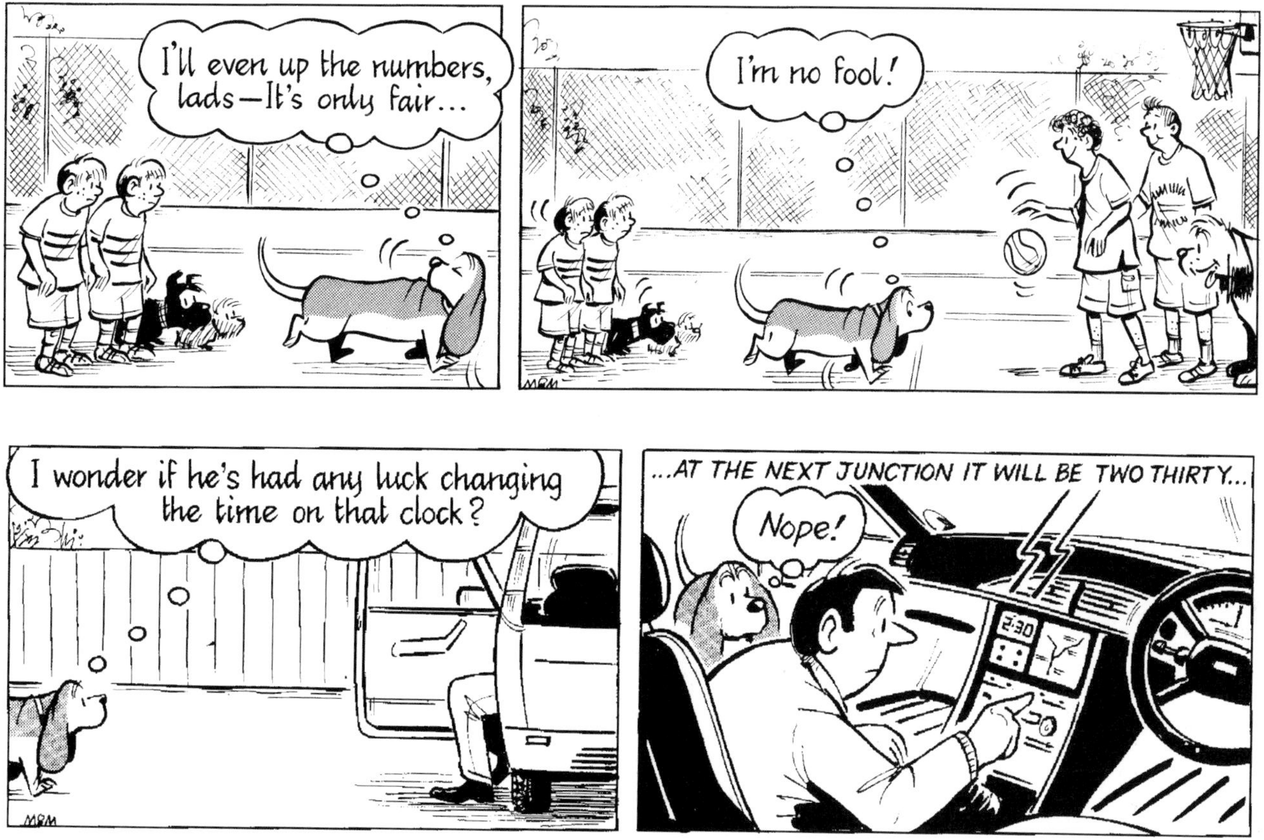
I'll even up the numbers, lads—It's only fair...
I'm no fool!
I wonder if he's had any luck changing the time on that clock?
...AT THE NEXT JUNCTION IT WILL BE TWO THIRTY...
Nope!
2:30

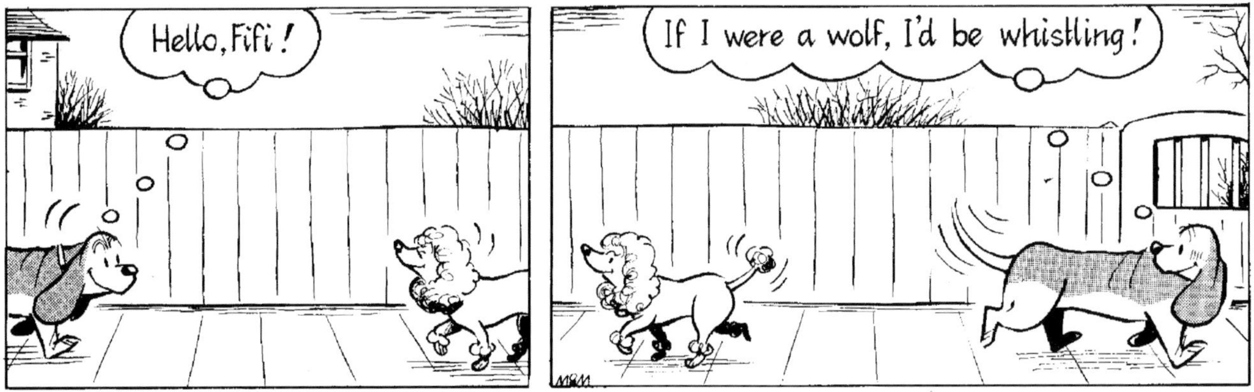
Hello, Fifi!
If I were a wolf, I'd be whistling!
M&M

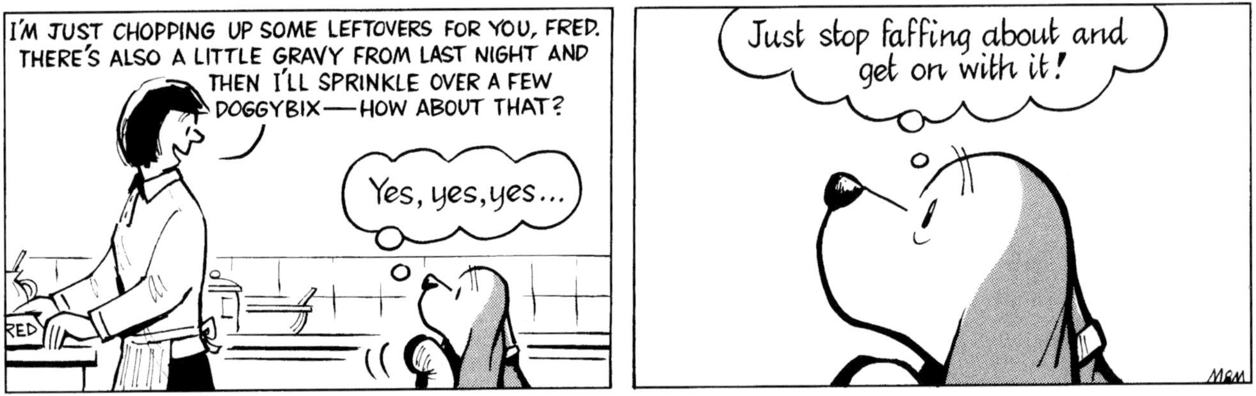
I'M JUST CHOPPING UP SOME LEFTOVERS FOR YOU, FRED. THERE'S ALSO A LITTLE GRAVY FROM LAST NIGHT AND THEN I'LL SPRINKLE OVER A FEW DOGGYBIX — HOW ABOUT THAT?
Yes, yes, yes...
Just stop faffing about and get on with it!
M&M

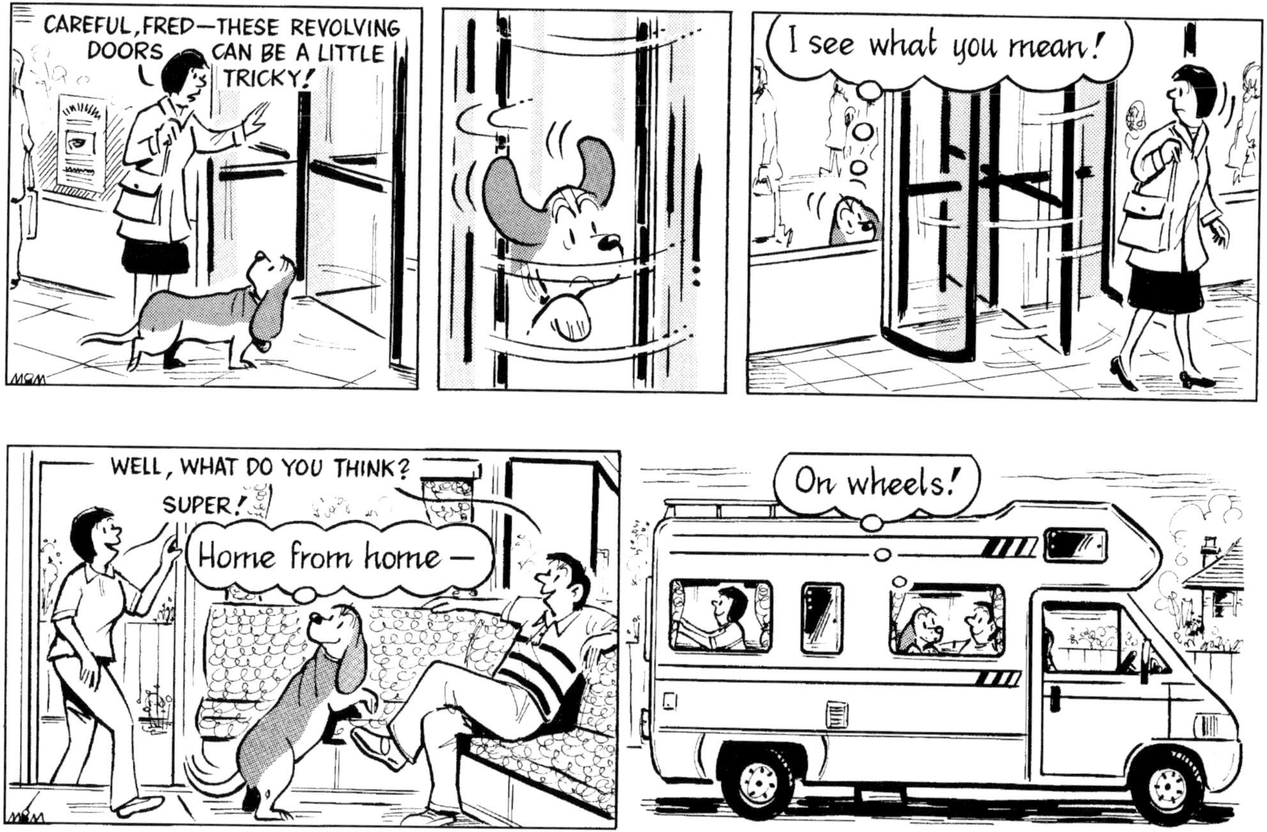
CAREFUL, FRED—THESE REVOLVING DOORS CAN BE A LITTLE TRICKY!
I see what you mean!
WELL, WHAT DO YOU THINK?
SUPER!
Home from home —
On wheels!

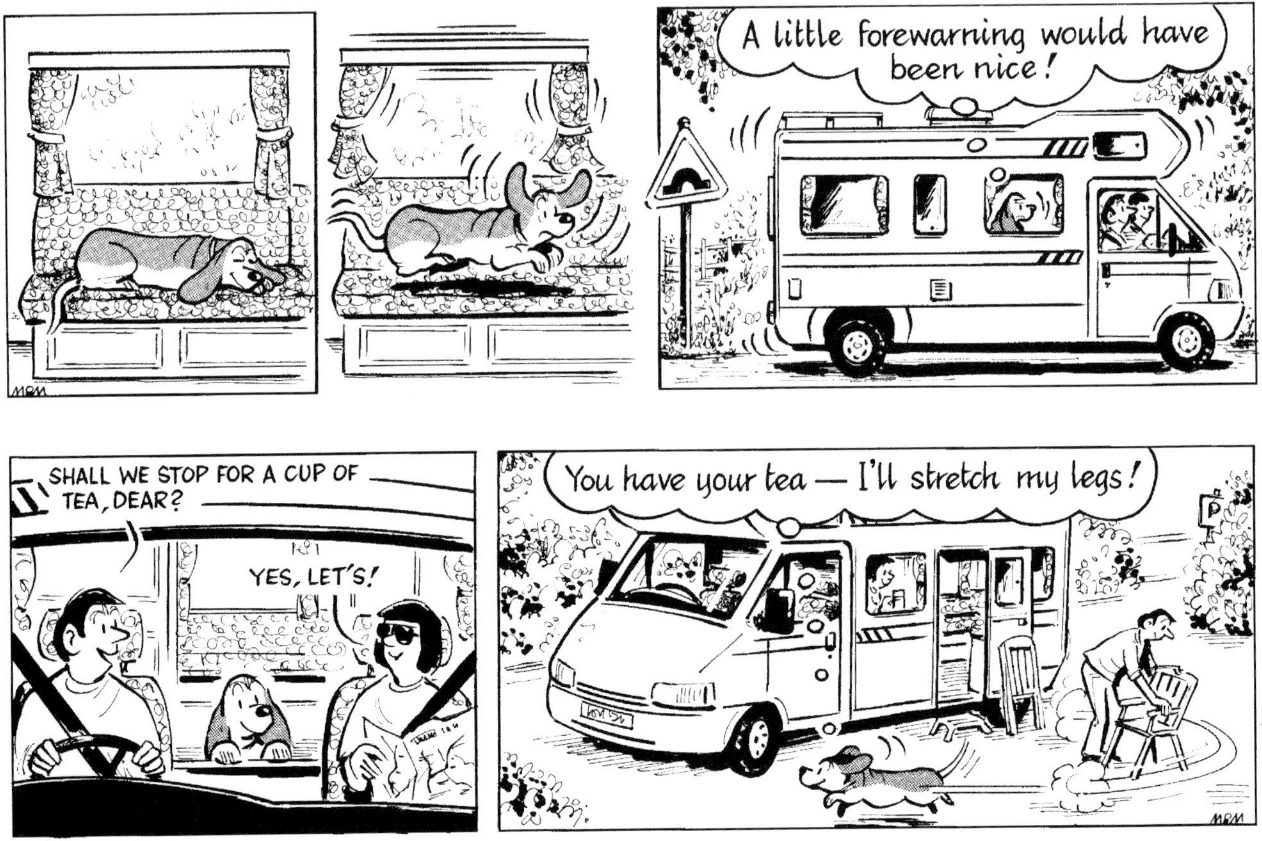
A little forewarning would have been nice!
SHALL WE STOP FOR A CUP OF TEA, DEAR?
YES, LET'S!
You have your tea — I'll stretch my legs!

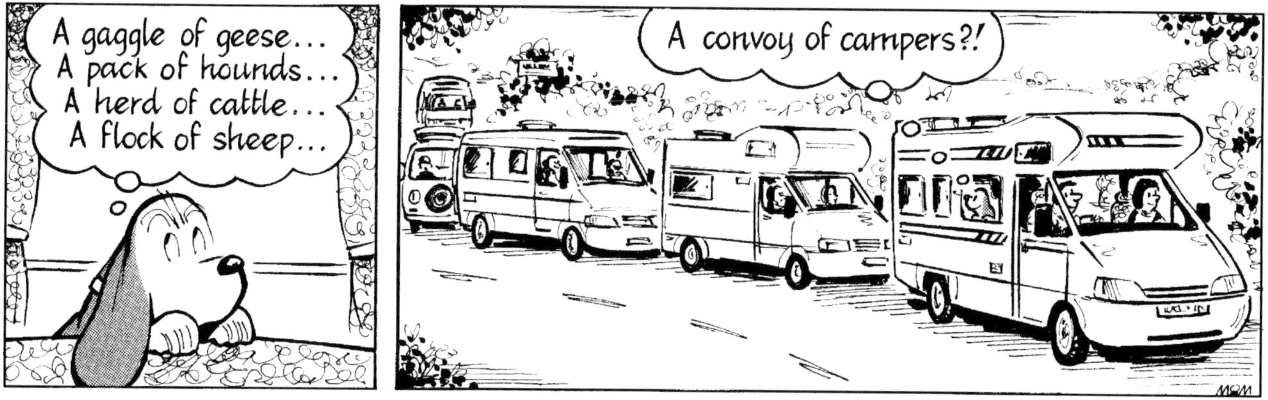
A gaggle of geese... A pack of hounds... A herd of cattle... A flock of sheep...
A convoy of campers?!

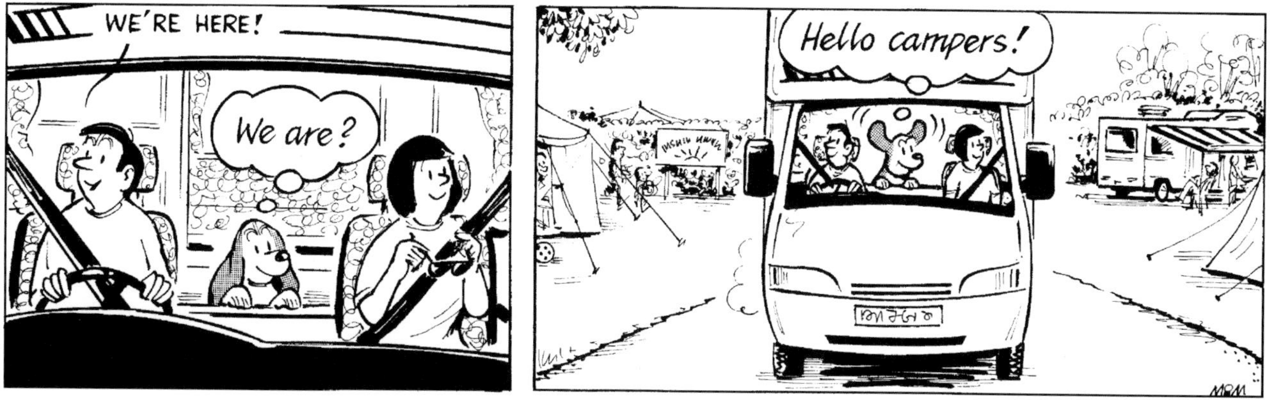
WE'RE HERE!
We are?
Hello campers!

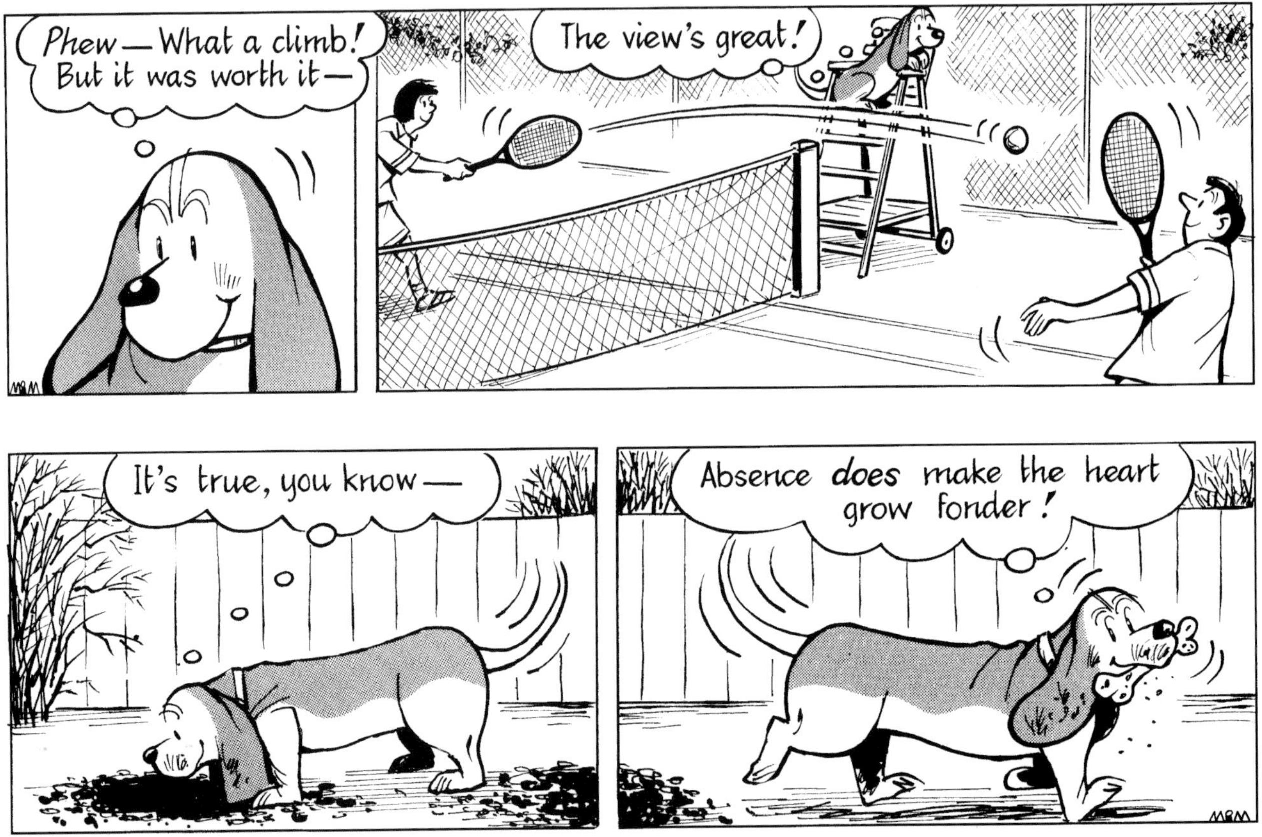
Phew — What a climb! But it was worth it —
MGM
The view's great!
It's true, you know —
Absence does make the heart grow fonder!
MGM

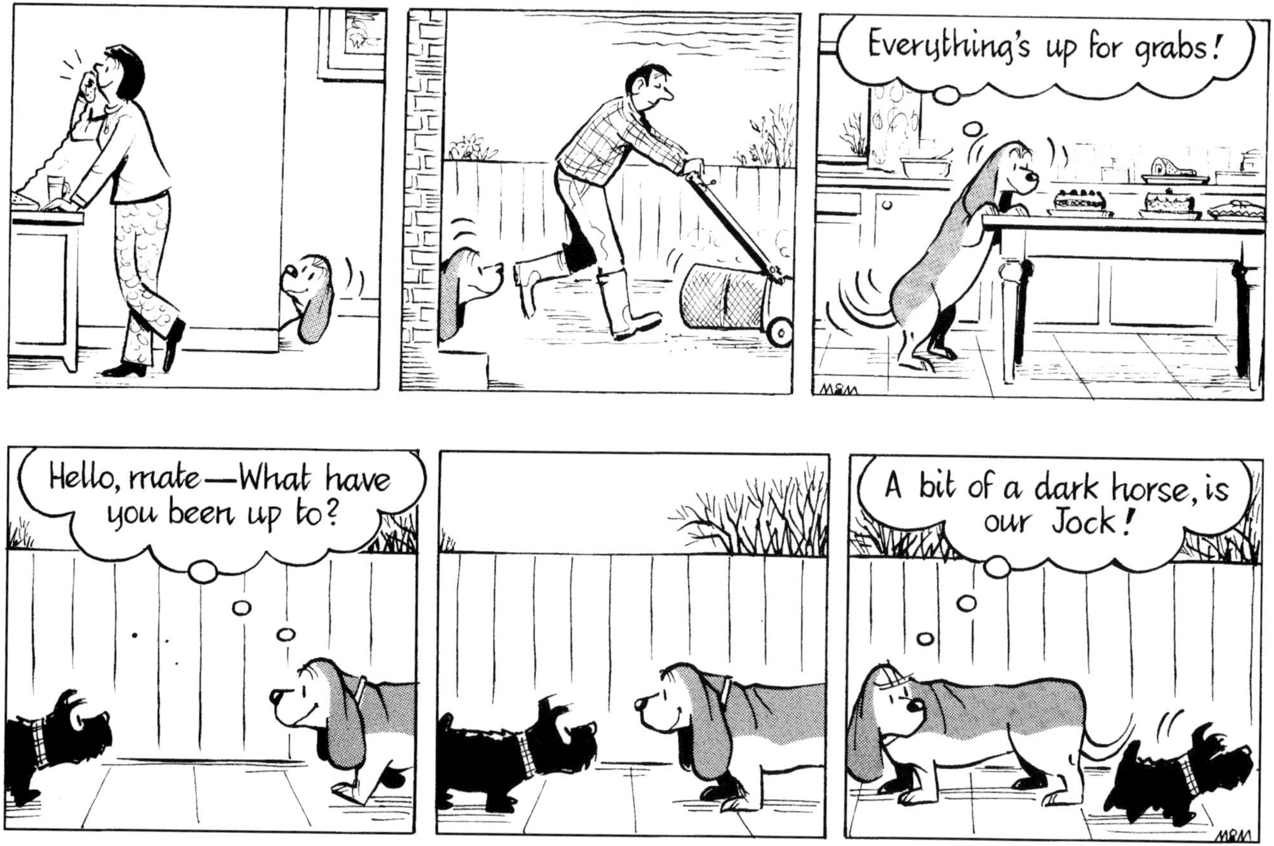
Everything's up for grabs!
MSM
Hello, mate—What have you been up to?
A bit of a dark horse, is our Jock!
MSM

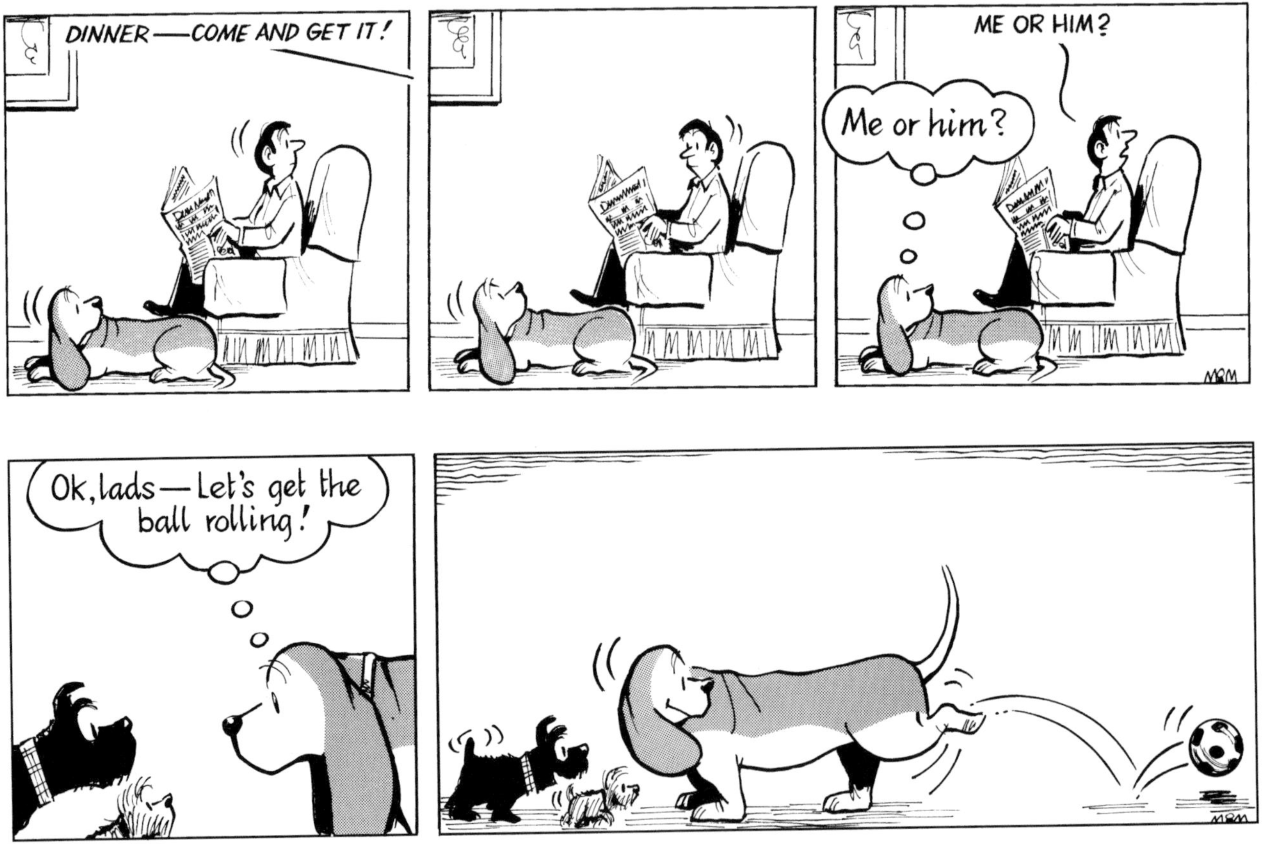
DINNER — COME AND GET IT!
ME OR HIM?
Me or him?
MSM
Ok, lads — Let's get the ball rolling!
MSM

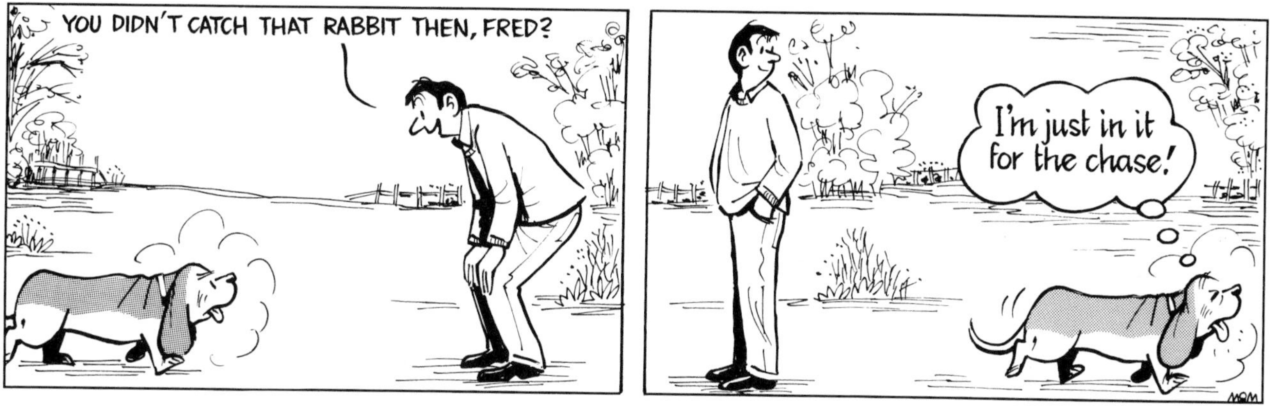
YOU DIDN'T CATCH THAT RABBIT THEN, FRED?
I'm just in it for the chase!

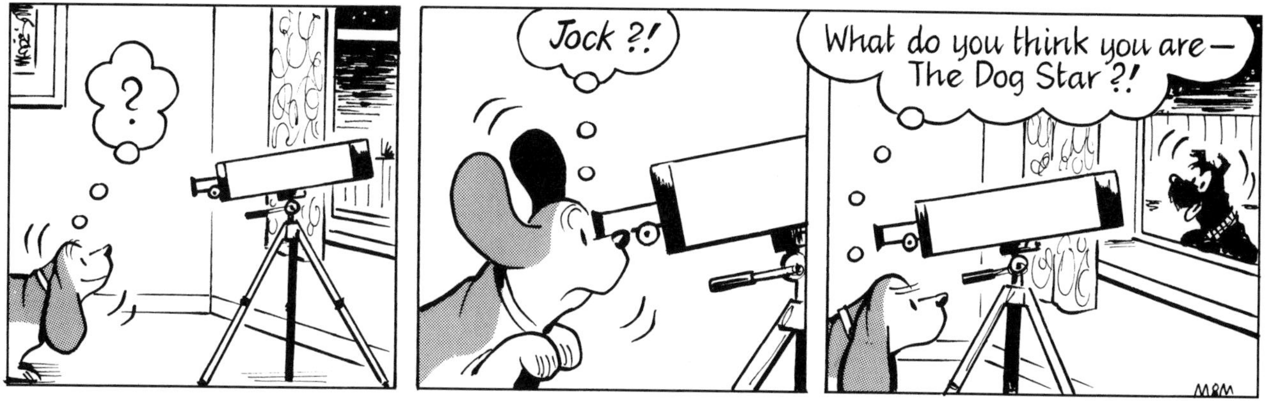
?
Jock ?!
What do you think you are— The Dog Star ?!

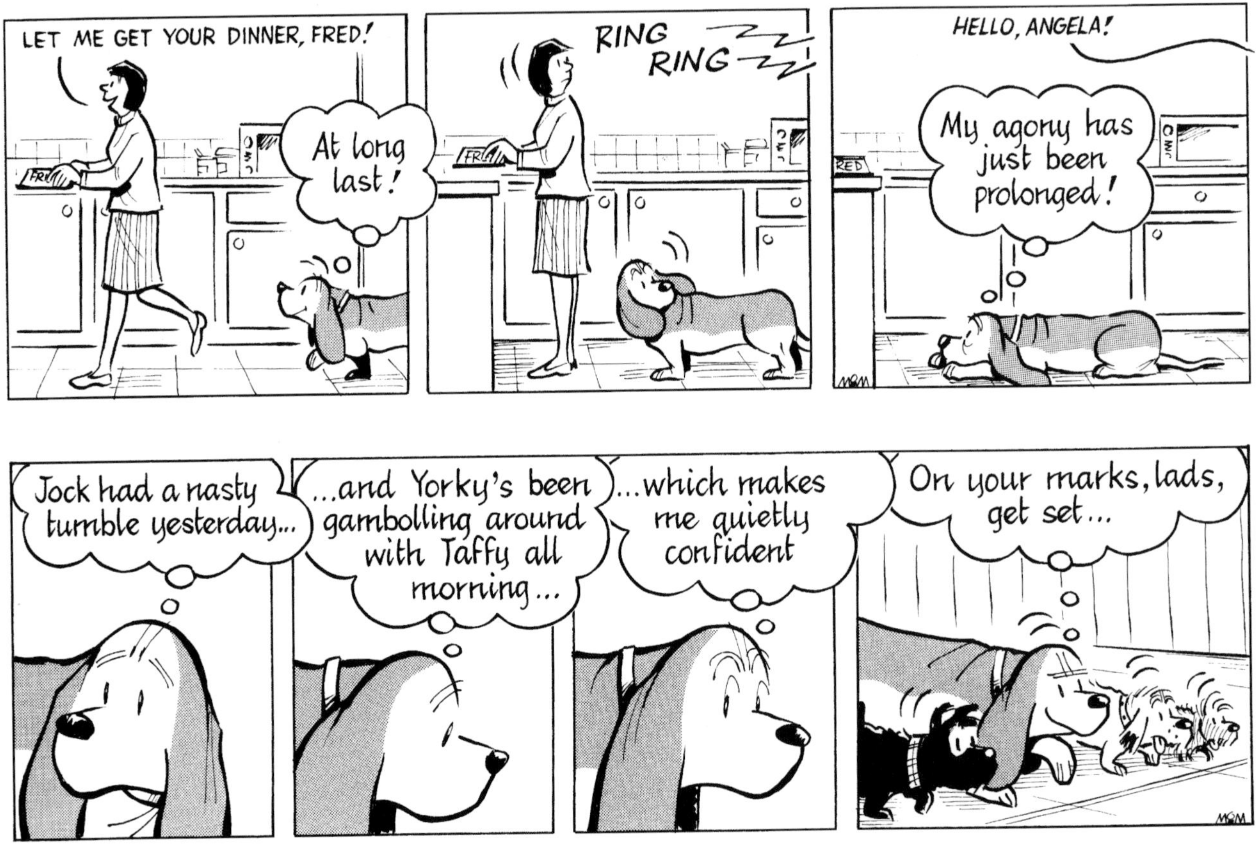
LET ME GET YOUR DINNER, FRED!
At long last!
RING RING
HELLO, ANGELA!
My agony has just been prolonged!
Jock had a nasty tumble yesterday...
...and Yorky's been gambolling around with Taffy all morning...
...which makes me quietly confident
On your marks, lads, get set...

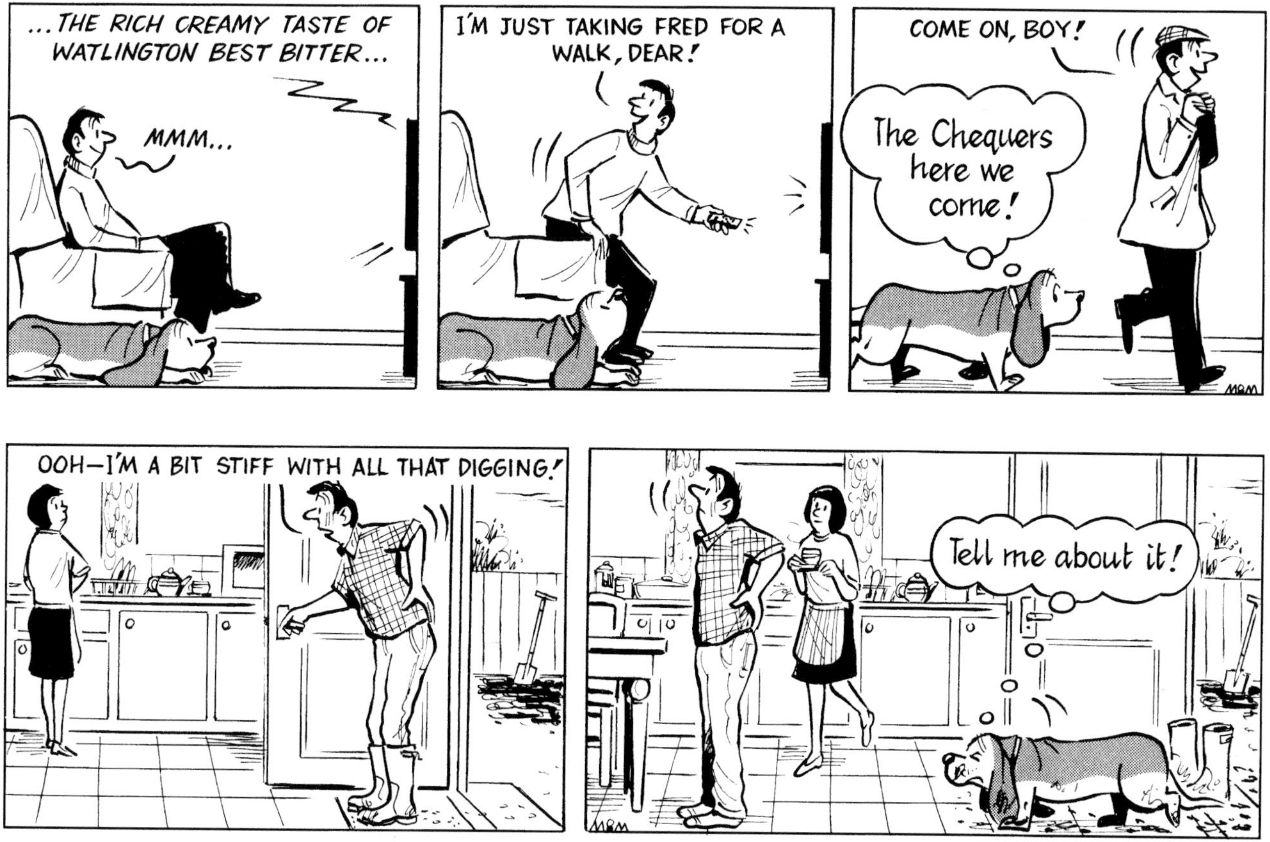
...THE RICH CREAMY TASTE OF WATLINGTON BEST BITTER...
MMM...
I'M JUST TAKING FRED FOR A WALK, DEAR!
COME ON, BOY!
The Chequers here we come!
OOH—I'M A BIT STIFF WITH ALL THAT DIGGING!
Tell me about it!

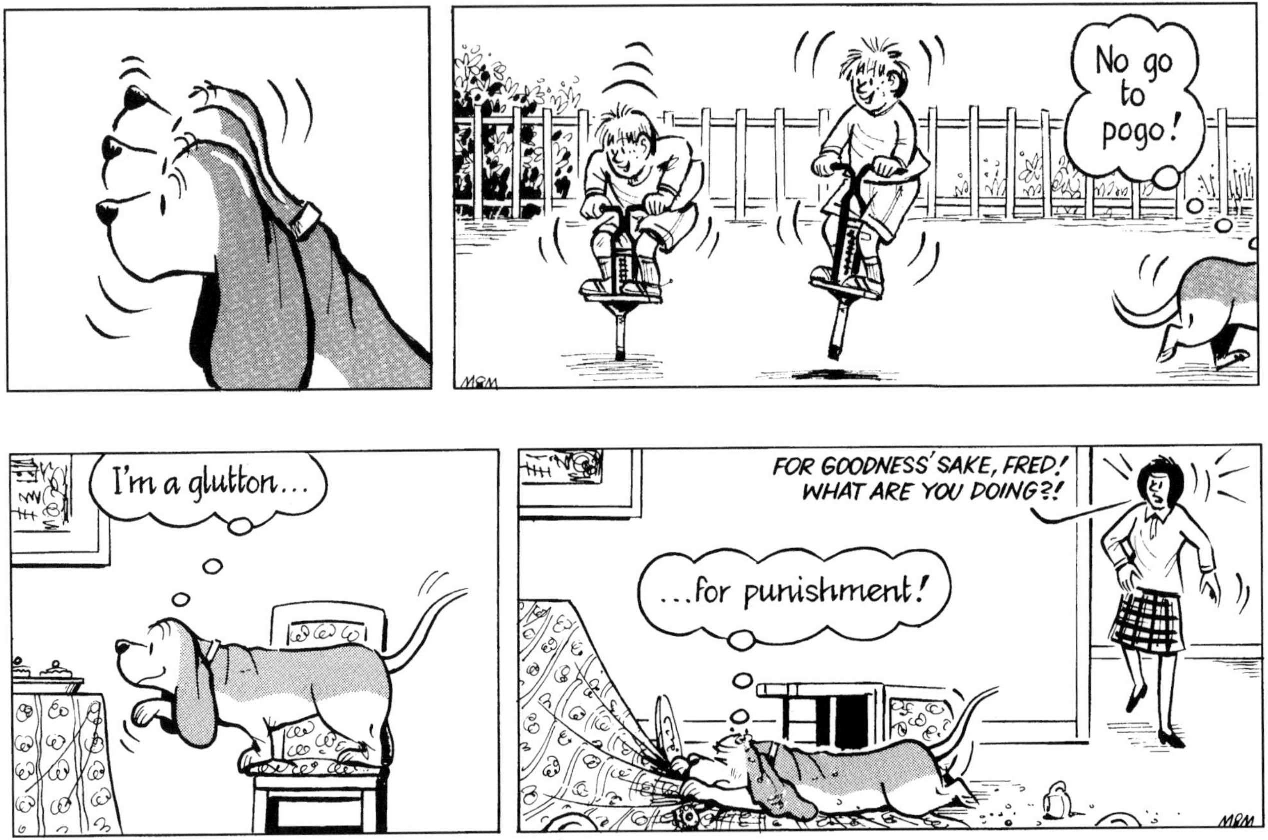
No go to pogo!
I'm a glutton...
FOR GOODNESS' SAKE, FRED! WHAT ARE YOU DOING?!
...for punishment!

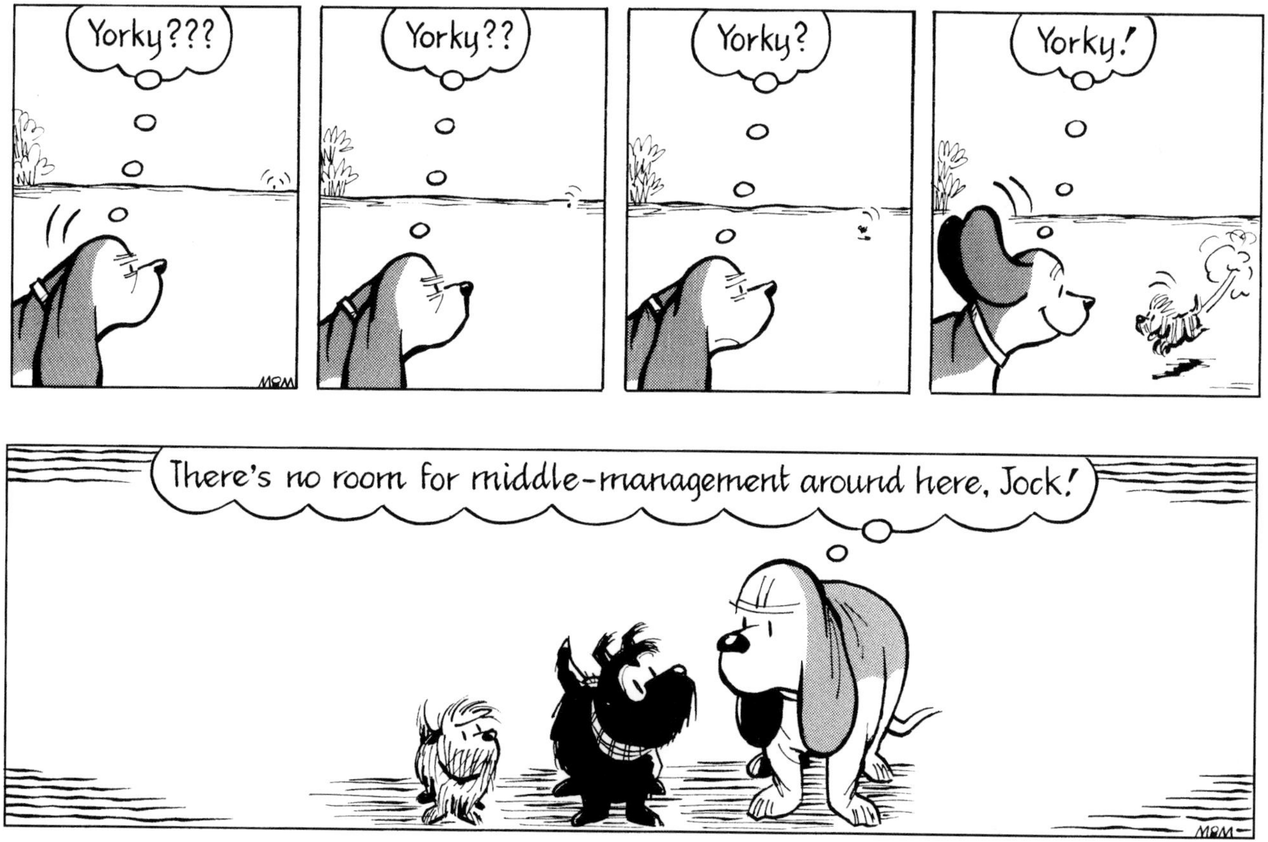
Yorky???
Yorky??
Yorky?
Yorky!
There's no room for middle-management around here, Jock!

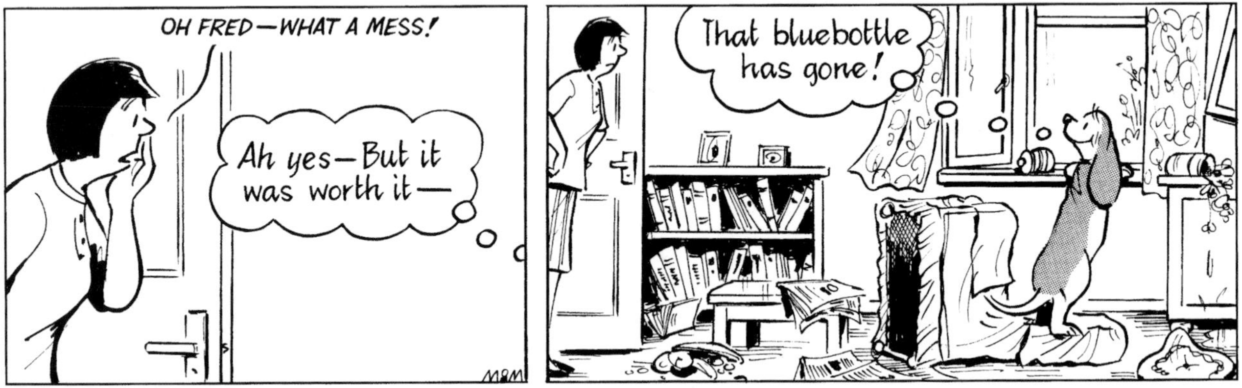
OH FRED—WHAT A MESS!
Ah yes—But it was worth it—
That bluebottle has gone!

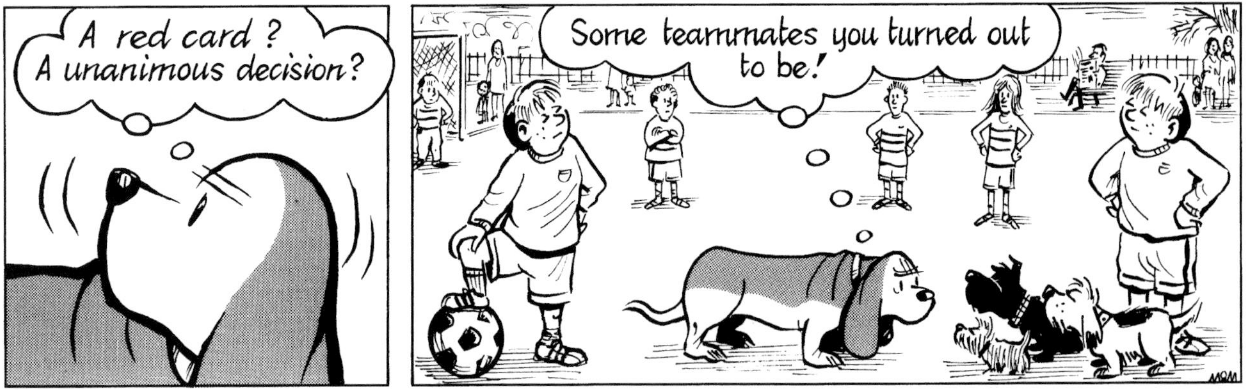
A red card ? A unanimous decision?
Some teammates you turned out to be!

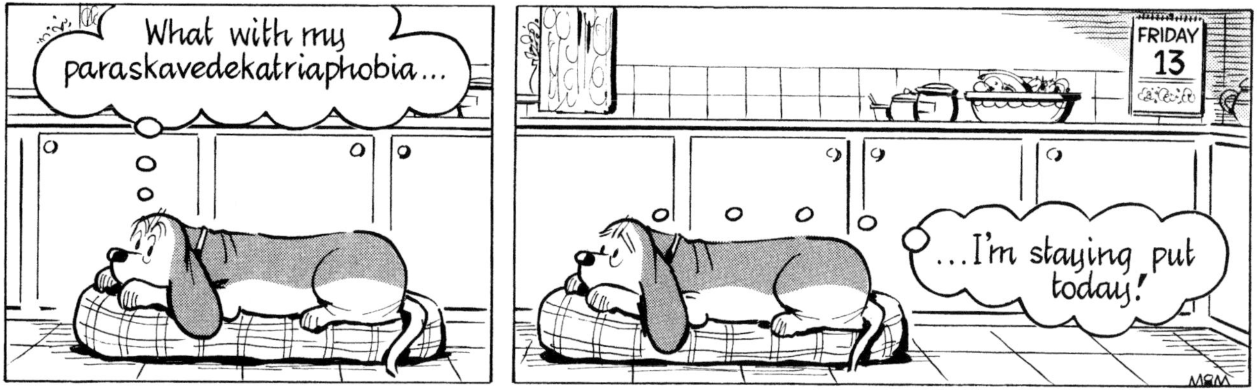
What with my paraskavedekatriaphobia...
FRIDAY 13
...I'm staying put today!

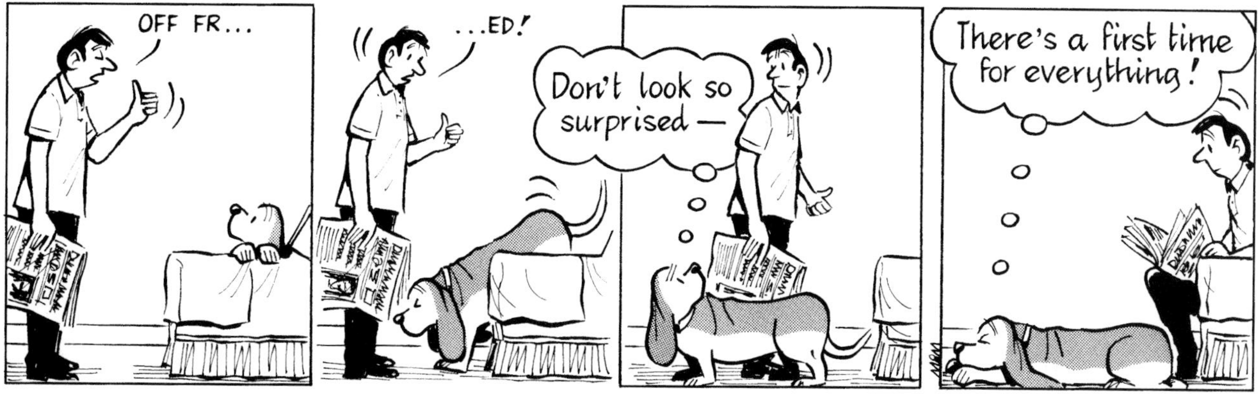
OFF FR...
...ED!
Don't look so surprised —
There's a first time for everything!

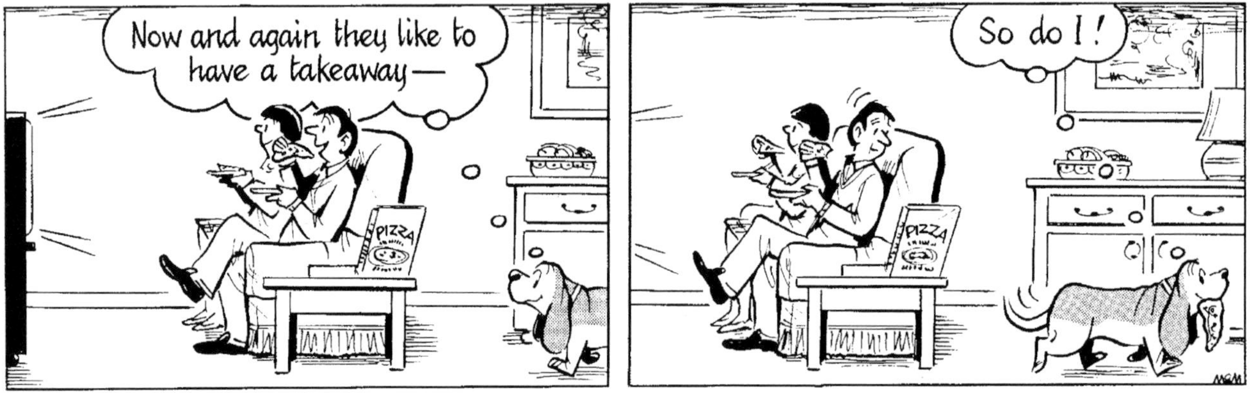
Now and again they like to have a takeaway—
PIZZA
So do I!
PIZZA

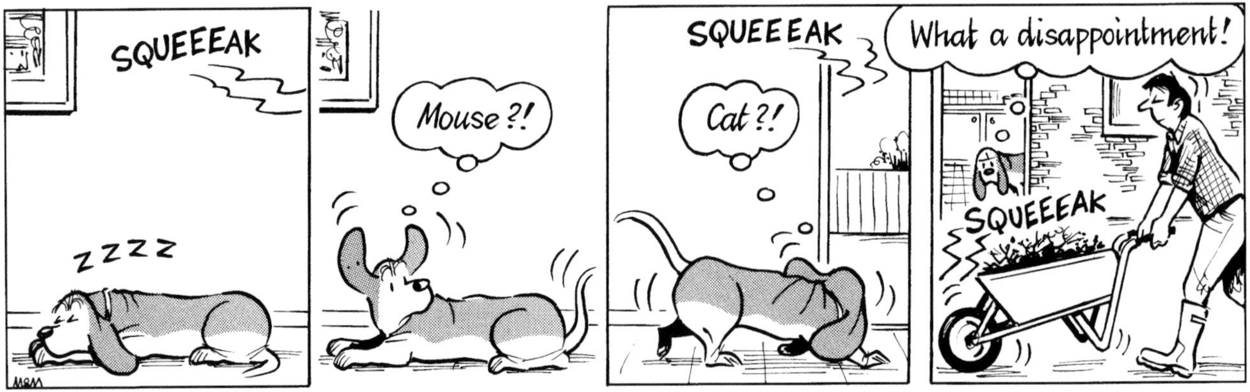
SQUEEEAK
ZZZZ
Mouse?!
SQUEEEAK
Cat?!
What a disappointment!
SQUEEEAK

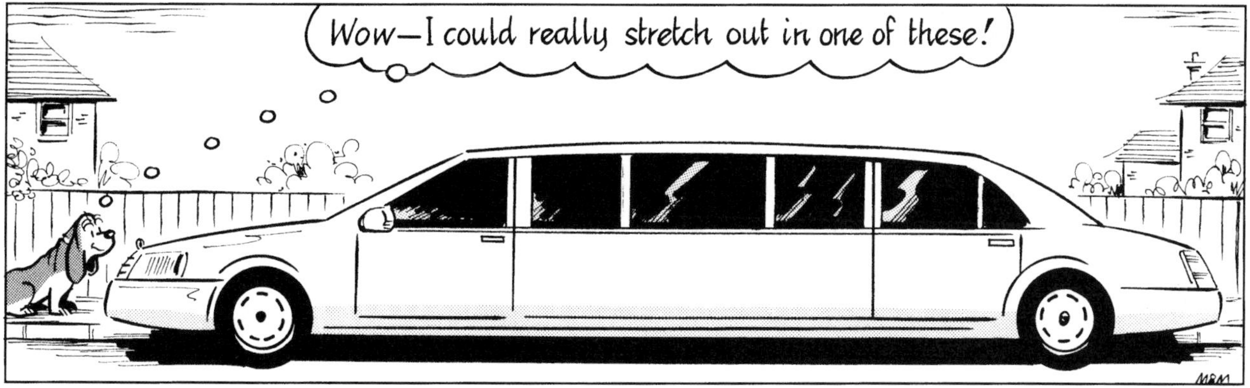
Wow—I could really stretch out in one of these!

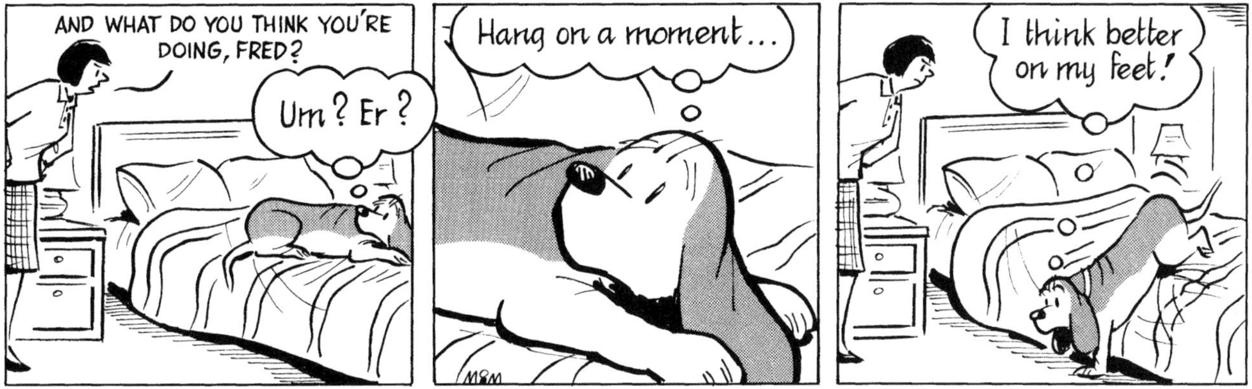
AND WHAT DO YOU THINK YOU'RE DOING, FRED?
Um? Er?
Hang on a moment...
I think better on my feet!

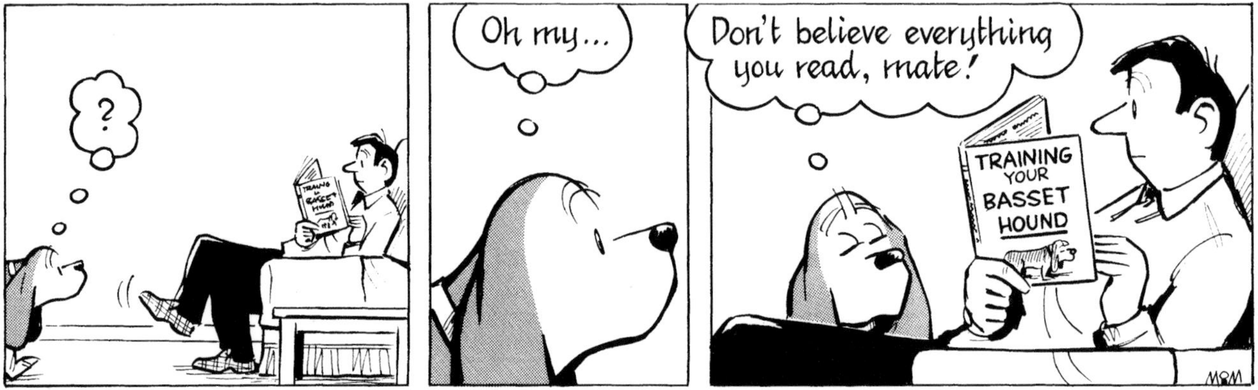
?
Oh my...
Don't believe everything you read, mate!
TRAINING YOUR BASSET HOUND

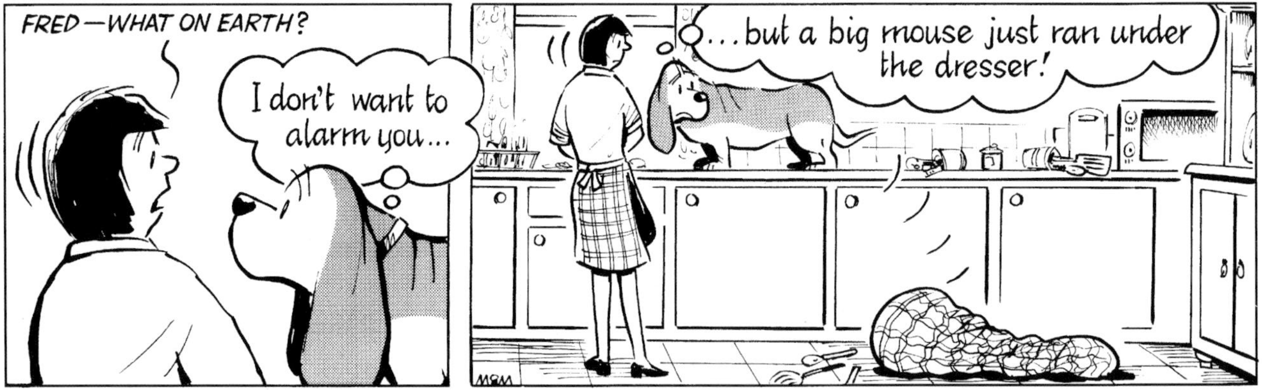
FRED—WHAT ON EARTH?
I don't want to alarm you...
...but a big mouse just ran under the dresser!

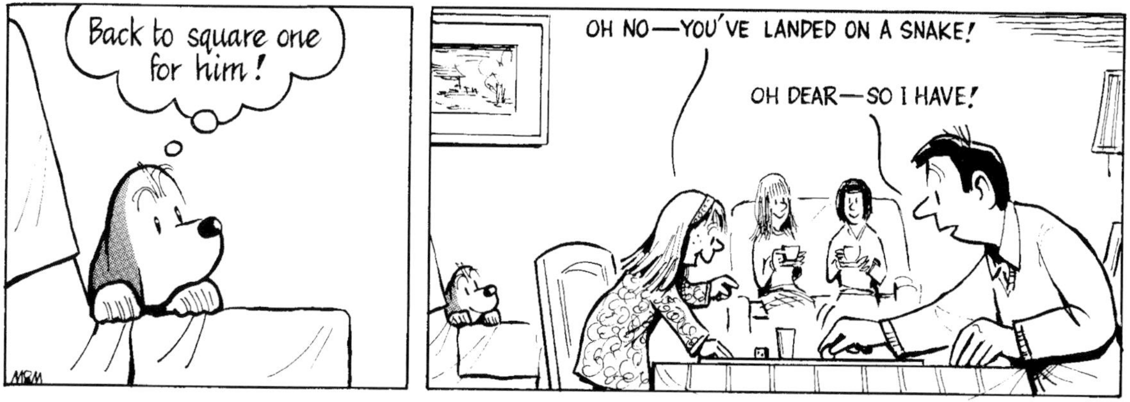
Back to square one for him!
OH NO—YOU'VE LANDED ON A SNAKE!
OH DEAR—SO I HAVE!

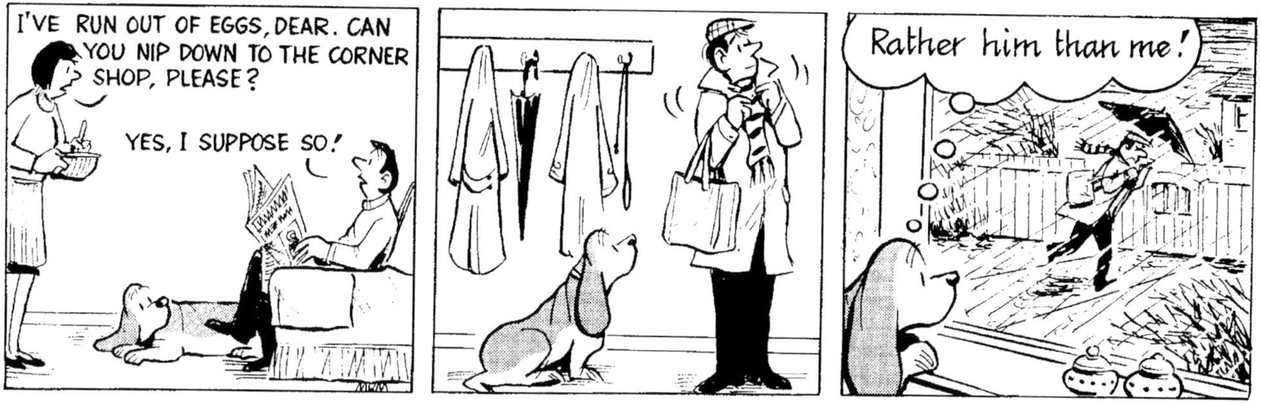
I'VE RUN OUT OF EGGS, DEAR. CAN YOU NIP DOWN TO THE CORNER SHOP, PLEASE?
YES, I SUPPOSE SO!
Rather him than me!

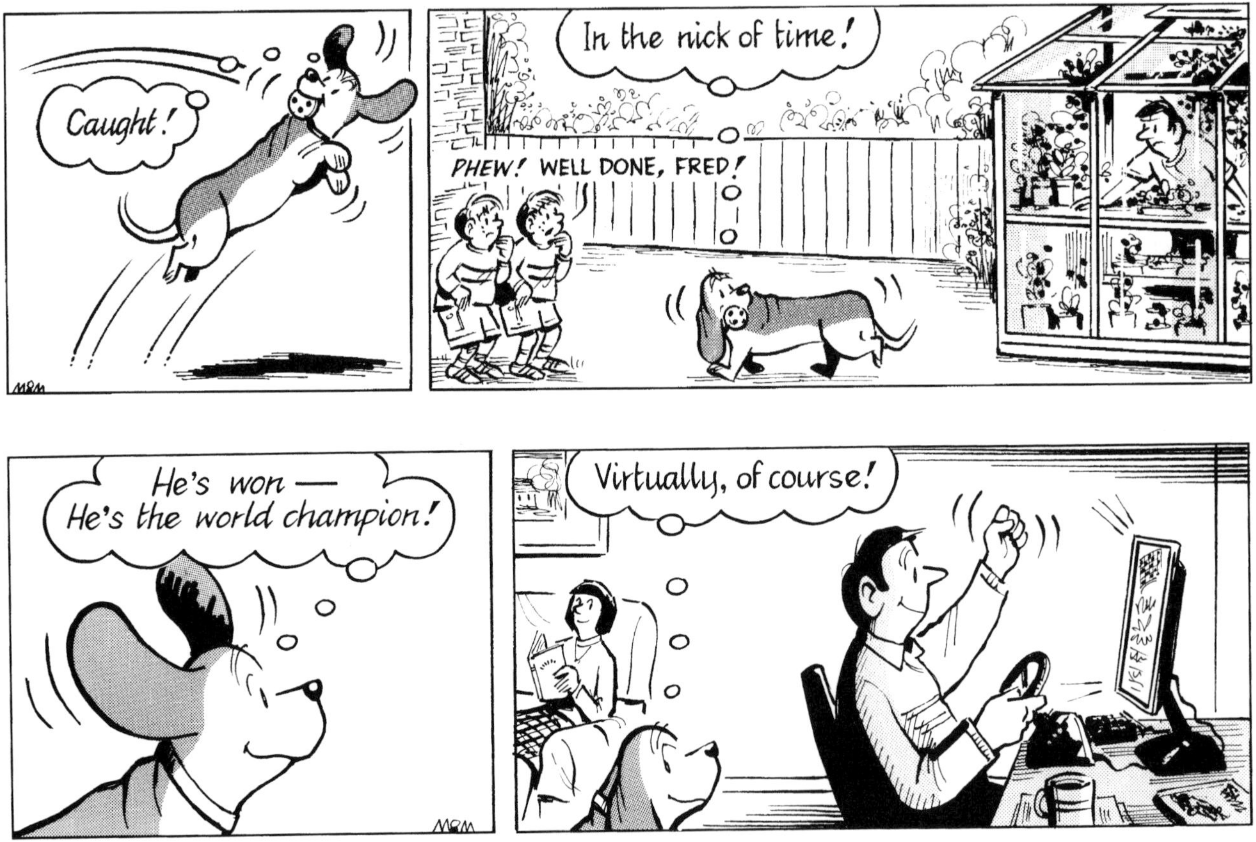
Caught!
In the nick of time!
PHEW! WELL DONE, FRED!
He's won —
He's the world champion!
Virtually, of course!

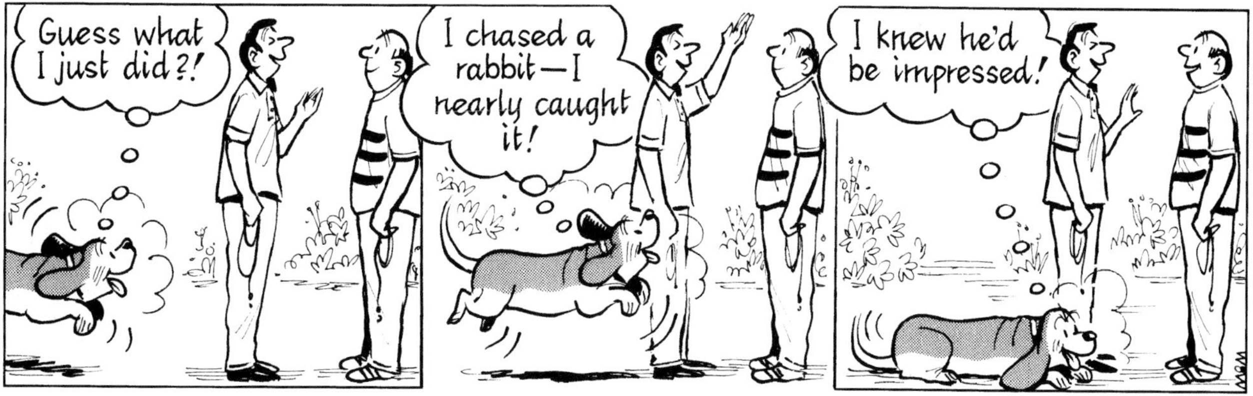

Guess what I just did?!
I chased a rabbit—I nearly caught it!
I knew he'd be impressed!

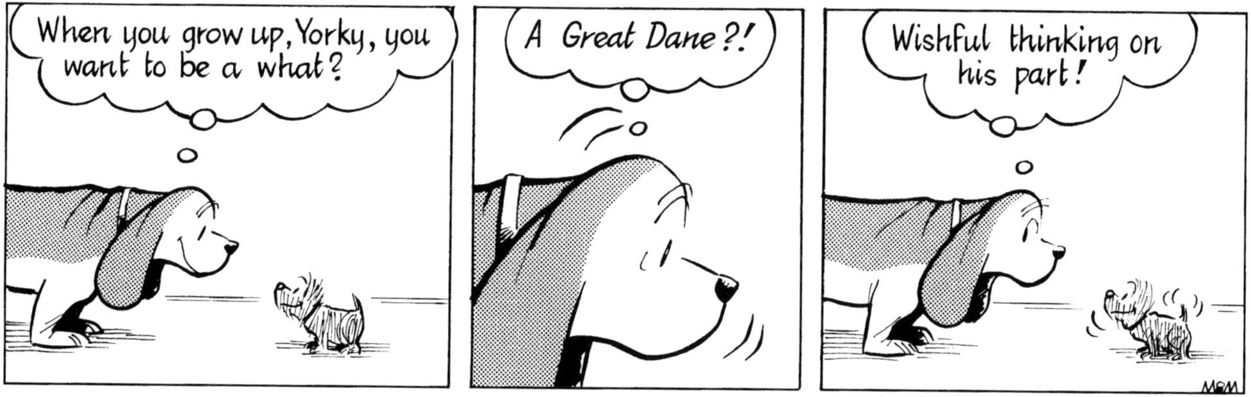

When you grow up, Yorky, you want to be a what?
A Great Dane?!
Wishful thinking on his part!

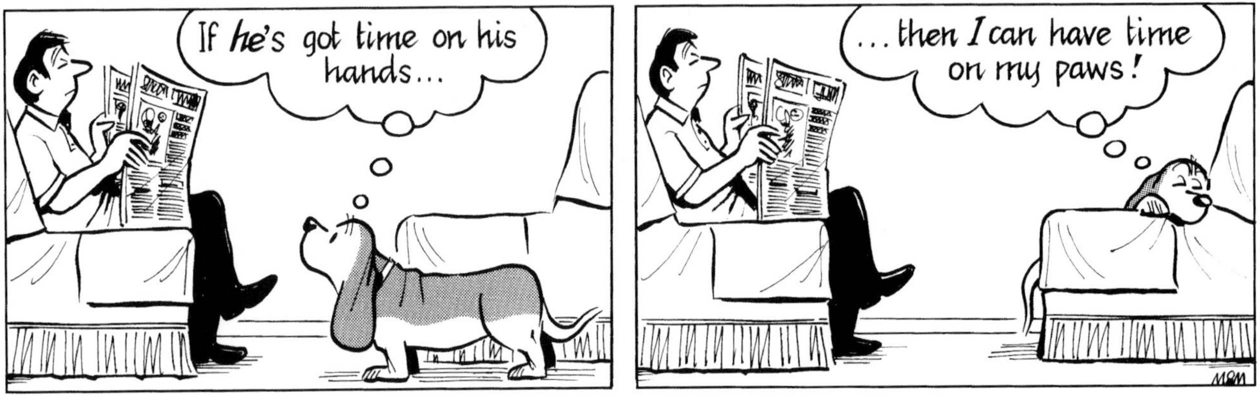
If *he*'s got time on his hands…
…then *I* can have time on my paws!

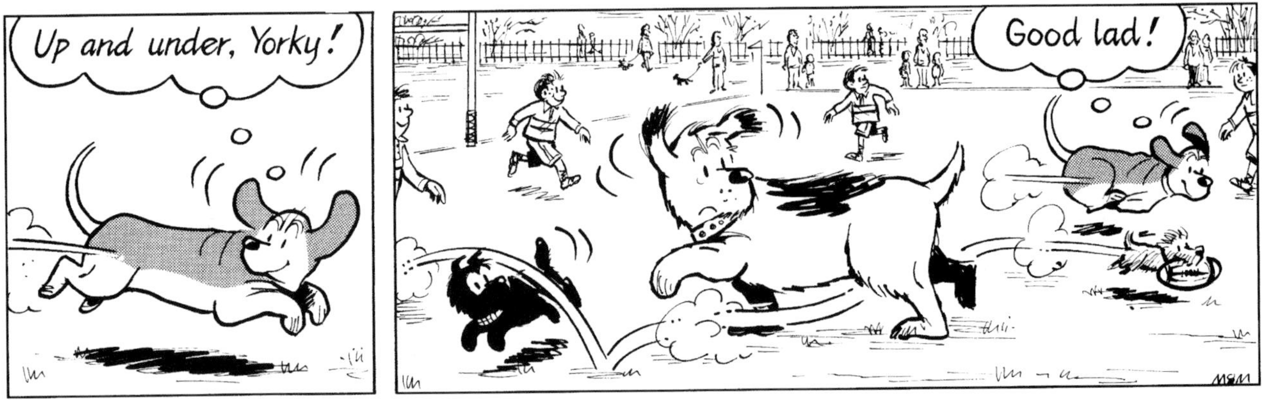
Up and under, Yorky!
Good lad!

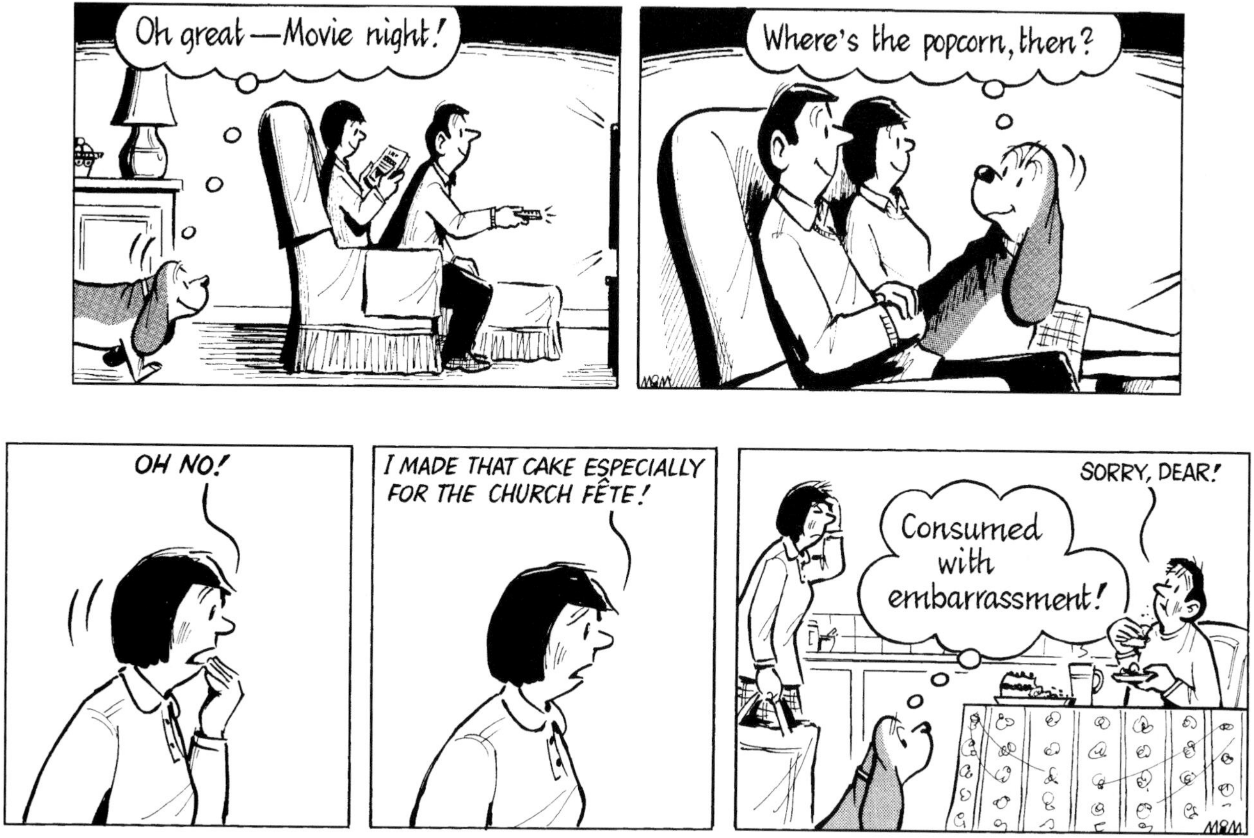
Oh great—Movie night!
Where's the popcorn, then?
OH NO!
I MADE THAT CAKE ESPECIALLY FOR THE CHURCH FÊTE!
Consumed with embarrassment!
SORRY, DEAR!
M&M
M&M

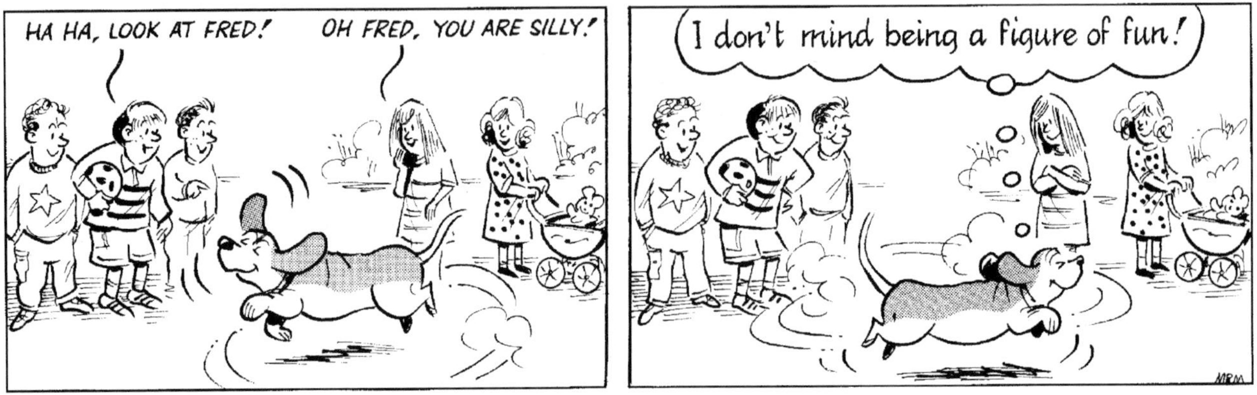
HA HA, LOOK AT FRED!
OH FRED, YOU ARE SILLY!
I don't mind being a figure of fun!

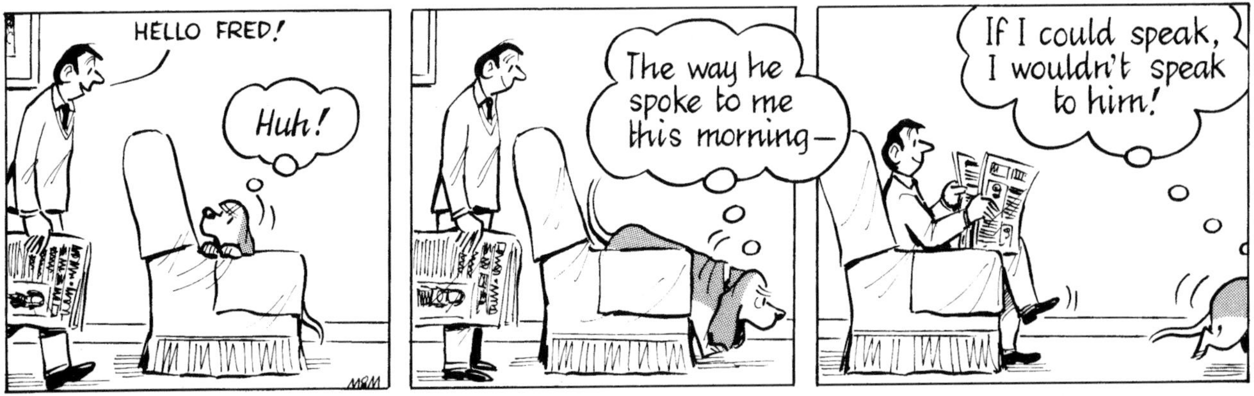
HELLO FRED!
Huh!
The way he spoke to me this morning—
If I could speak, I wouldn't speak to him!

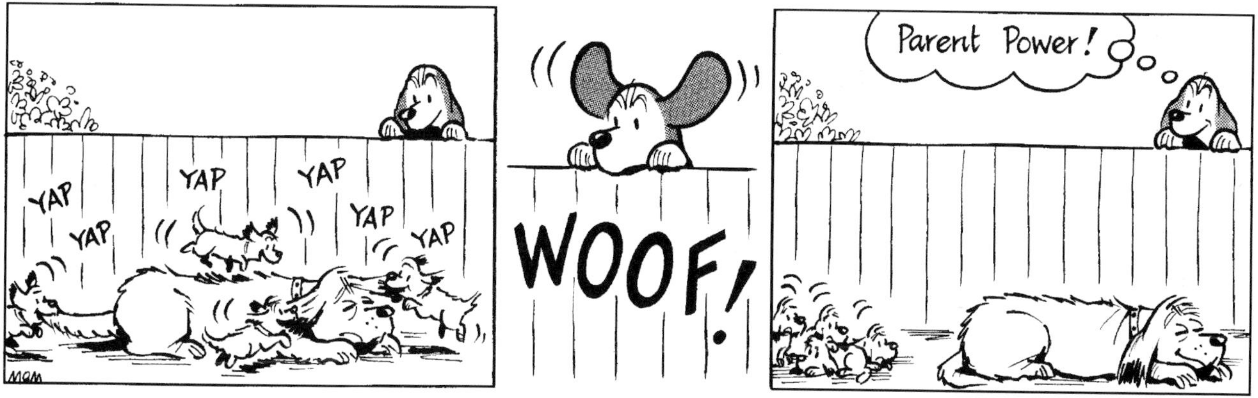
YAP
YAP
YAP
YAP
YAP
YAP
WOOF!
Parent Power!

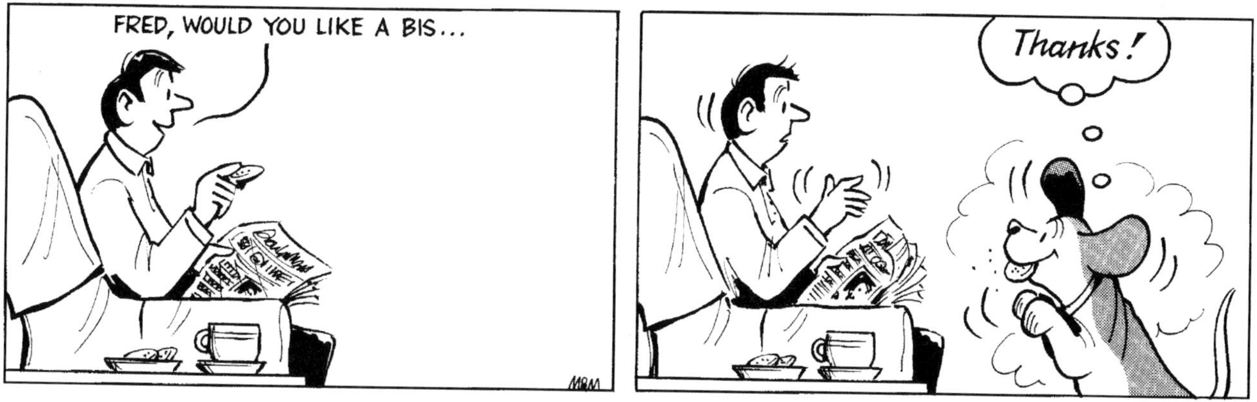
FRED, WOULD YOU LIKE A BIS...
Thanks!

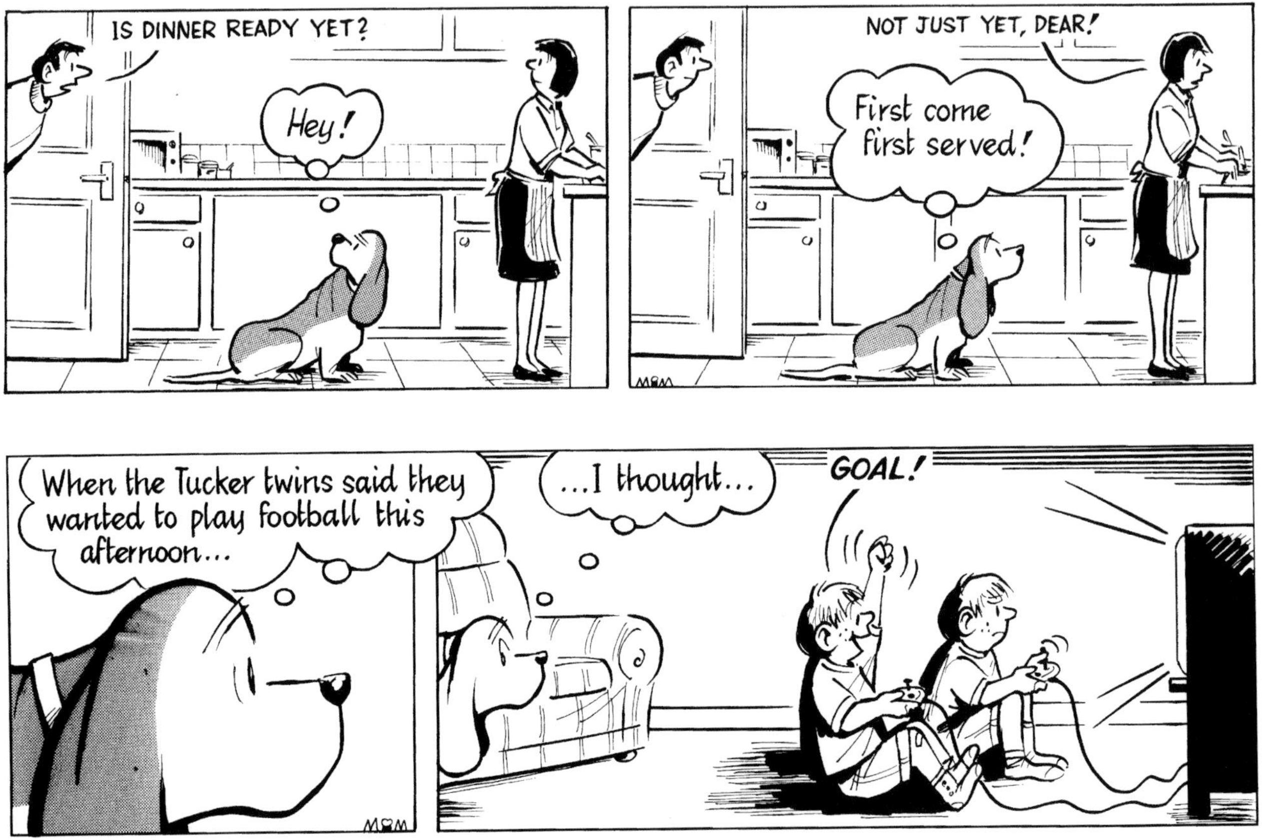
IS DINNER READY YET?
Hey!
NOT JUST YET, DEAR!
First come first served!
When the Tucker twins said they wanted to play football this afternoon...
...I thought...
GOAL!

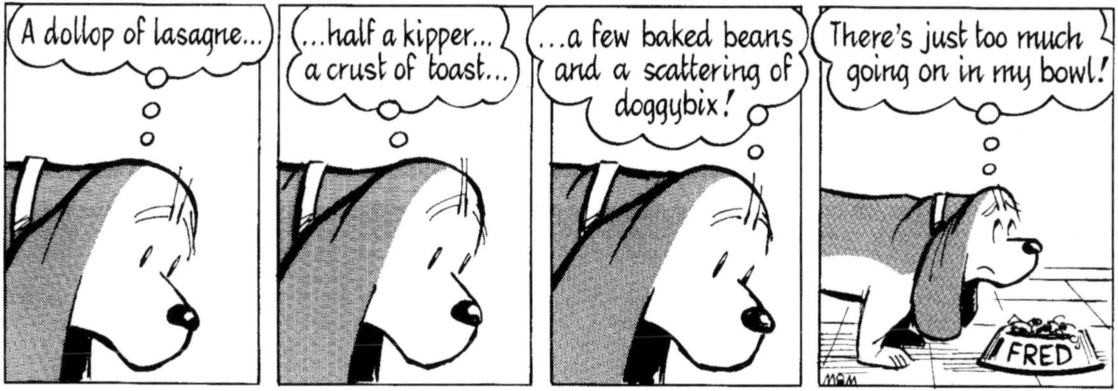
A dollop of lasagne...
...half a kipper... a crust of toast...
...a few baked beans and a scattering of doggybix!
There's just too much going on in my bowl!
FRED

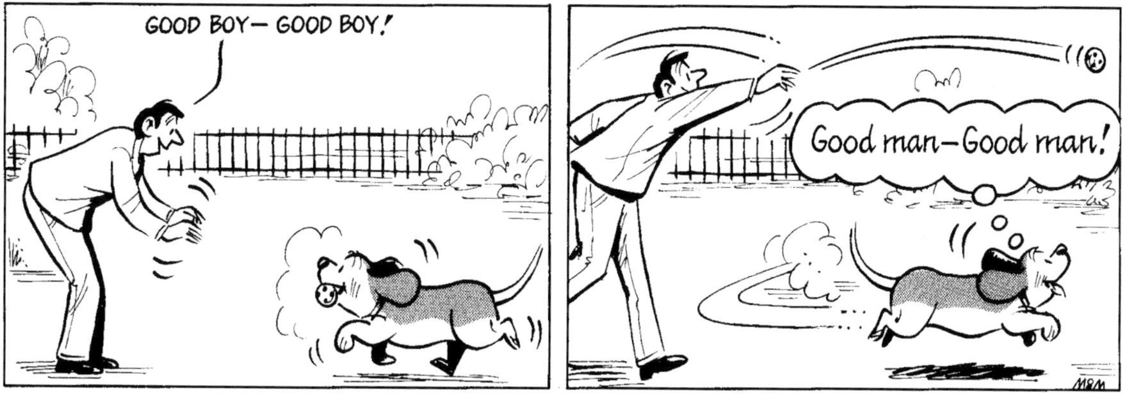
GOOD BOY— GOOD BOY!
Good man—Good man!

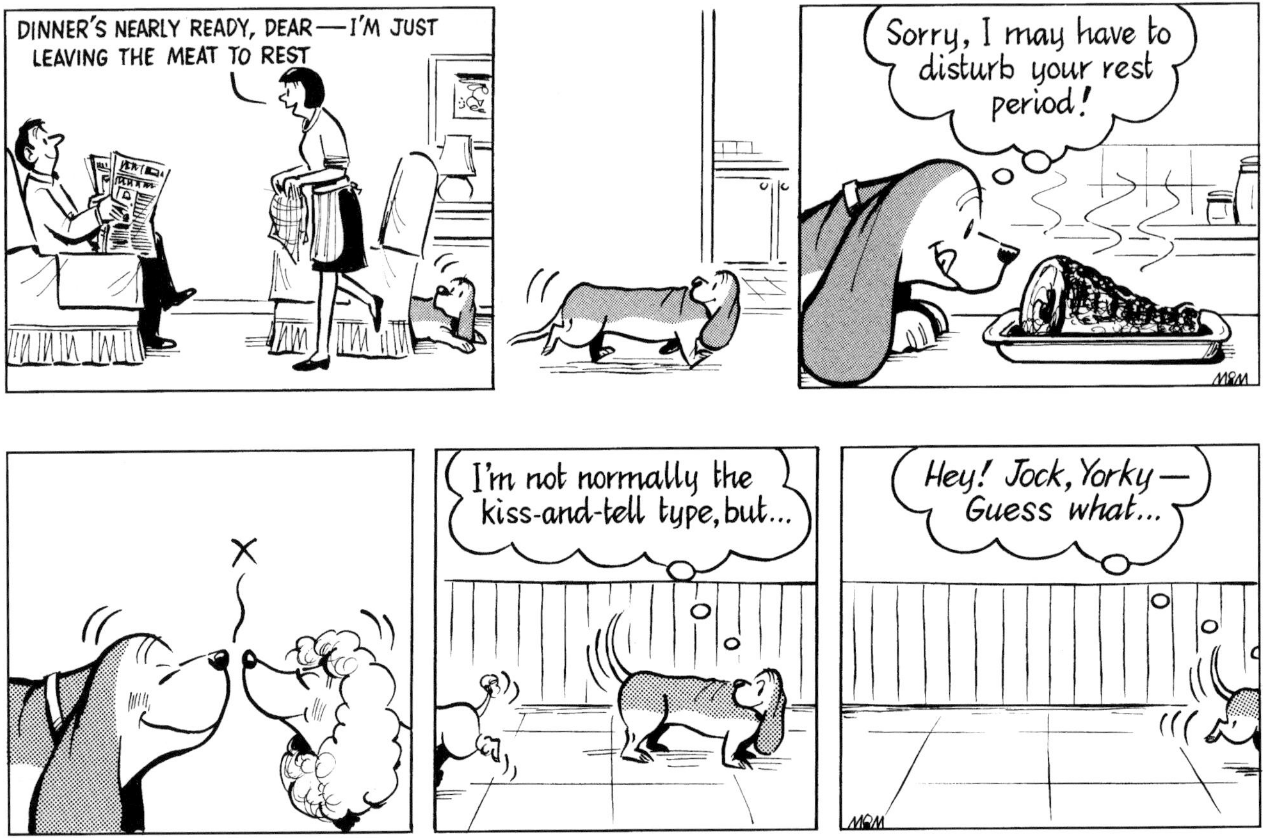
DINNER'S NEARLY READY, DEAR—I'M JUST LEAVING THE MEAT TO REST
Sorry, I may have to disturb your rest period!
MGM
I'm not normally the kiss-and-tell type, but...
Hey! Jock, Yorky— Guess what...
MGM

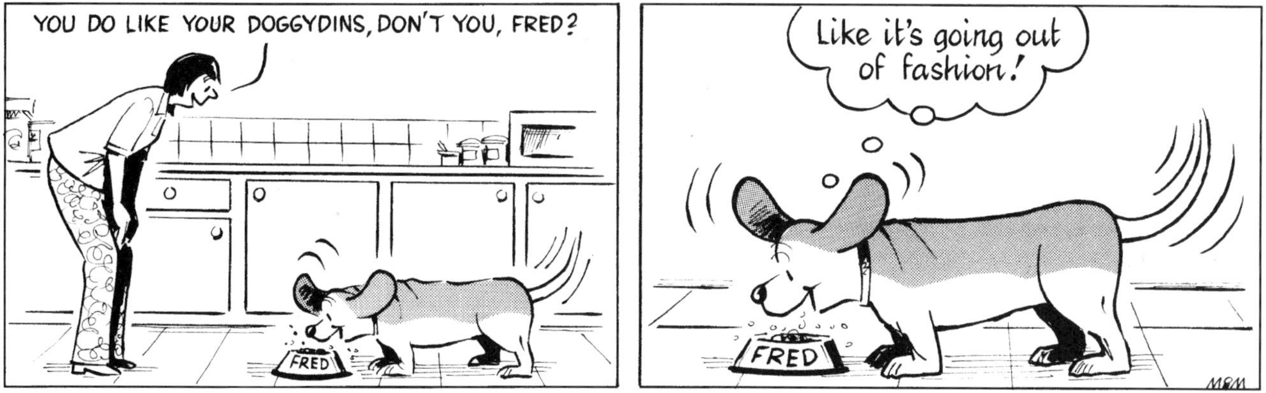
YOU DO LIKE YOUR DOGGYDINS, DON'T YOU, FRED?
FRED
Like it's going out of fashion!
FRED

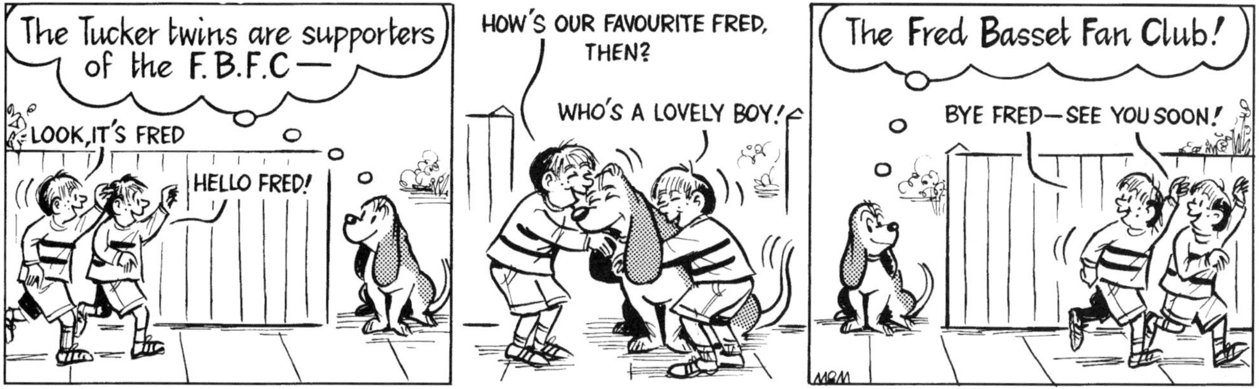
The Tucker twins are supporters of the F.B.F.C —
LOOK, IT'S FRED
HELLO FRED!
HOW'S OUR FAVOURITE FRED, THEN?
WHO'S A LOVELY BOY!
The Fred Basset Fan Club!
BYE FRED—SEE YOU SOON!

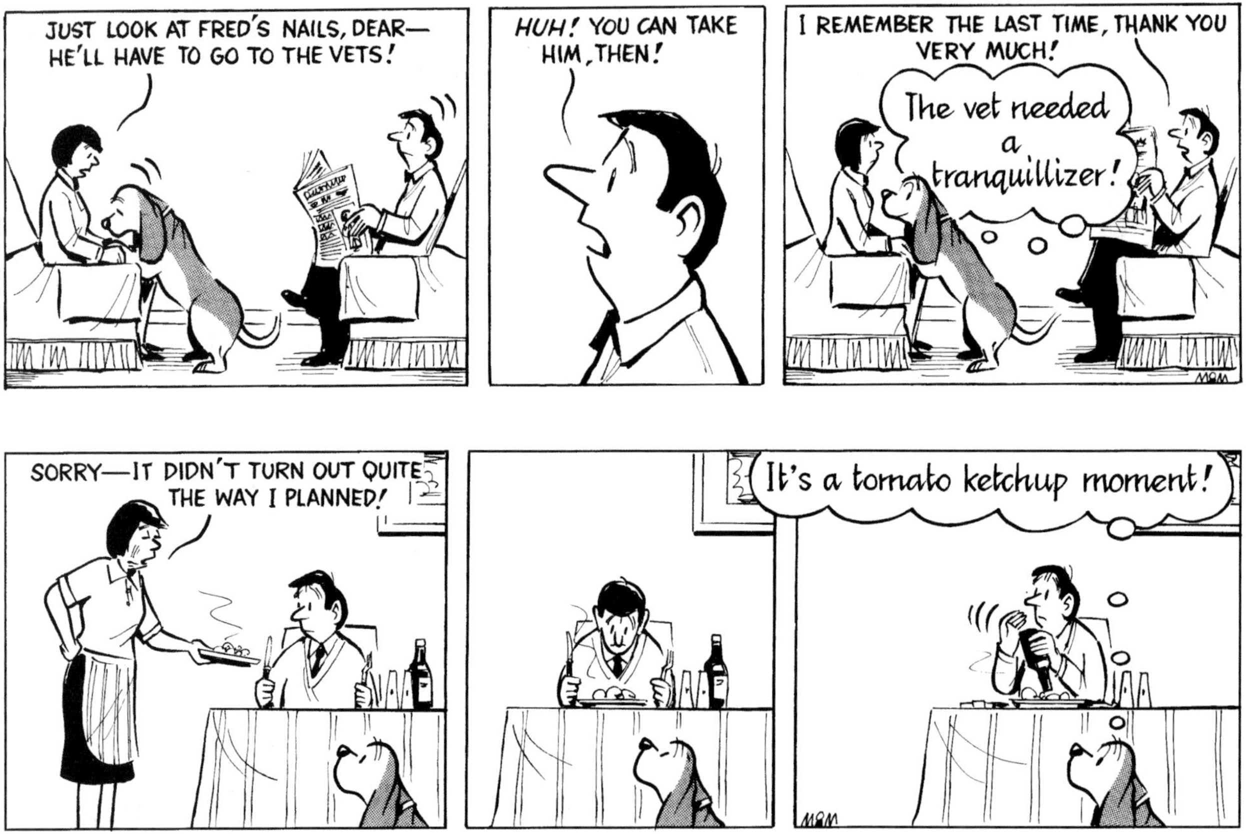
JUST LOOK AT FRED'S NAILS, DEAR— HE'LL HAVE TO GO TO THE VETS!
HUH! YOU CAN TAKE HIM, THEN!
I REMEMBER THE LAST TIME, THANK YOU VERY MUCH!
The vet needed a tranquillizer!
MGM
SORRY—IT DIDN'T TURN OUT QUITE THE WAY I PLANNED!
It's a tomato ketchup moment!
MGM

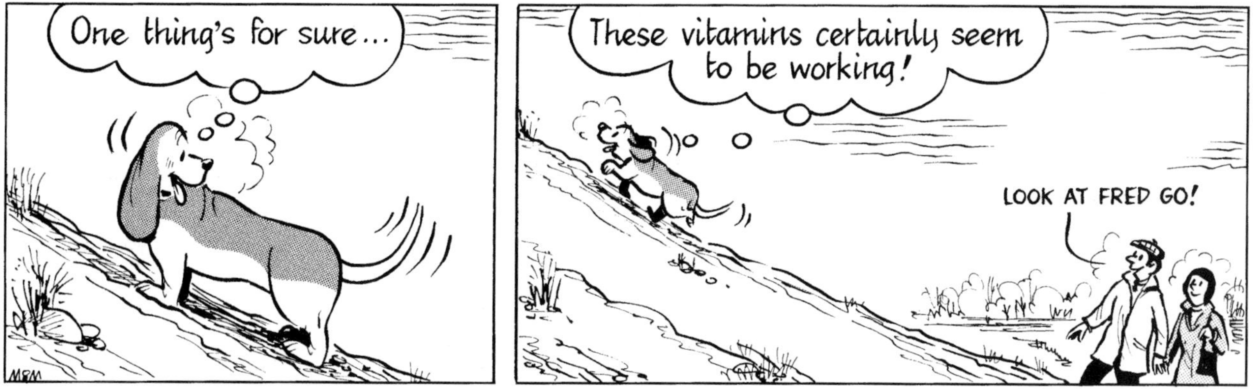
One thing's for sure...
These vitamins certainly seem to be working!
LOOK AT FRED GO!

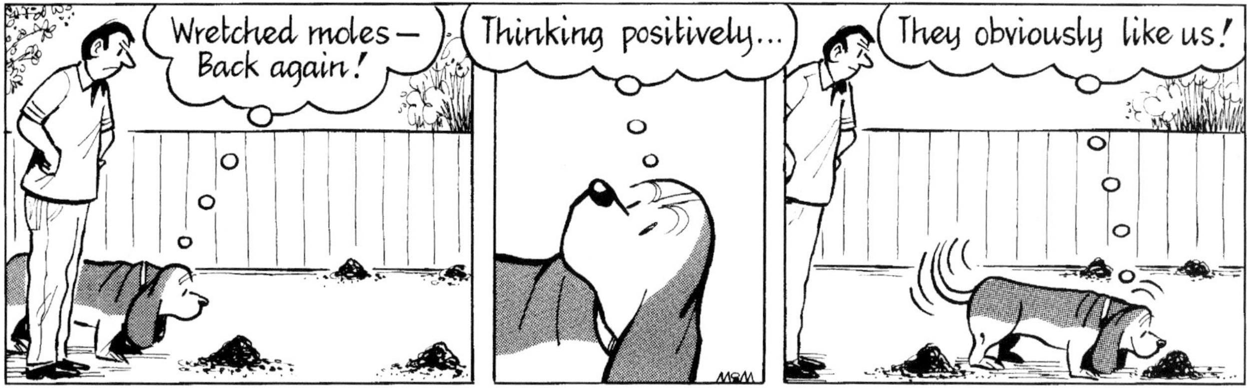
Wretched moles—
Back again!
Thinking positively...
They obviously like us!

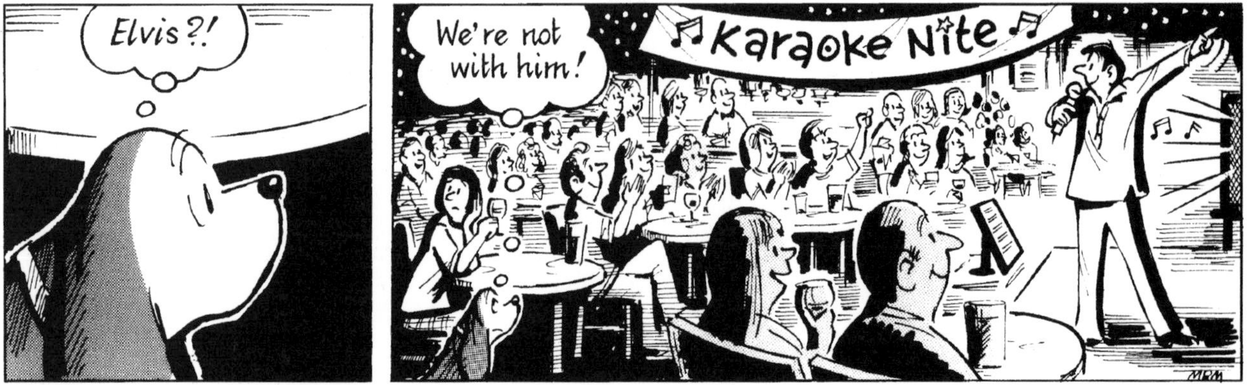
Elvis?!
We're not with him!
Karaoke Nite
MRM

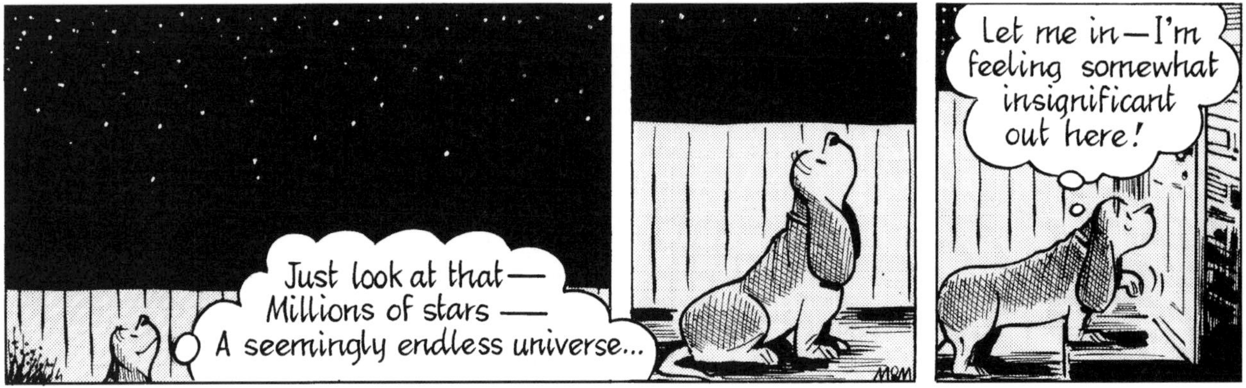
Just look at that—
Millions of stars —
A seemingly endless universe...
MRM
Let me in—I'm feeling somewhat insignificant out here!

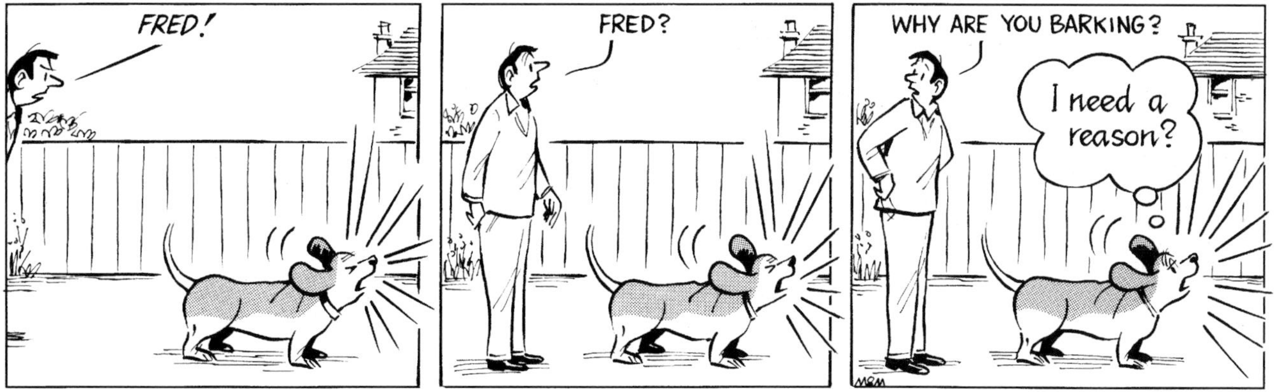
FRED!
FRED?
WHY ARE YOU BARKING?
I need a reason?

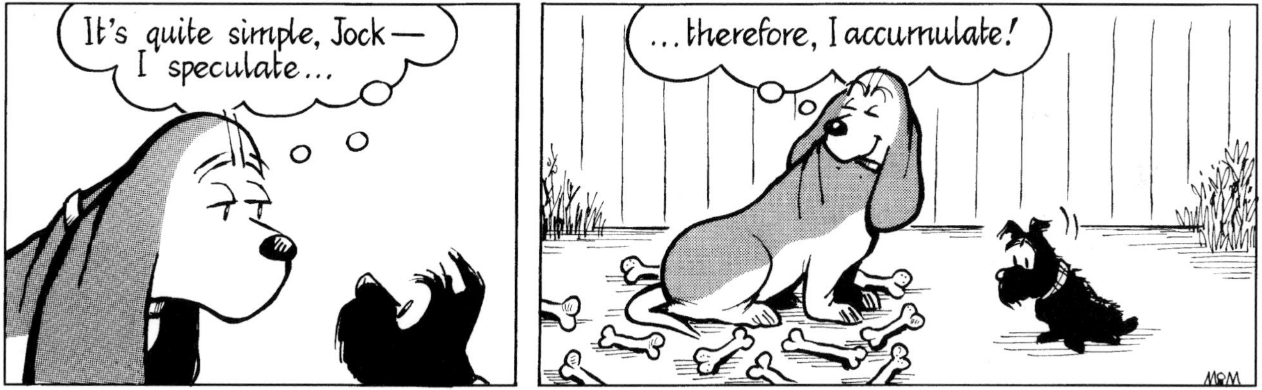
It's quite simple, Jock— I speculate...
...therefore, I accumulate!

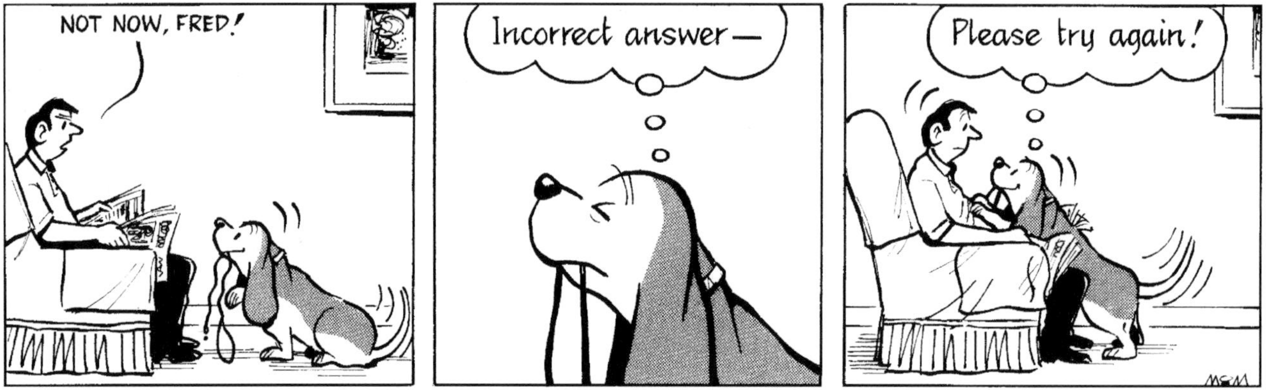
NOT NOW, FRED!
Incorrect answer—
Please try again!

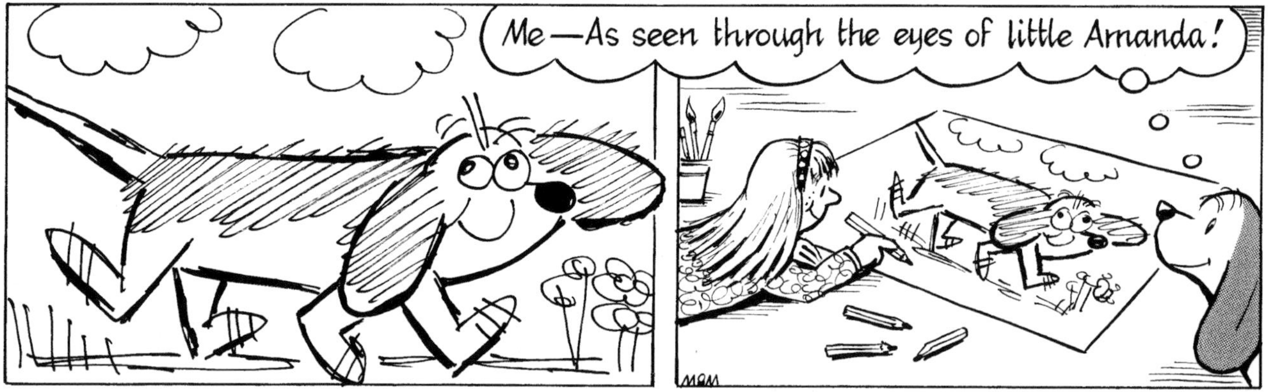
Me—As seen through the eyes of little Amanda!

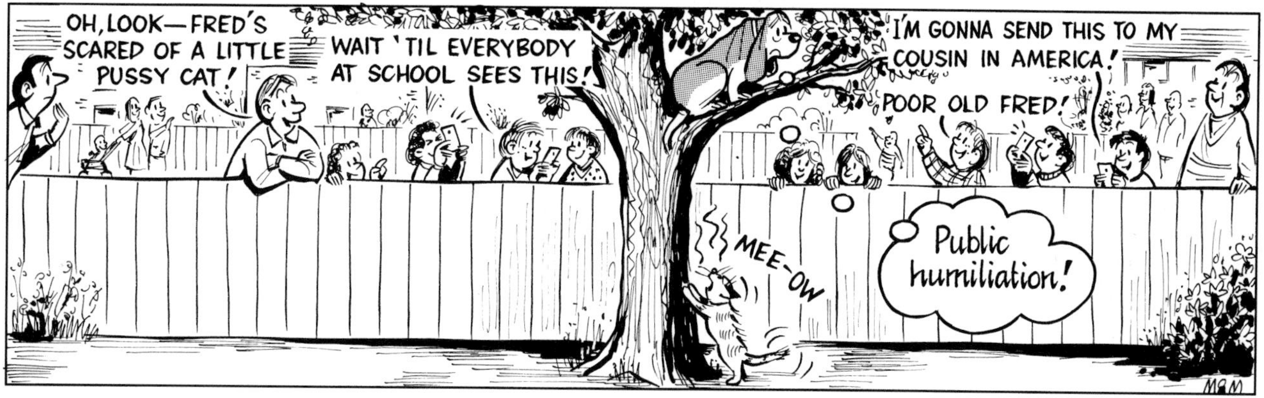
OH, LOOK—FRED'S SCARED OF A LITTLE PUSSY CAT!
WAIT 'TIL EVERYBODY AT SCHOOL SEES THIS!
I'M GONNA SEND THIS TO MY COUSIN IN AMERICA!
POOR OLD FRED!
MEE-OW
Public humiliation!
M&M

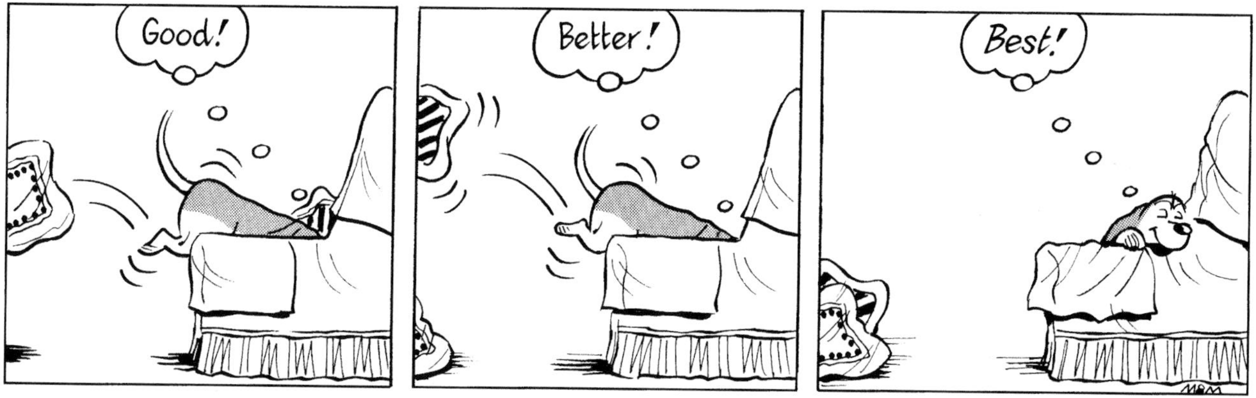
Good!
Better!
Best!
M&M

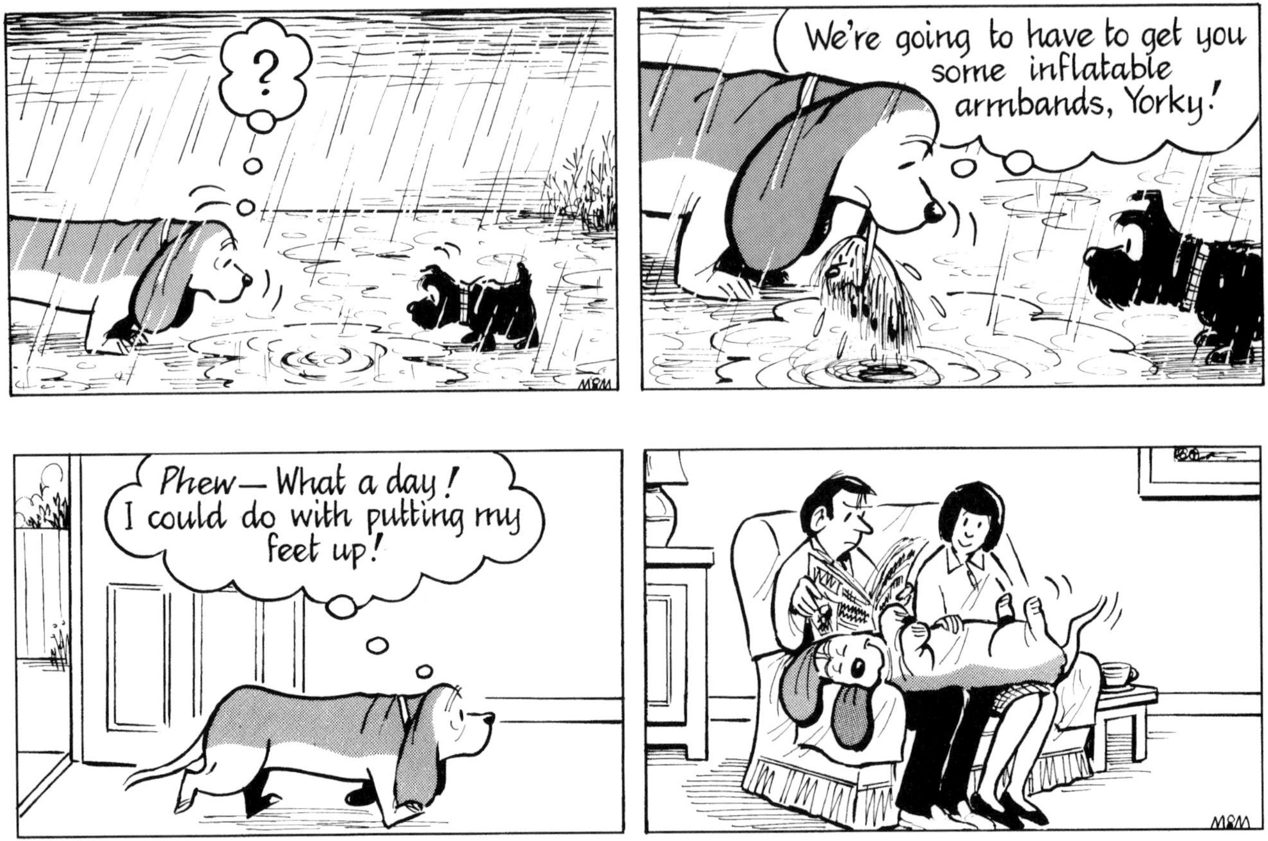
?
We're going to have to get you some inflatable armbands, Yorky!
Phew— What a day! I could do with putting my feet up!

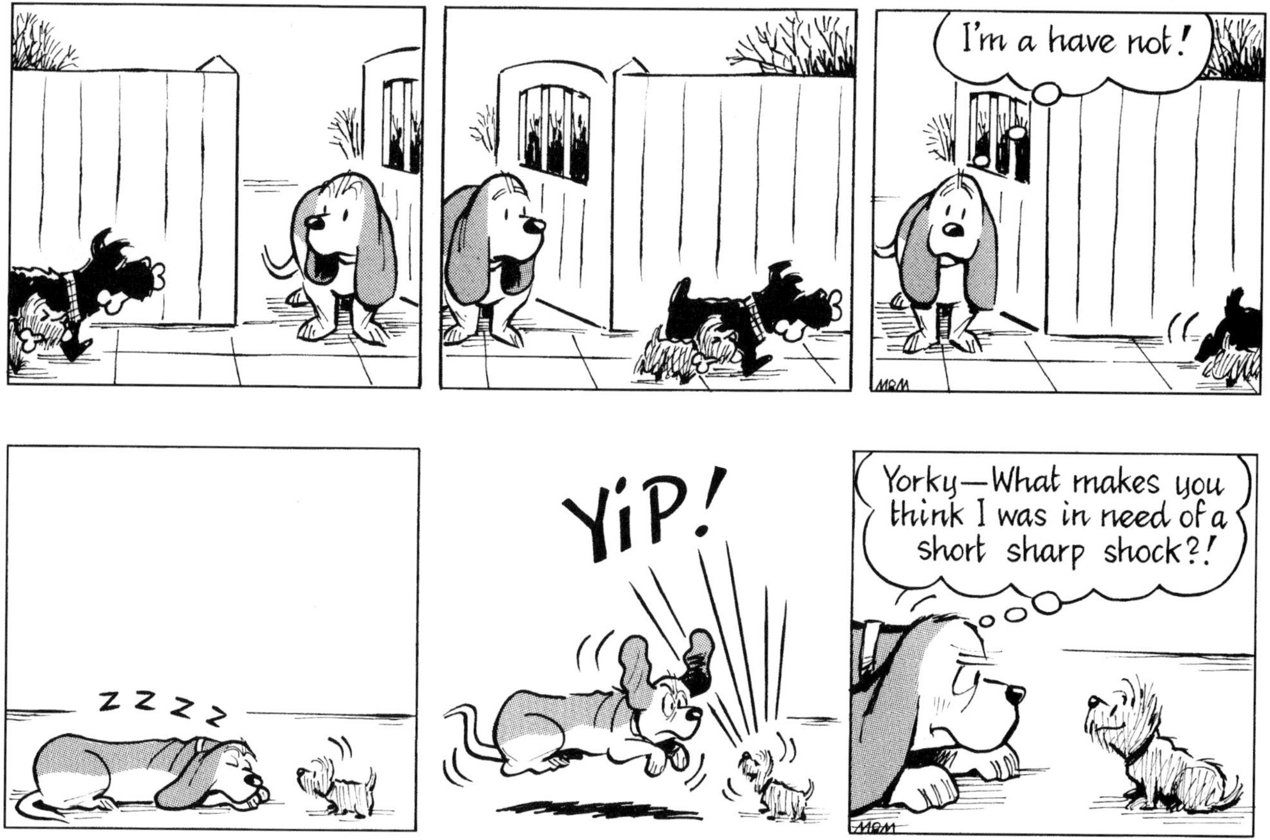
I'm a have not!
MGM
ZZZZ
YiP!
Yorky—What makes you think I was in need of a short sharp shock?!
MGM

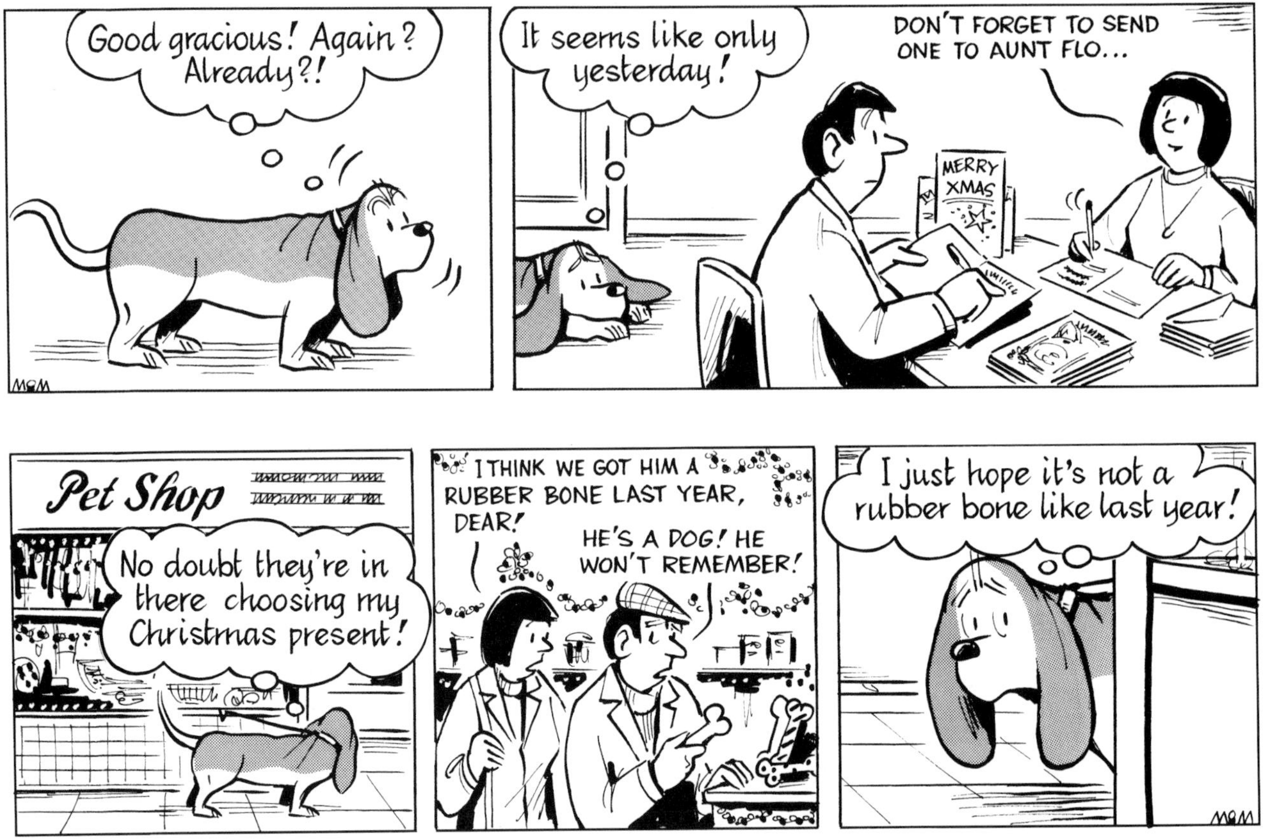
Good gracious! Again? Already?!
MOM
It seems like only yesterday!
DON'T FORGET TO SEND ONE TO AUNT FLO...
MERRY XMAS
Pet Shop
No doubt they're in there choosing my Christmas present!
I THINK WE GOT HIM A RUBBER BONE LAST YEAR, DEAR!
HE'S A DOG! HE WON'T REMEMBER!
I just hope it's not a rubber bone like last year!
MOM

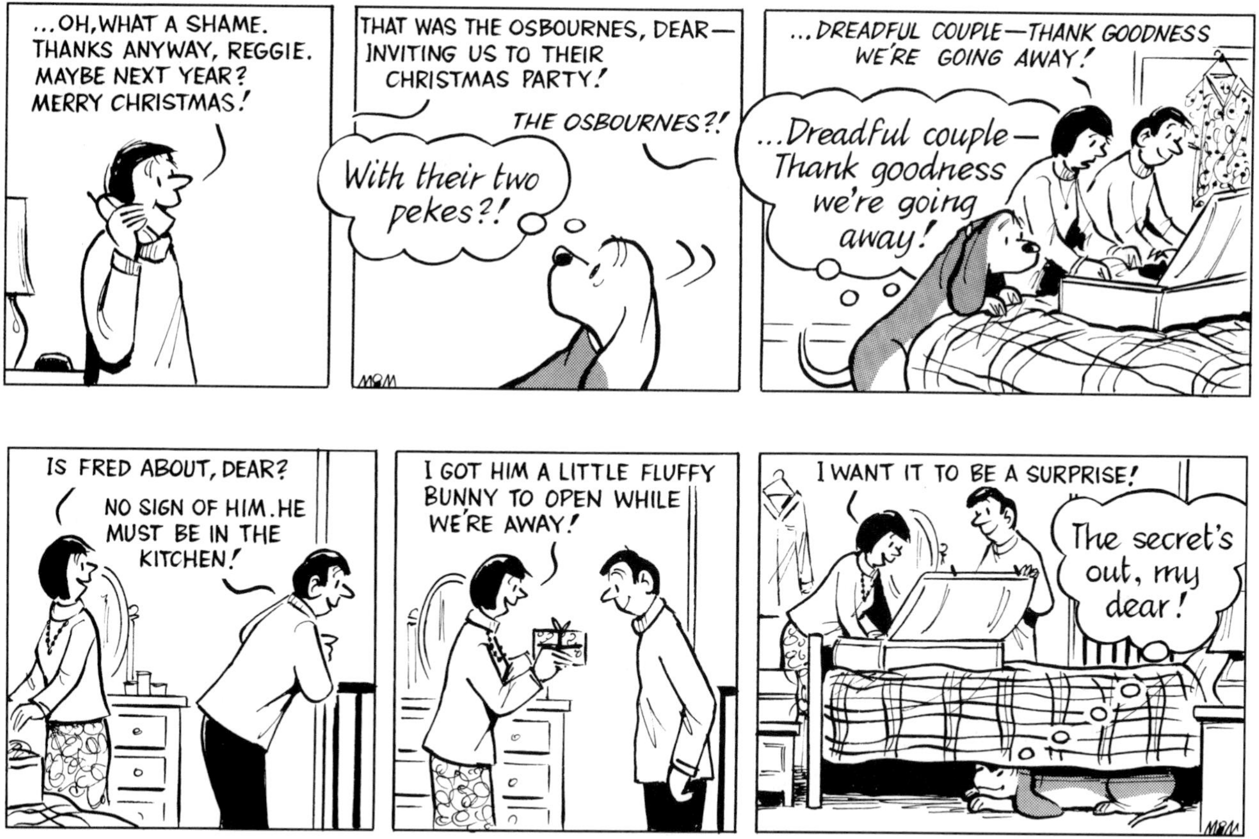
...OH, WHAT A SHAME. THANKS ANYWAY, REGGIE. MAYBE NEXT YEAR? MERRY CHRISTMAS!
THAT WAS THE OSBOURNES, DEAR— INVITING US TO THEIR CHRISTMAS PARTY!
THE OSBOURNES?!
With their two pekes?!
M&M
...DREADFUL COUPLE—THANK GOODNESS WE'RE GOING AWAY!
...Dreadful couple— Thank goodness we're going away!
IS FRED ABOUT, DEAR?
NO SIGN OF HIM. HE MUST BE IN THE KITCHEN!
I GOT HIM A LITTLE FLUFFY BUNNY TO OPEN WHILE WE'RE AWAY!
I WANT IT TO BE A SURPRISE!
The secret's out, my dear!
M&M

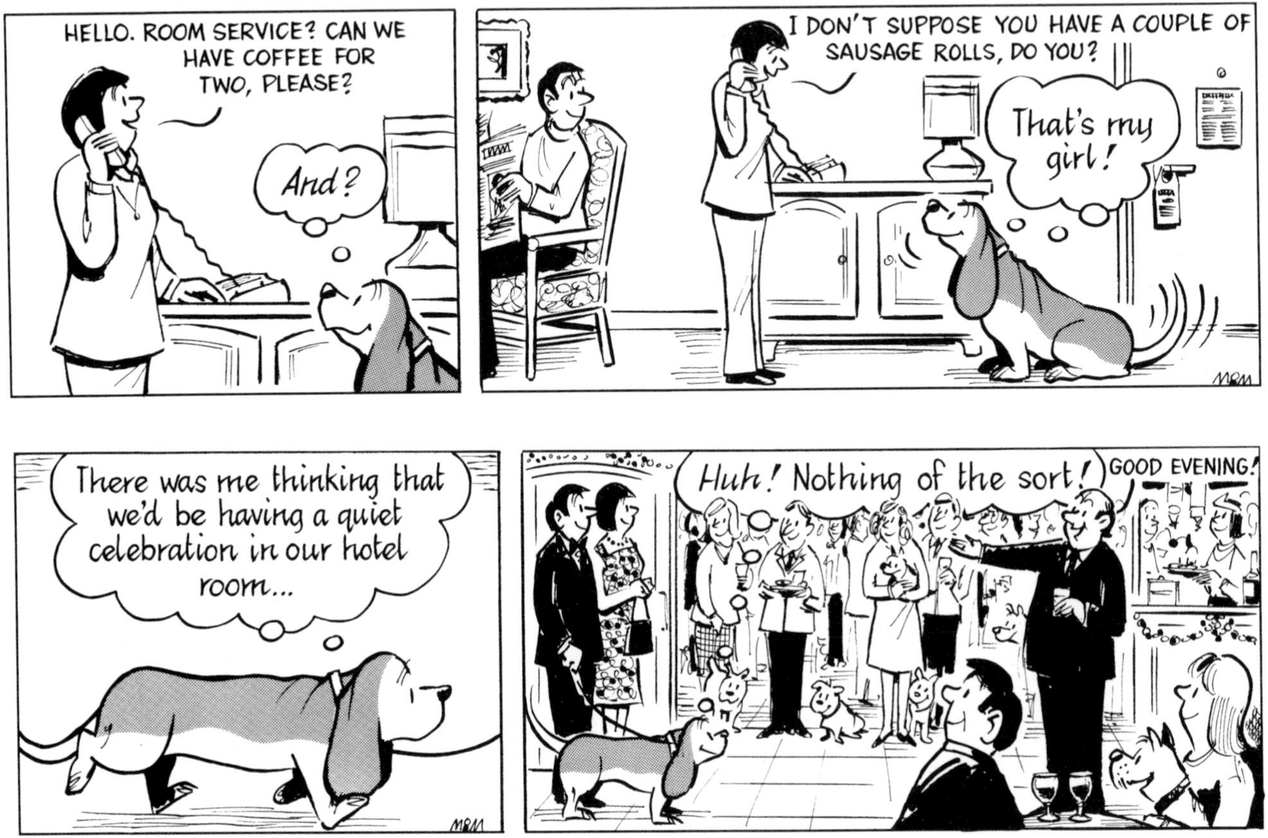
HELLO. ROOM SERVICE? CAN WE HAVE COFFEE FOR TWO, PLEASE?
And?
I DON'T SUPPOSE YOU HAVE A COUPLE OF SAUSAGE ROLLS, DO YOU?
That's my girl!
There was me thinking that we'd be having a quiet celebration in our hotel room...
Huh! Nothing of the sort!
GOOD EVENING!

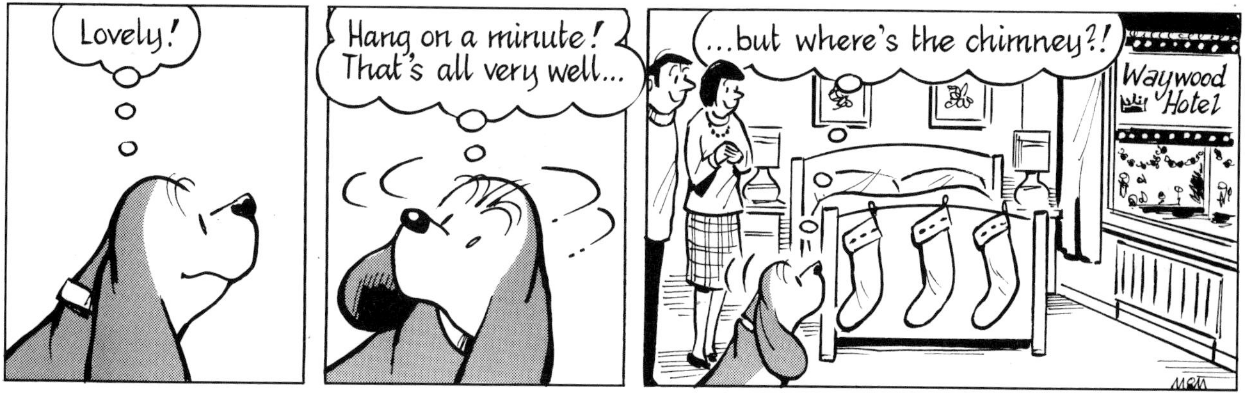
Lovely!
Hang on a minute! That's all very well...
...but where's the chimney?!
Waywood Hotel

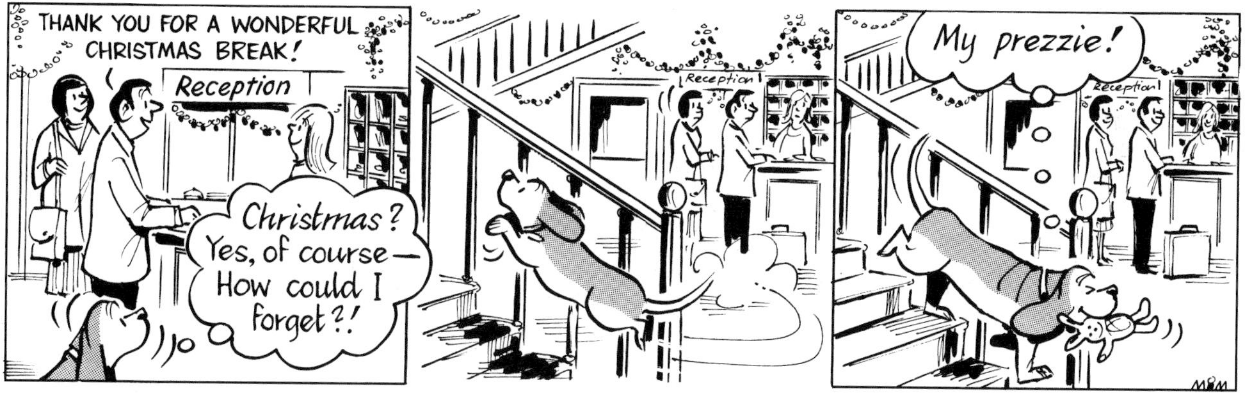
THANK YOU FOR A WONDERFUL CHRISTMAS BREAK!
Reception
Christmas? Yes, of course— How could I forget?!
Reception
Reception
My prezzie!

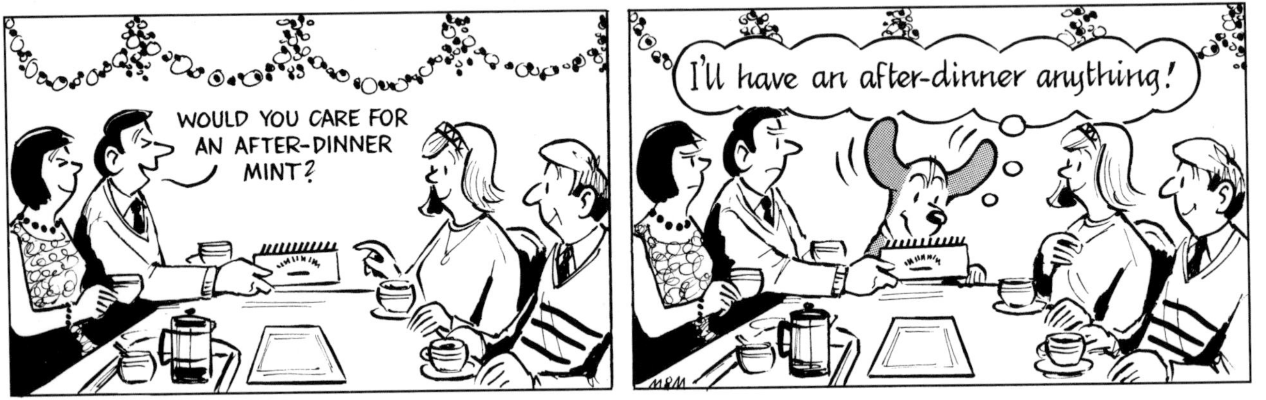
WOULD YOU CARE FOR AN AFTER-DINNER MINT?
I'll have an after-dinner anything!
M&M

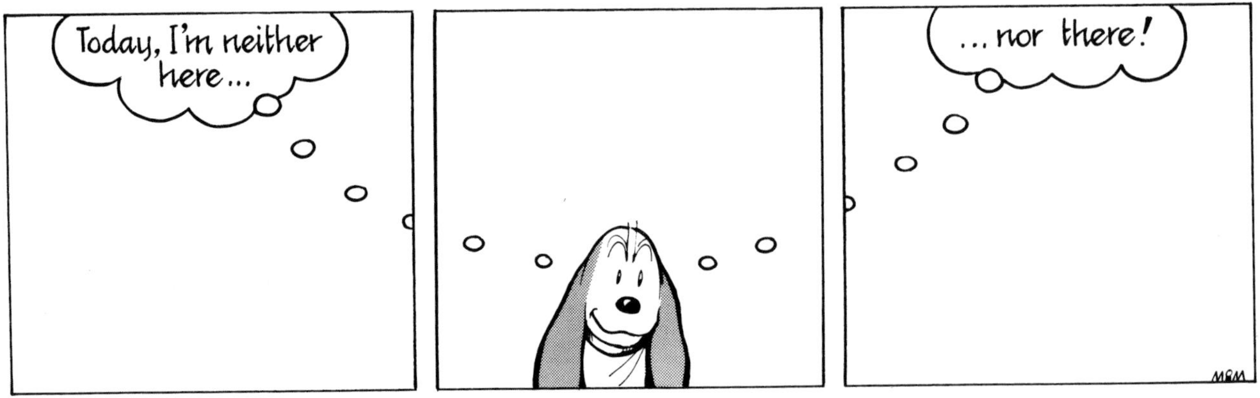
Today, I'm neither here...
...nor there!
M&M